Erin and Adam,

Merry Christmas! I lov[illegible] has many of our favorite cocktails and many more to try. We so appreciate your friendship and all our great memories. We look forward to many more.

Love you!

The Richards

2022

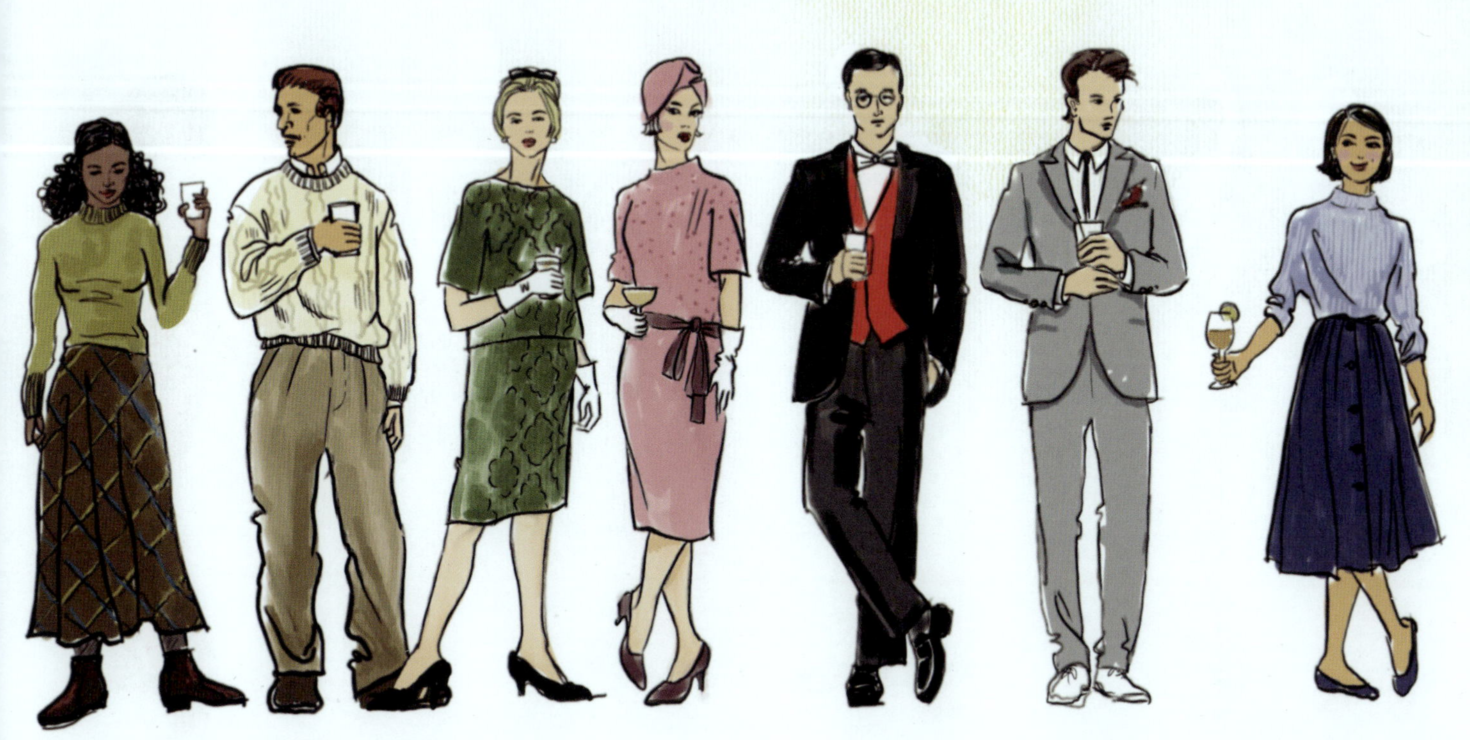

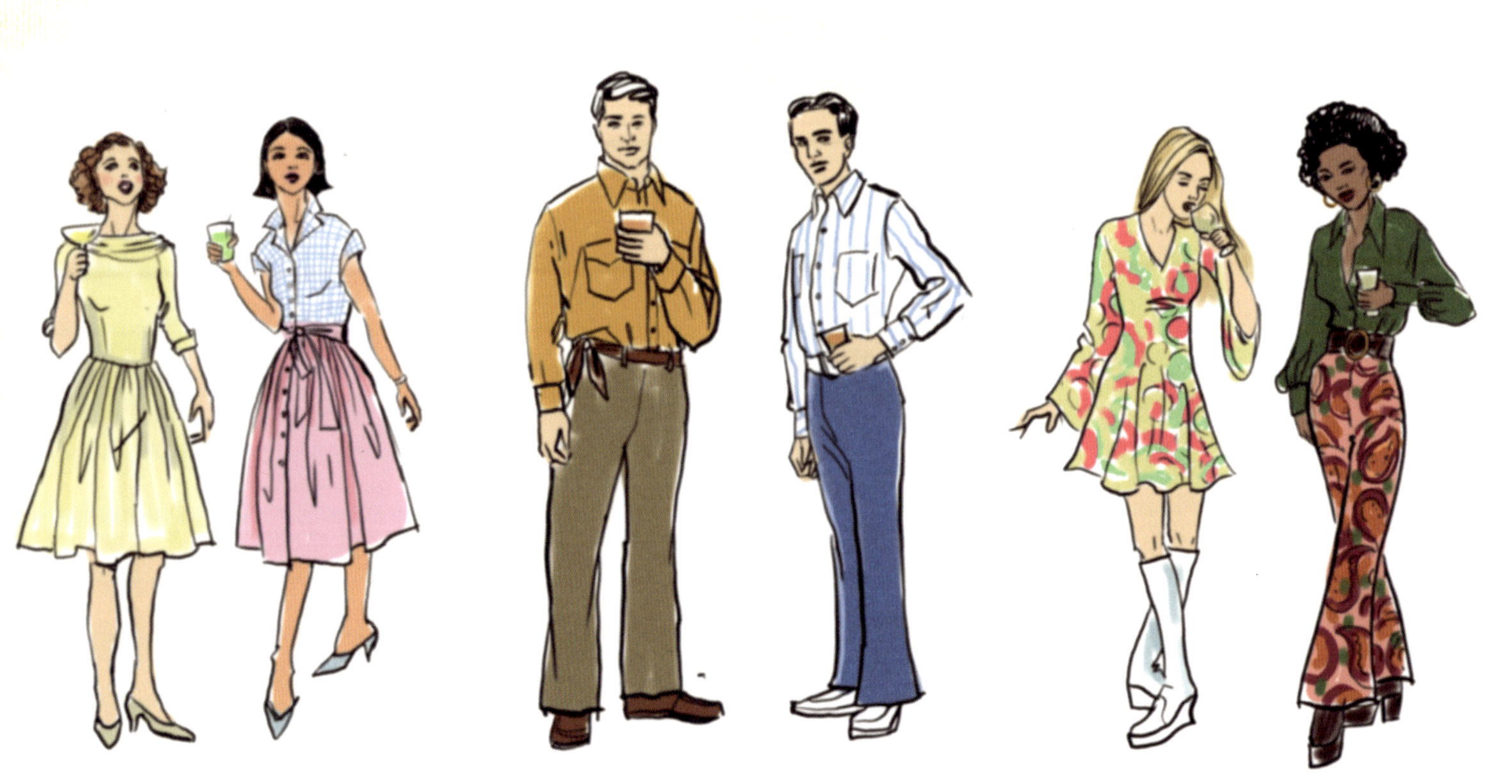

THE Illustrated Cocktail

The "Art" of Mixology

Rachel K Miller

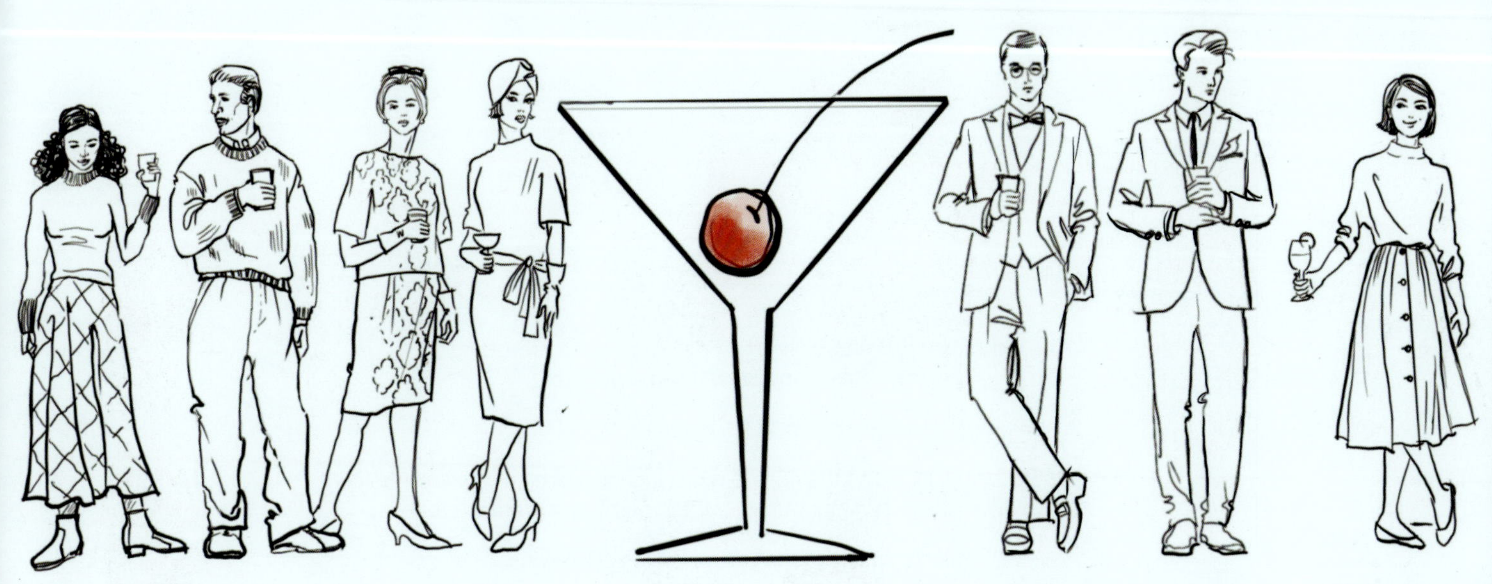

Additional Text and Editing by Francesca Hess Kranzberg
Book Design by Steven Jurgensmeyer

Manufactured in the United States of America

ISBN 978 0 578 90558 7

For
Abigail & Tamara

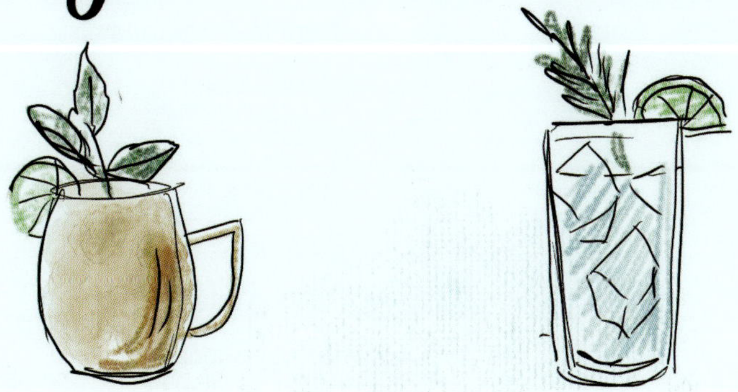

CONTENTS

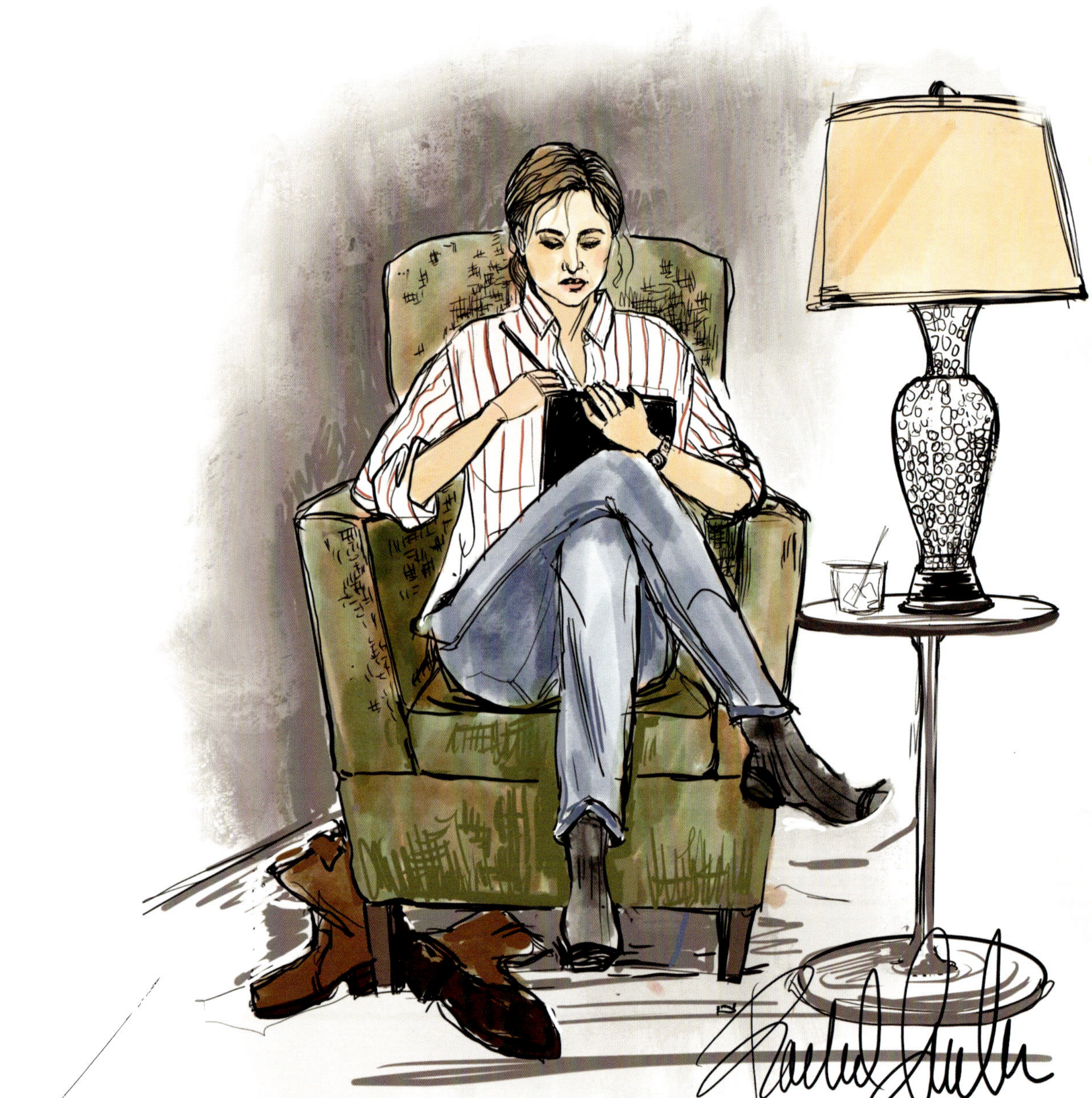

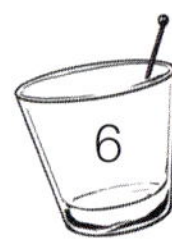

Introduction

Full disclosure: I am neither a bartender nor an expert at making drinks. But I do enjoy a cocktail before or after dinner.

What I am is an artist. I studied painting in college and have worked as an artist and designer my whole career. I am always drawing. I can not just sit still and rest. I have a constant urge to pick up a pen, brush or, more recently, an iPad, and create. I would fill the Instagram feed with sketches about my everyday life.

My friends and followers were enjoying my drawings, and then I started illustrating cocktail recipes. The response was overwhelming. Something that I had drawn on a whim really hit a chord. I started receiving requests for prints, and suggestions that I put the recipes together into a book.

What I discovered is that preparing a cocktail is a lot like creating a book. You gather your ingredients and make them into a wonderful and satisfying whole. You take your time and enjoy the process. You admire your handiwork. You indulge… slowly enjoying the drink and the experience.

Remember, it's quality, not quantity. Drink responsibly.

"There is no bad whiskey. There are only some whiskeys that aren't as good as others."

—Raymond Chandler

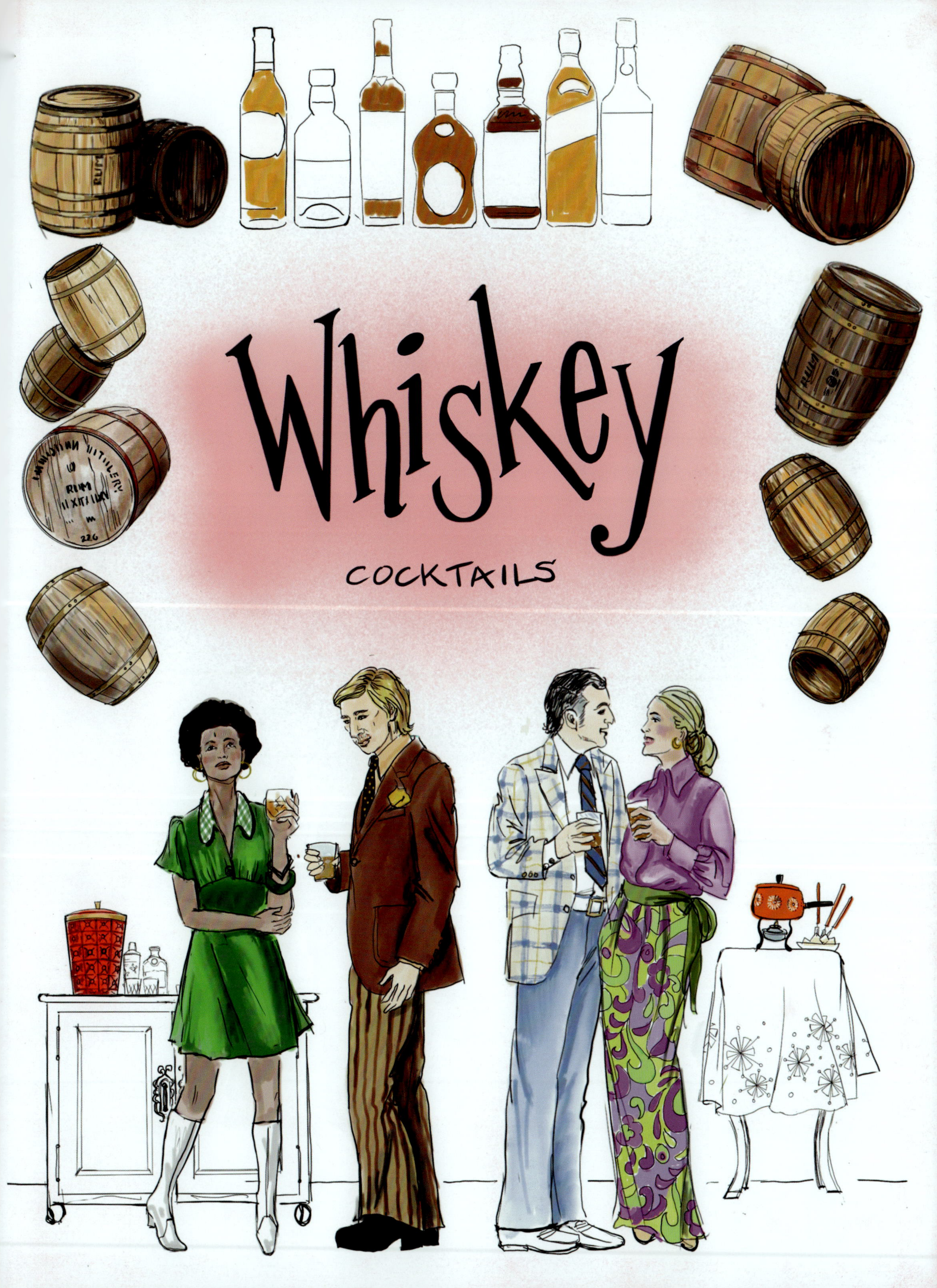
Whiskey
COCKTAILS
RUM
RUM

Blood & Sand

Do you know anything about Rudolph Valentino? He was a famous silent picture movie star who died tragically at the age of 31. He was a sex symbol, women loved him, he was married twice and had countless affairs. The movie *Blood and Sand* is one of his greatest performances. While this cocktail is named for the movie, the blood also refers to the juice of the blood orange used in the drink. Let's just call it a sexy, mysterious drink.

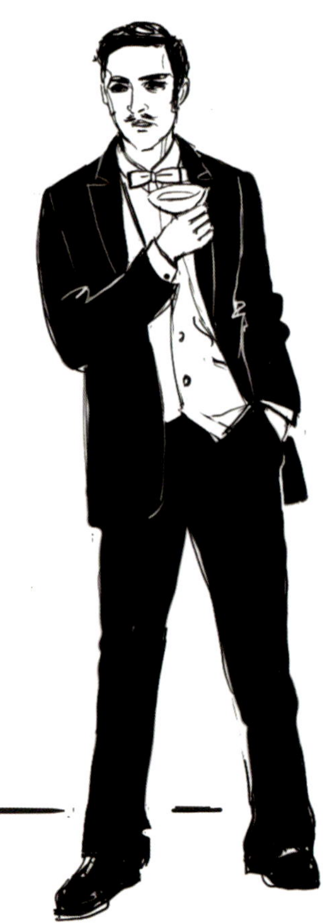

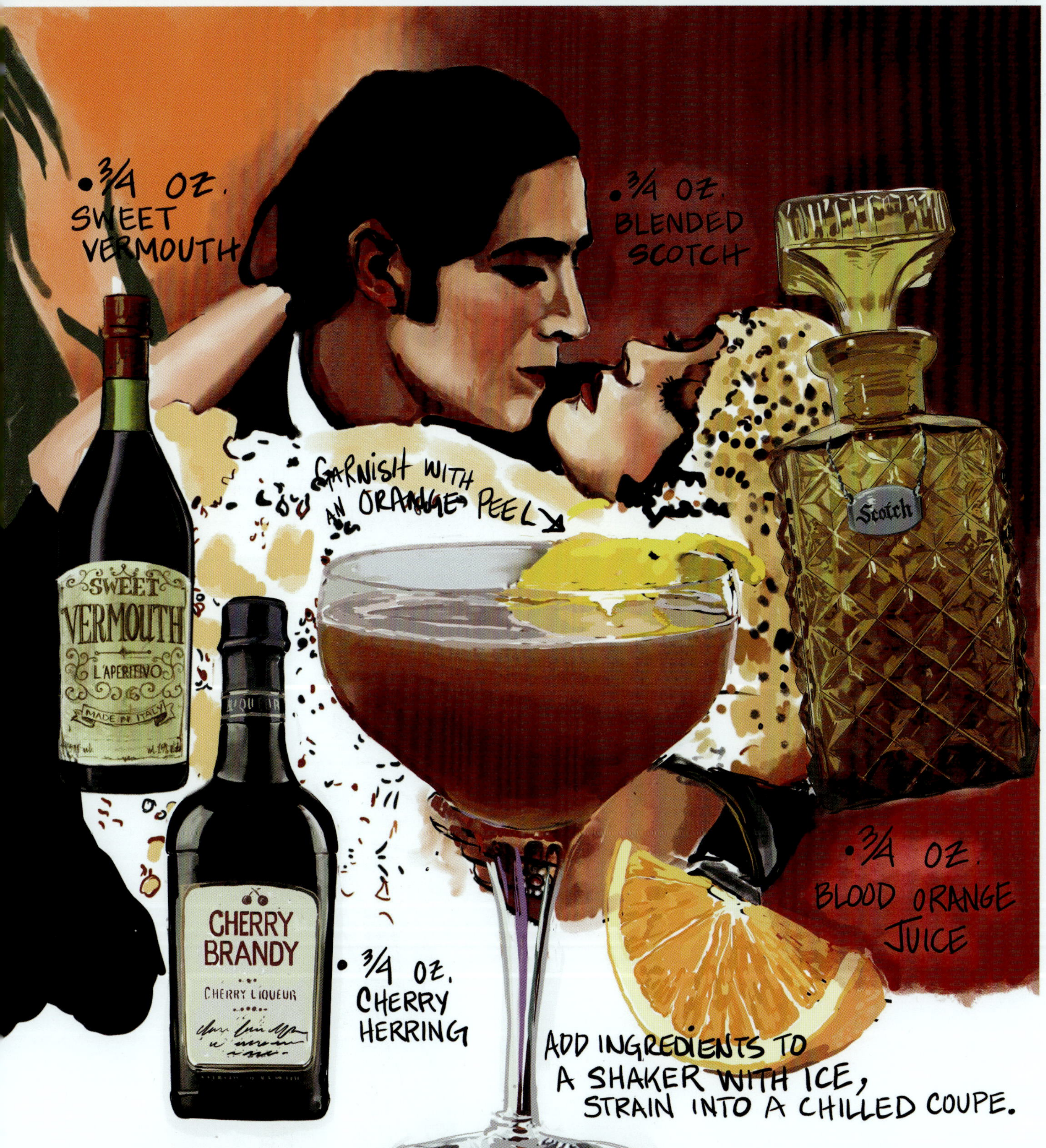
• 3/4 OZ. SWEET VERMOUTH
• 3/4 OZ. BLENDED SCOTCH
SWEET VERMOUTH
L'APERITIVO
MADE IN ITALY
Scotch
GARNISH WITH AN ORANGE PEEL
CHERRY BRANDY
CHERRY LIQUEUR
• 3/4 OZ. BLOOD ORANGE JUICE
• 3/4 OZ. CHERRY HERRING
ADD INGREDIENTS TO A SHAKER WITH ICE, STRAIN INTO A CHILLED COUPE.

Blood & Sand

Boulevardier

One of my favorite movies is the classic, *An American in Paris*. It's about a sexy American Artist, Gene Kelly, who falls in love with a beautiful Parisian girl, Leslie Caron. The music is by George Gershwin, and it is directed by Vincent Minelli, how much classier can you get? The boulevardier cocktail was invented by an American living in Paris, Erskine Gwynne. Gwynne was a writer who founded a monthly magazine called the Boulevardier, published from 1927-1932.

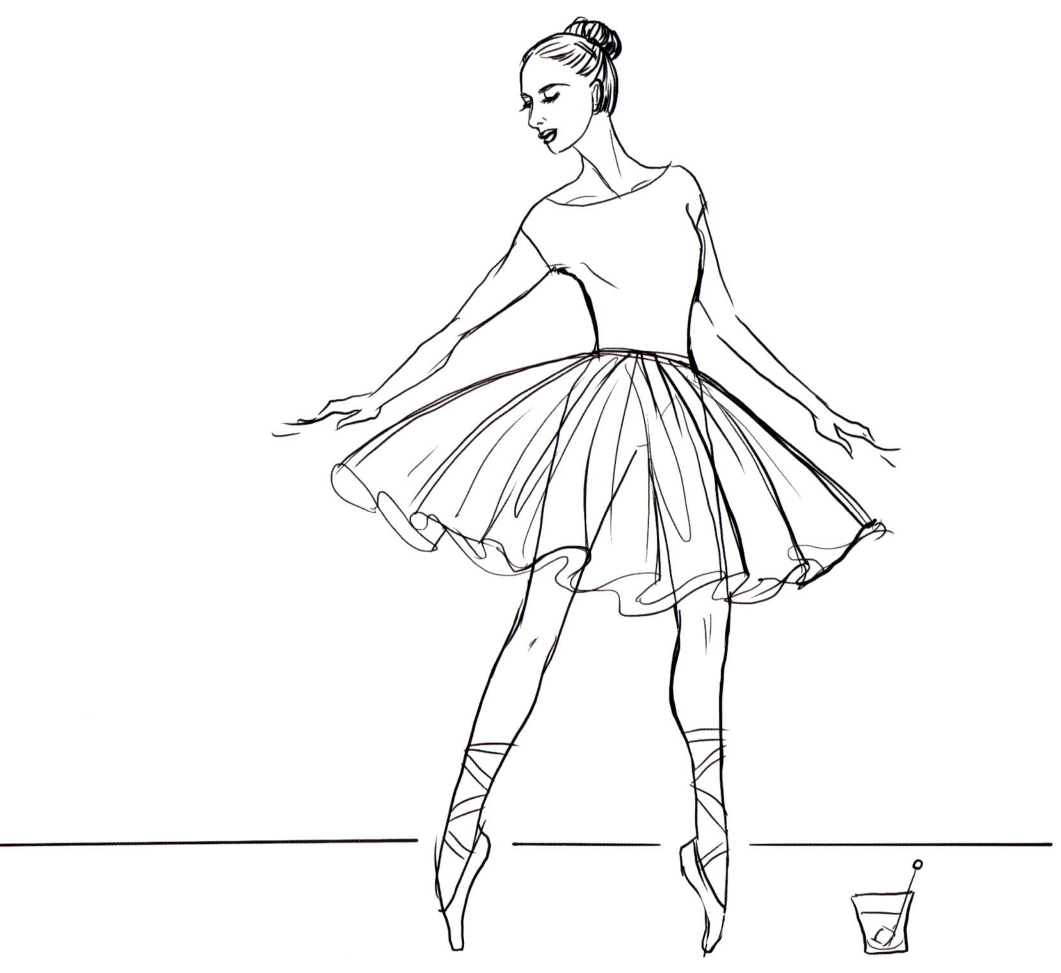

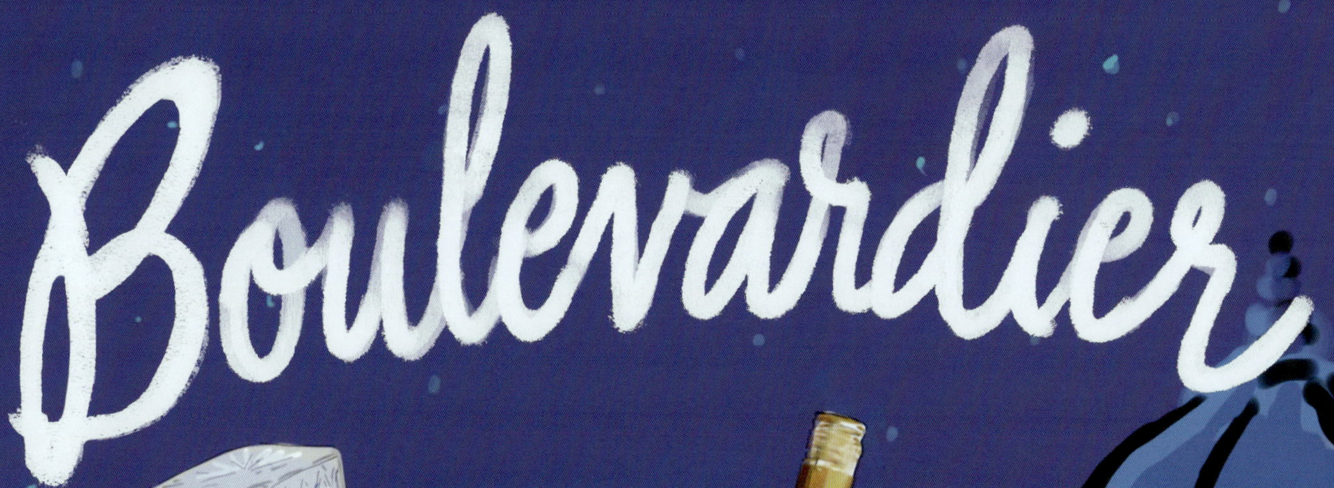

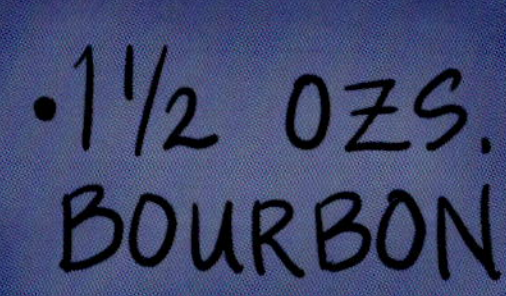

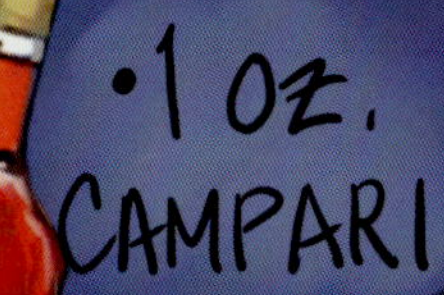

•1 OZ.
SWEET
VERMOUTH

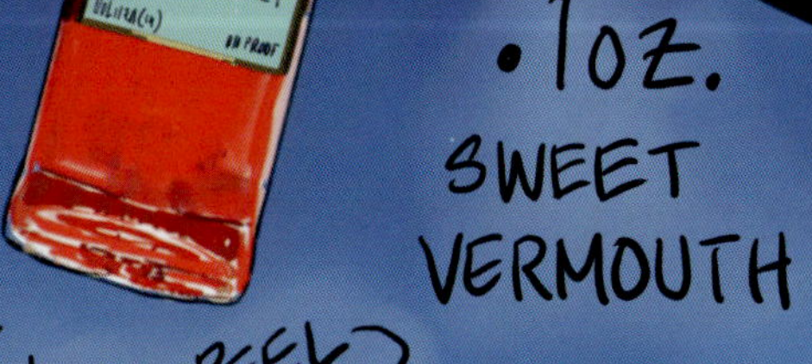

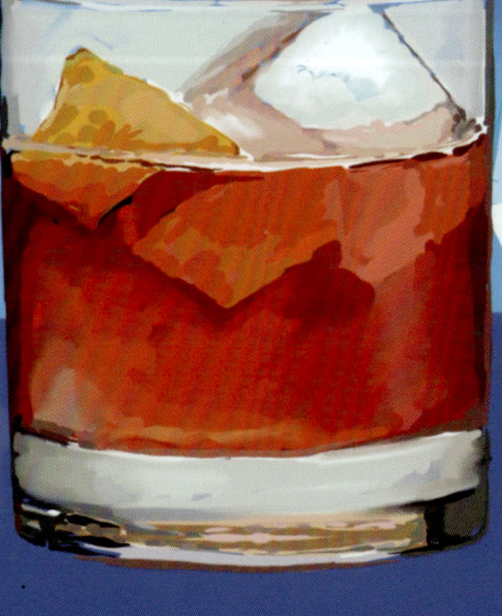

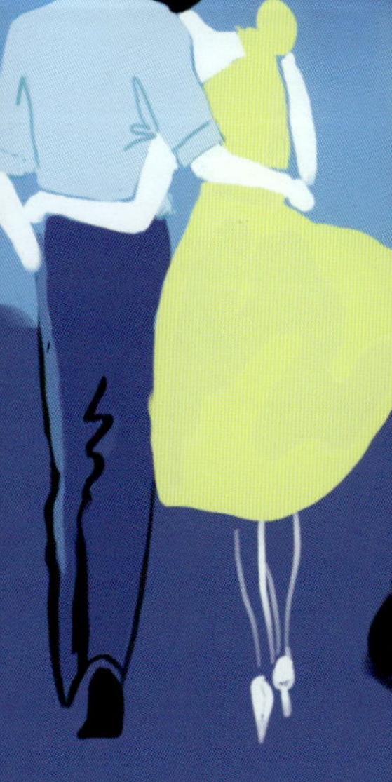

STIR WITH ICE IN A MIXING GLASS. STRAIN INTO WHISKEY GLASS WITH FRESH ICE.

Easy Spiked Cider

Autumn is apple season. Every part of the country has their local favorite pick-your-own orchard where you can gather fresh apples and pick up some cider. Local cider is the best. But, it's fun to make it a bit more interesting by adding some bourbon and honey and stirring it up with a cinnamon stick. What a cozy feeling. It makes a chilly night so much warmer.

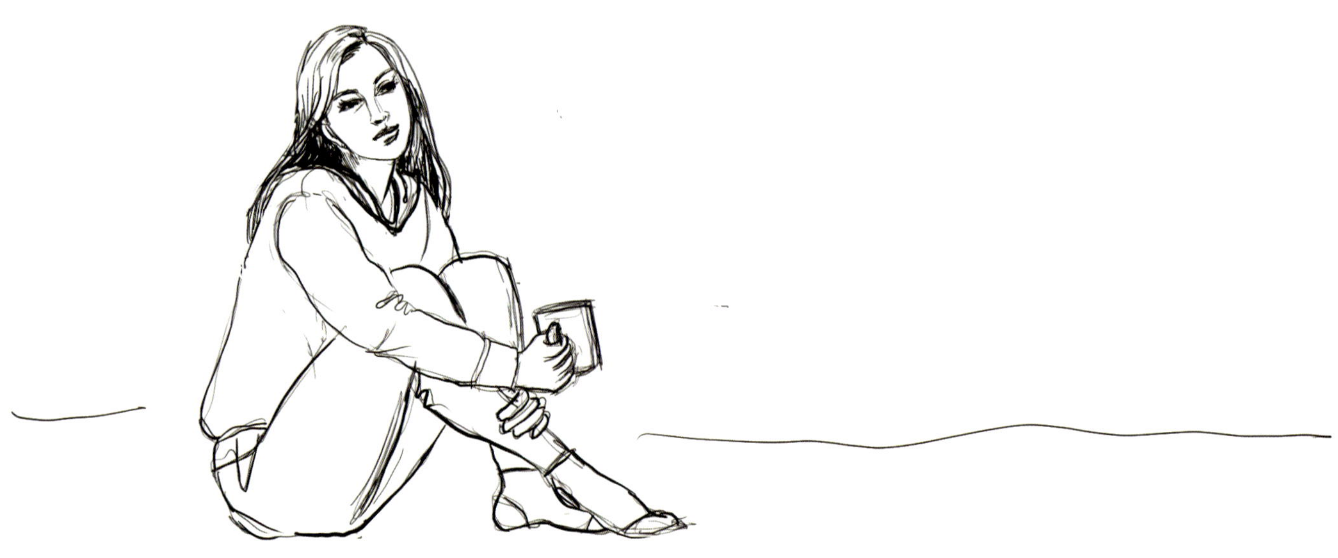

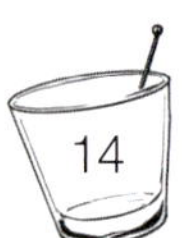

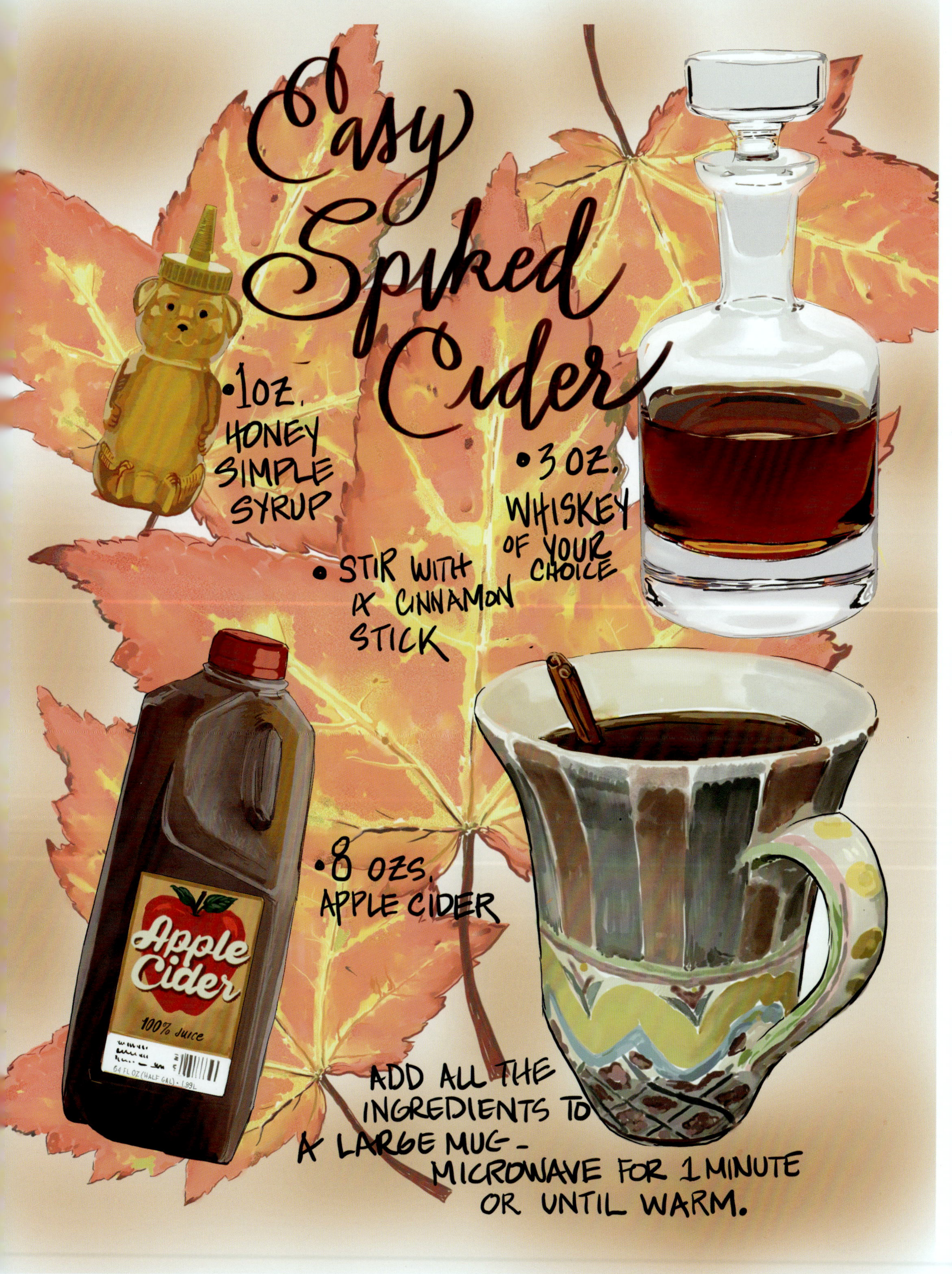

Easy Spiked Cider
•1oz. HONEY SIMPLE SYRUP
•3oz. WHISKEY OF YOUR CHOICE
• STIR WITH A CINNAMON STICK
•8 ozs. APPLE CIDER
Apple Cider
100% Juice
64 FL OZ (HALF GAL) • 1.89L
ADD ALL THE INGREDIENTS TO A LARGE MUG - MICROWAVE FOR 1 MINUTE OR UNTIL WARM.

Irish Coffee

It's cold outside. Snowing, the sky is gray, and it's one of those days where you want nothing more than to just stay inside, curled up in a warm blanket, with that book you have been wanting to read (or a show to binge watch) and a nice, hot beverage. Something with cream and coffee… and more. And if that "more" makes your coffee beverage an Irish Coffee, so much the better.

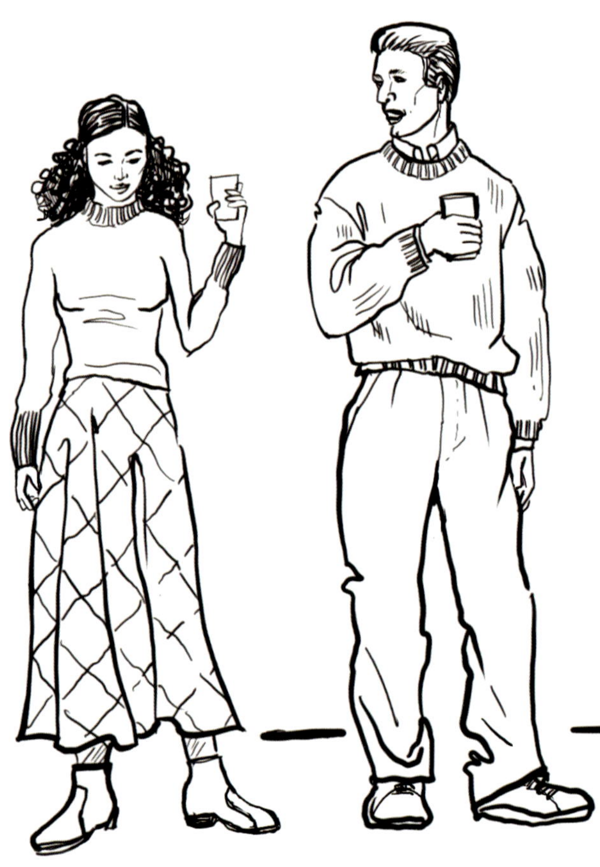

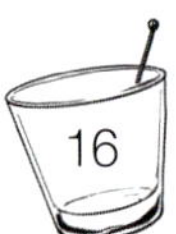

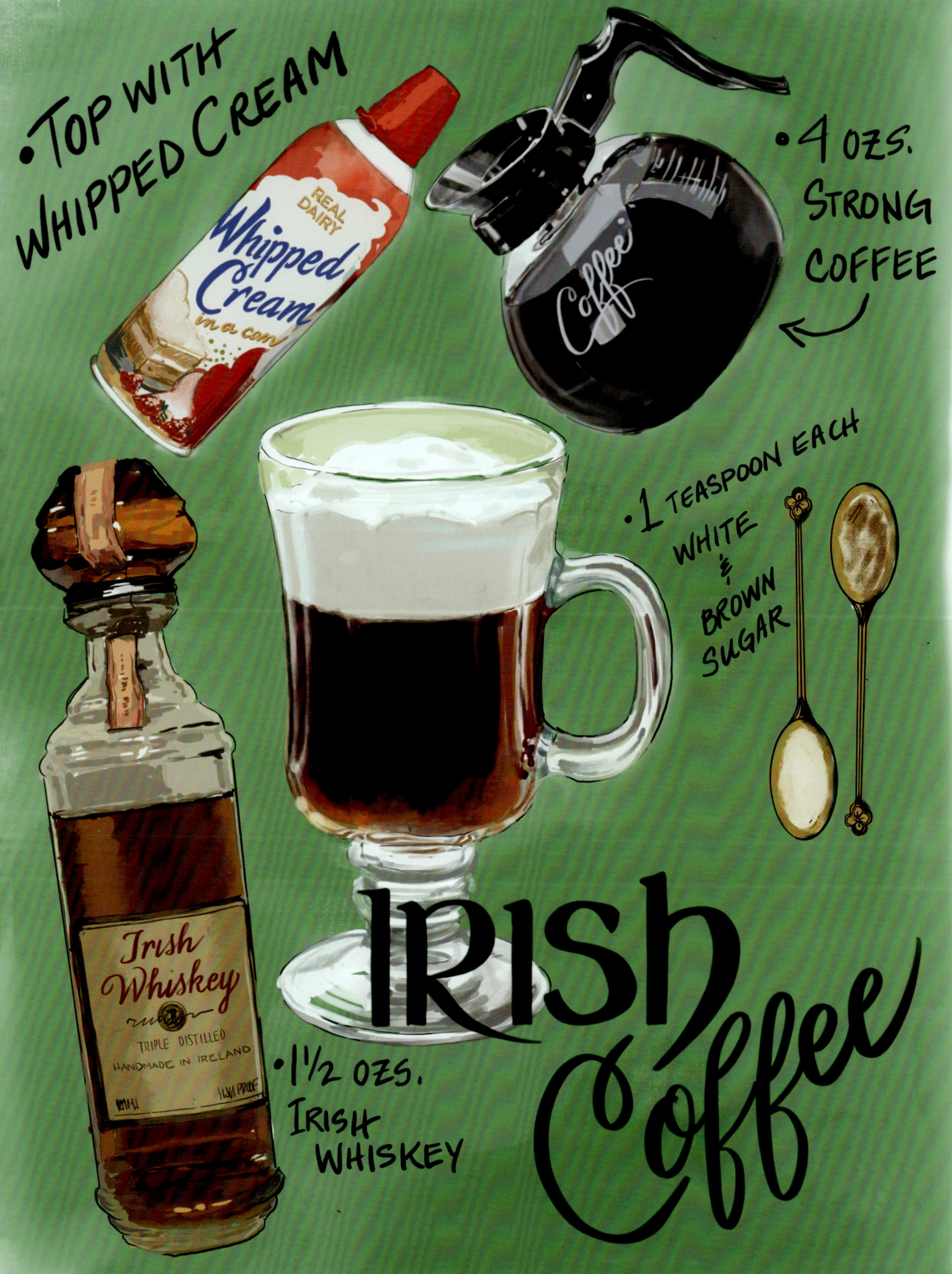

•TOP WITH WHIPPED CREAM
REAL DAIRY
Whipped Cream
in a can
Coffee
•4 OZS. STRONG COFFEE
•1 TEASPOON EACH WHITE & BROWN SUGAR
Irish Whiskey
TRIPLE DISTILLED
HANDMADE IN IRELAND
•1½ OZS. IRISH WHISKEY
IRISH Coffee

Lynchburg Lemonade

My dad was in the business of selling decorated glassware. He worked with some exceptionally fine distilleries, one of which was Jack Daniels. Back in the 1970's my dad decided to take the family on a road trip to Lynchburg Tennessee, where this famous whiskey is made. He had to meet with his client, and we got a tour of the plant. After that, we were served a glass of lemonade. Just. Lemonade. Lynchburg, believe it or not, is a dry county.

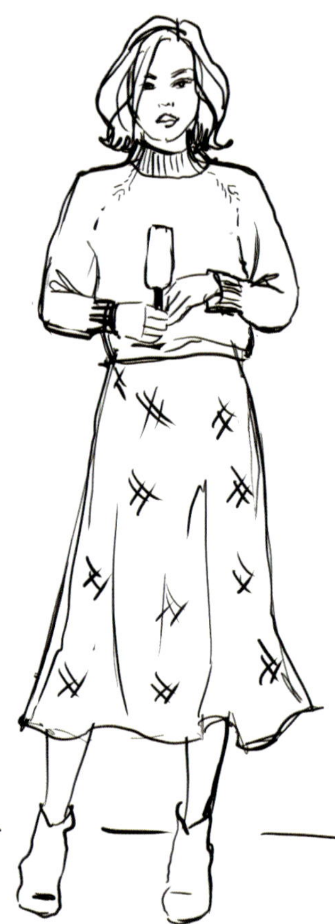

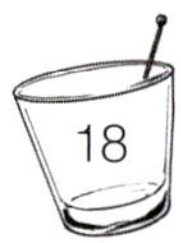

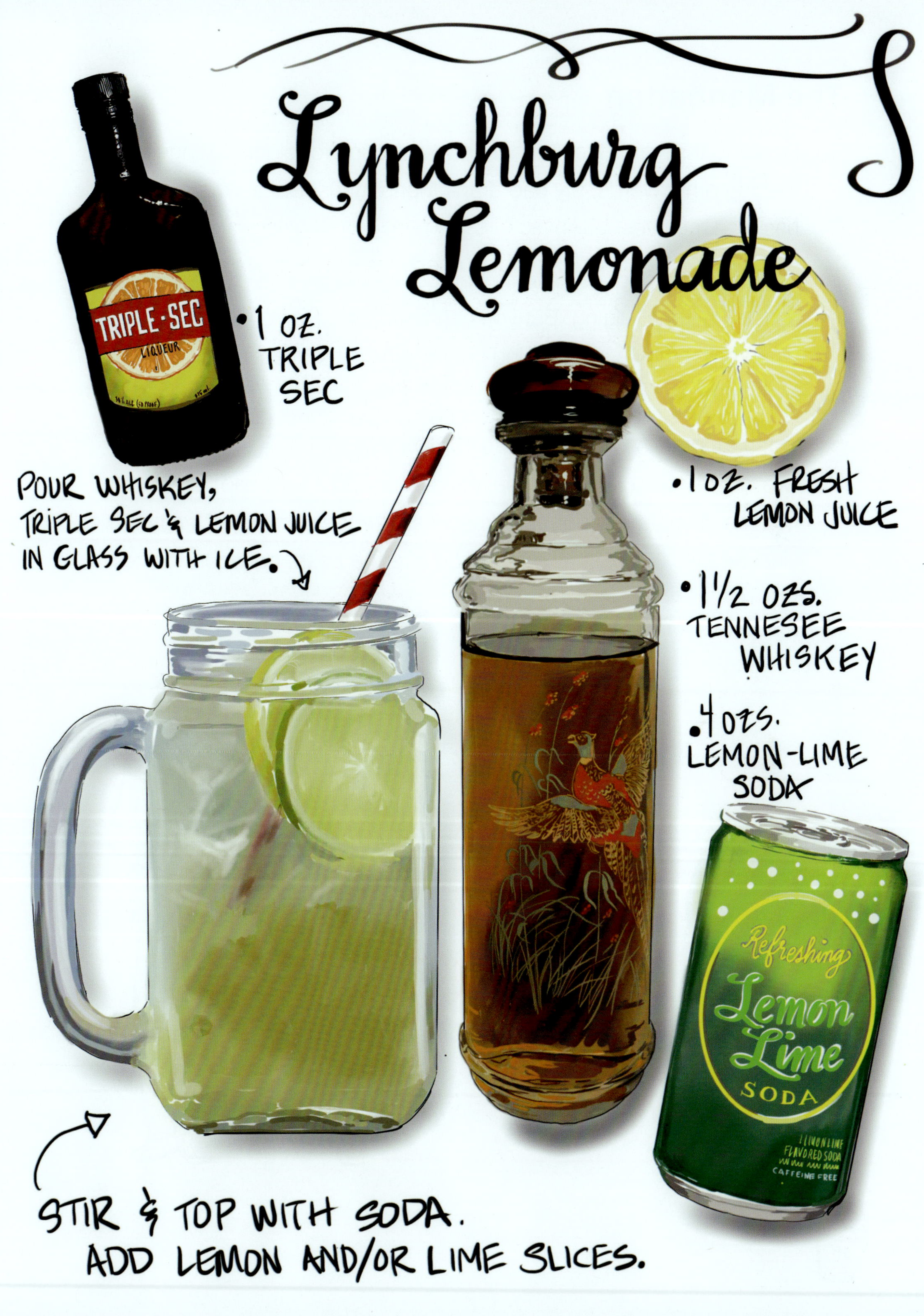
Lynchburg Lemonade
TRIPLE-SEC
LIQUEUR
•1 OZ. TRIPLE SEC
POUR WHISKEY, TRIPLE SEC & LEMON JUICE IN GLASS WITH ICE.
•1 OZ. FRESH LEMON JUICE
•1½ OZS. TENNESEE WHISKEY
•4 OZS. LEMON-LIME SODA
Refreshing
Lemon Lime
SODA
CAFFEINE FREE
STIR & TOP WITH SODA.
ADD LEMON AND/OR LIME SLICES.

The Manhattan

I used to think that the Manhattan was a drink for older, distinguished men. In other words, my dad drank Manhattans. But it's deep rich flavor has won me over.

It is also named for my favorite borough of my favorite city. It is as iconic as the Flatiron Building. But you can't drink the Flatiron Building, even when topped by a maraschino cherry, which is a must garnish for a Manhattan.

Tip: Vermouth is primarily made from wine, so it has a short shelf life, two weeks tops. Store it in the refrigerator and it will keep for up to two months. If you are in doubt of freshness, try the sniff test. If it smells like vinegar, then it is past its prime. Add it to the trash, not your cocktail.

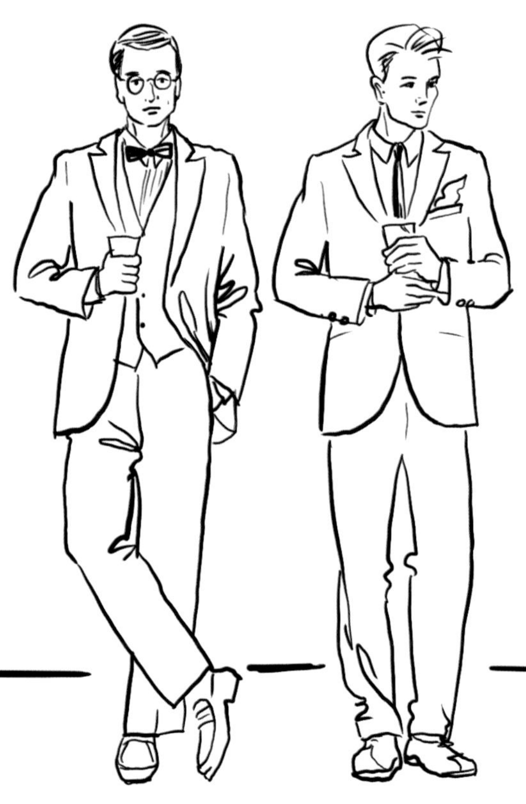

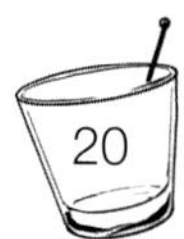

COMBINE WHISKEY, VERMOUTH, & BITTERS IN A MIXING GLASS WITH ICE. STIR GENTLY & STRAIN INTO A CHILLED COCKTAIL GLASS & ADD A CHERRY.

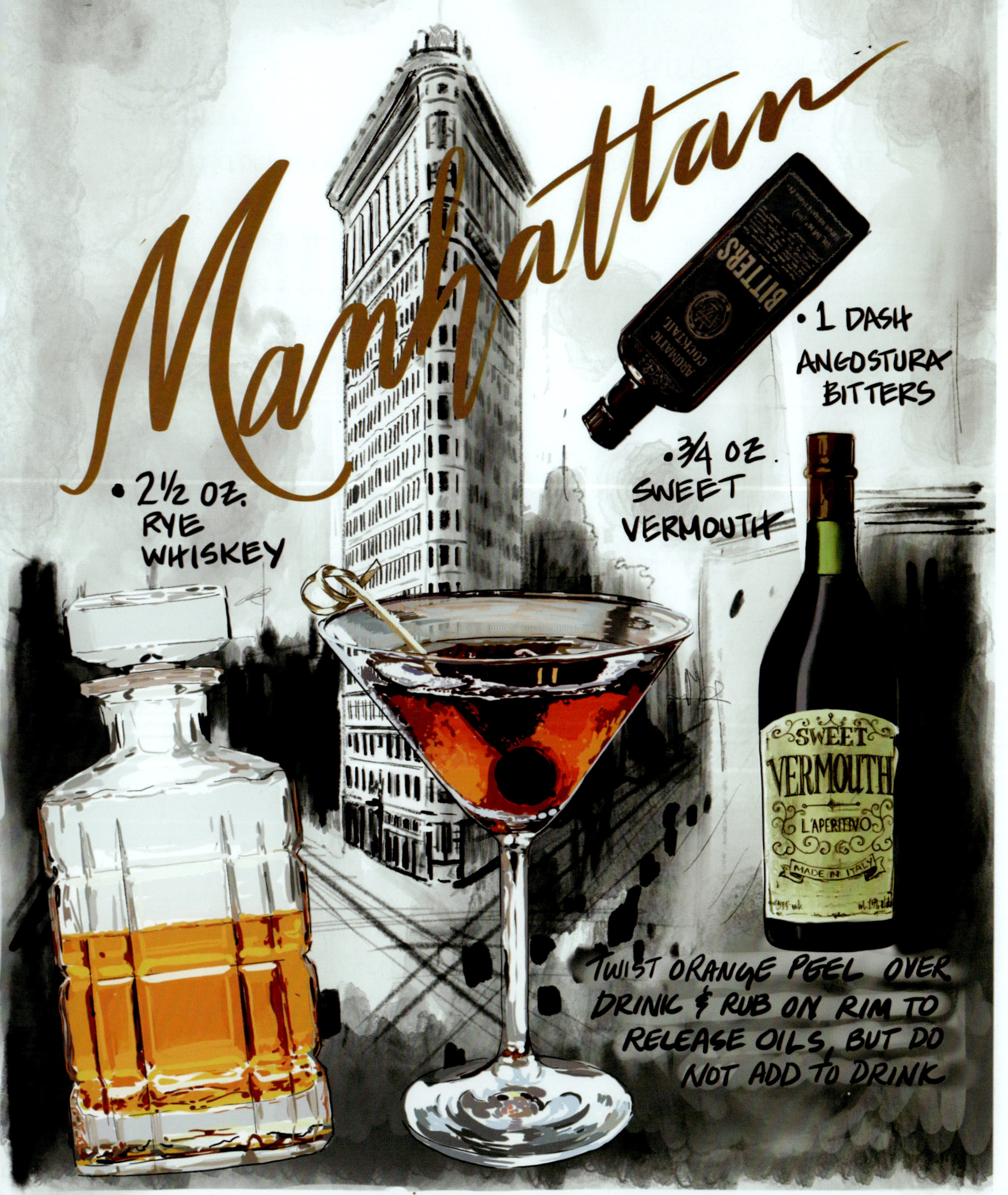

Mint Julep

The Kentucky Derby is known for thoroughbred horses, big parties, even bigger hats, and the Mint Julep. The Mint Julep is a mix of Kentucky Bourbon, fresh mint, simple syrup, and lots of ice. It is traditionally served in a silver cup because metal cups keep the drink icy longer and it's hot in Louisville in May. I may be watching the race on my TV, but I'm enjoying the Mint Julep with the rest of America.

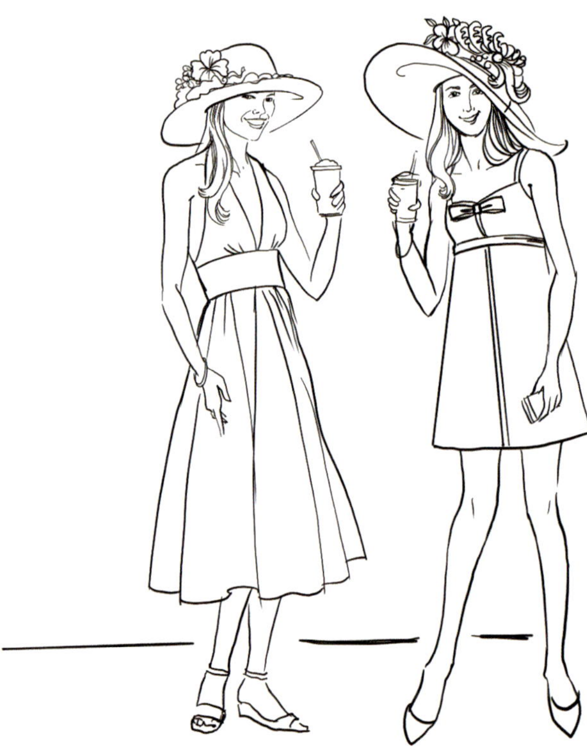

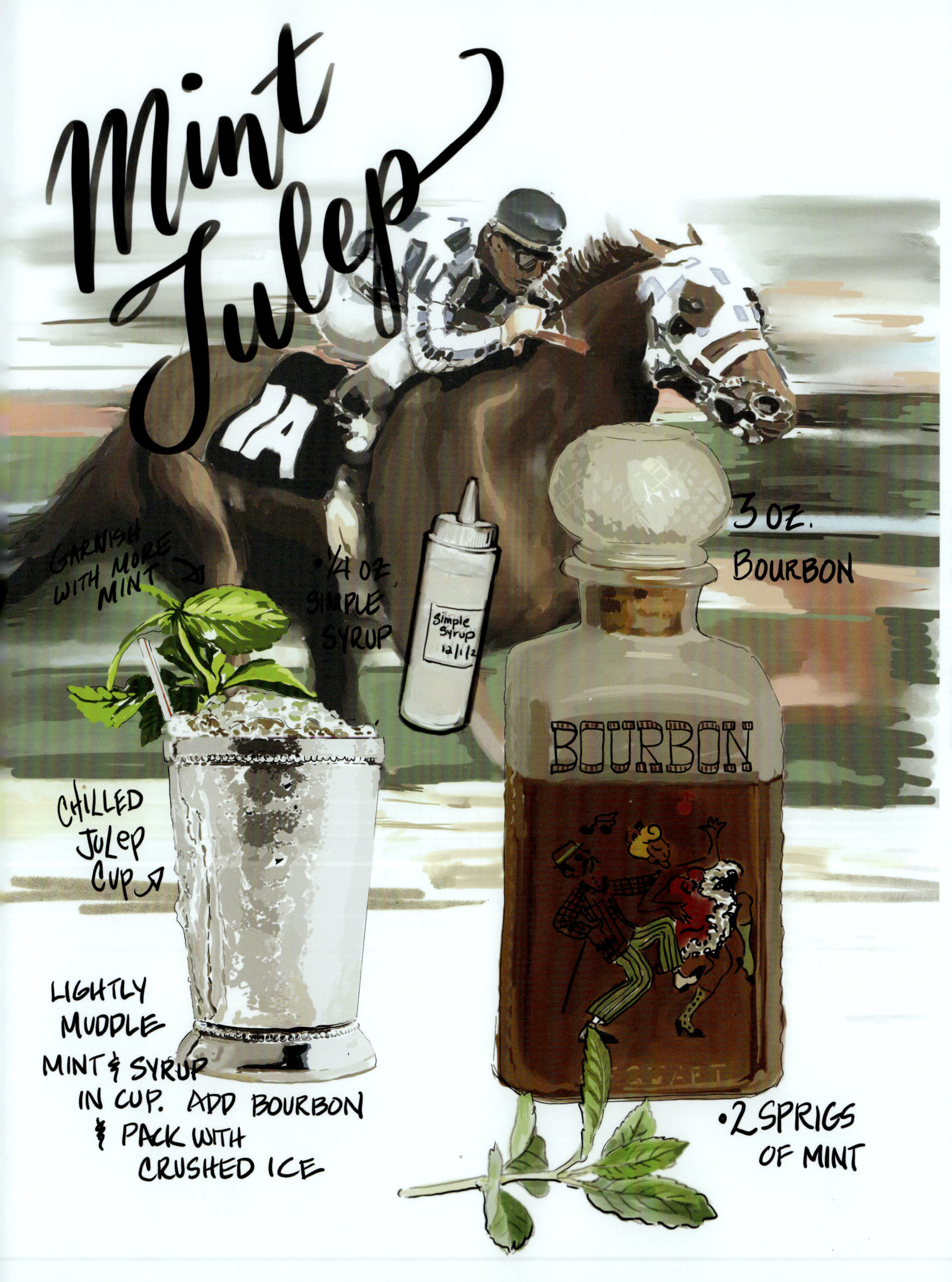
Mint Julep
GARNISH WITH MORE MINT
•1/4 OZ. SIMPLE SYRUP
Simple Syrup 12/1/12
3 OZ. BOURBON
BOURBON
CHILLED JULEP CUP
LIGHTLY MUDDLE MINT & SYRUP IN CUP. ADD BOURBON & PACK WITH CRUSHED ICE
•2 SPRIGS OF MINT

Old Fashioned

This is where this whole project started. I was binge watching *Mad Men* and Don Draper ordered this classic cocktail. I started to draw. I found myself drawing the recipe for the Old Fashioned, inspired by the mid-century motifs of one of television's most stylish — and stylized — shows. This is still one of my favorite drawings.

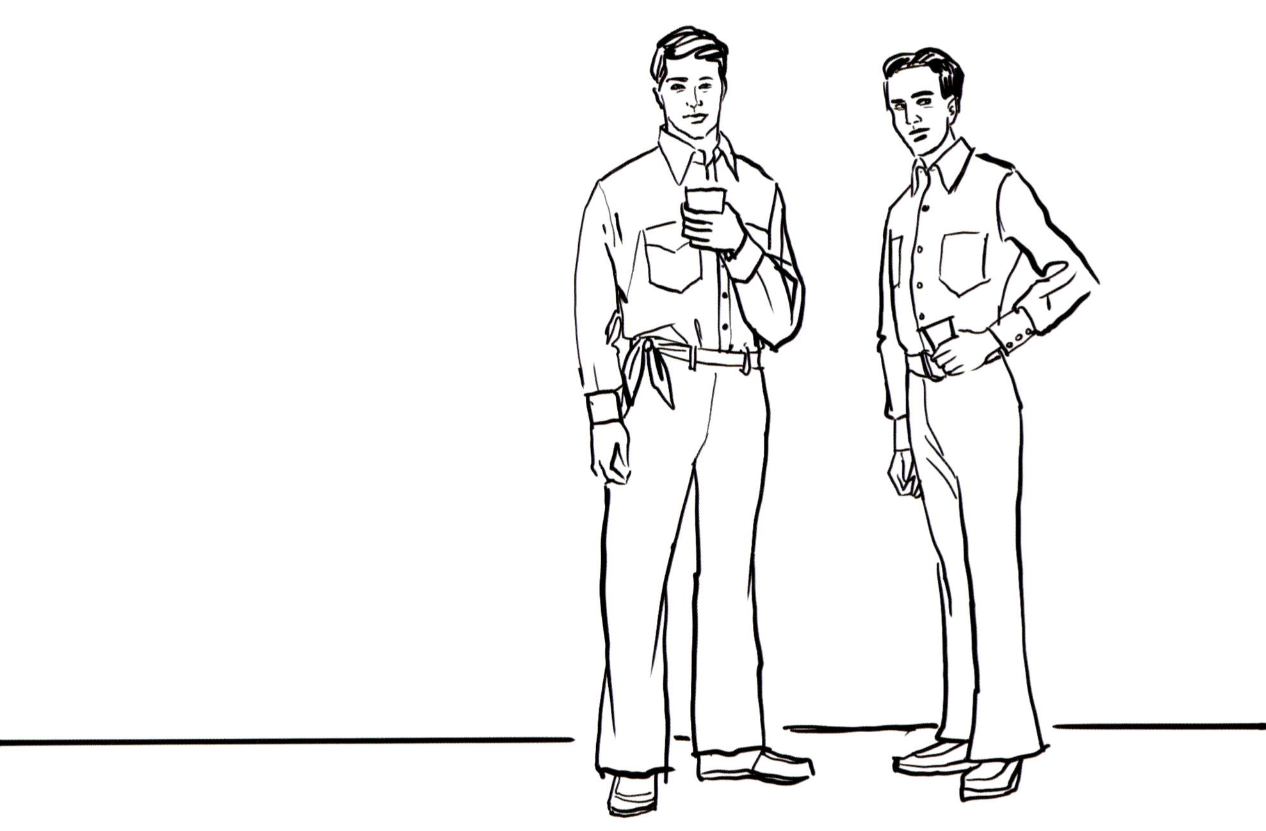

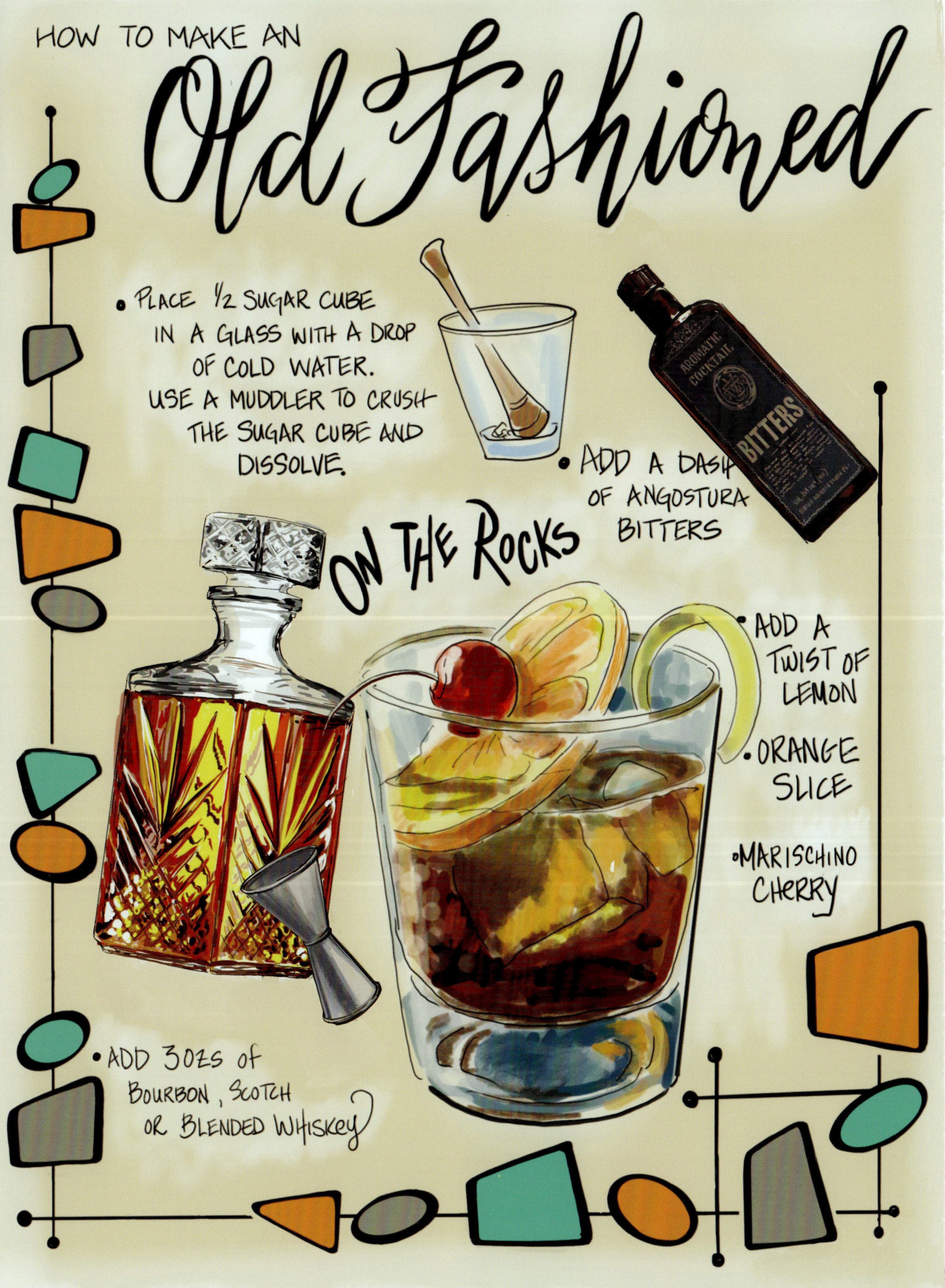
HOW TO MAKE AN
Old Fashioned
• PLACE 1/2 SUGAR CUBE IN A GLASS WITH A DROP OF COLD WATER. USE A MUDDLER TO CRUSH THE SUGAR CUBE AND DISSOLVE.
AROMATIC COCKTAIL
BITTERS
• ADD A DASH OF ANGOSTURA BITTERS
ON THE ROCKS
• ADD A TWIST OF LEMON
• ORANGE SLICE
• MARISCHINO CHERRY
• ADD 3OZS OF BOURBON, SCOTCH OR BLENDED WHISKEY

Penicillin

Ginger is a wonder. It has amazing qualities. It aids in digestion and is good for your heart and lungs. Honey has been used for centuries to help fight colds. Add a couple of different kinds of scotch and some lemon juice to the mix and you have a cure. I know, I'm no doctor but what could it hurt? But please never mix alcohol with medication. That goes without saying.

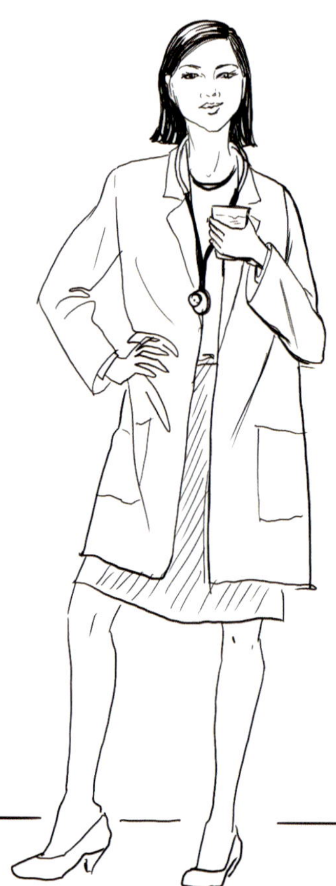

PENICILLIN

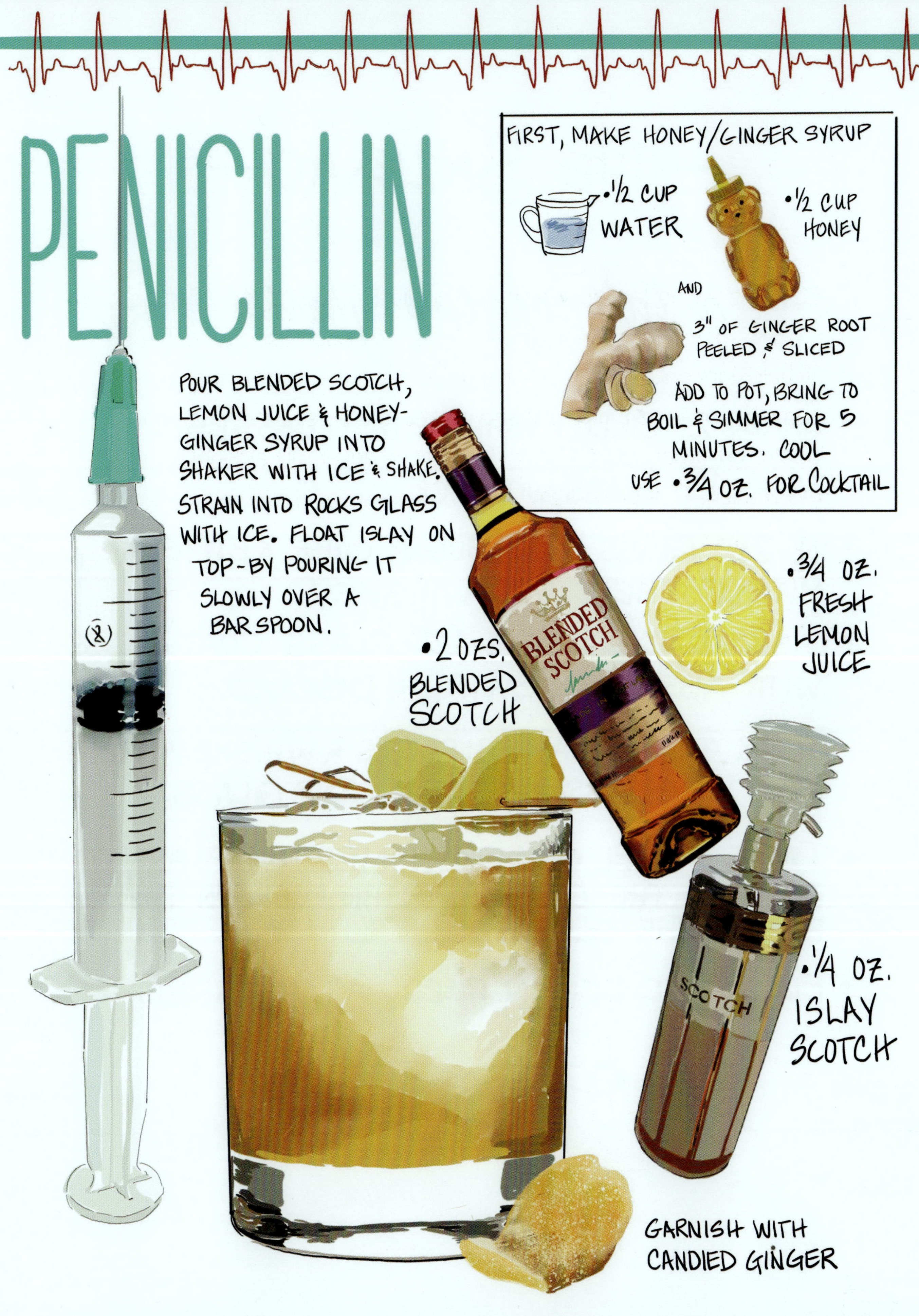

FIRST, MAKE HONEY/GINGER SYRUP
•1/2 CUP WATER
•1/2 CUP HONEY
AND
3" OF GINGER ROOT PEELED & SLICED
ADD TO POT, BRING TO BOIL & SIMMER FOR 5 MINUTES. COOL
USE •3/4 OZ. FOR COCKTAIL
POUR BLENDED SCOTCH, LEMON JUICE & HONEY-GINGER SYRUP INTO SHAKER WITH ICE & SHAKE. STRAIN INTO ROCKS GLASS WITH ICE. FLOAT ISLAY ON TOP-BY POURING IT SLOWLY OVER A BAR SPOON.
•2 OZS. BLENDED SCOTCH
BLENDED SCOTCH
•3/4 OZ. FRESH LEMON JUICE
SCOTCH
•1/4 OZ. ISLAY SCOTCH
GARNISH WITH CANDIED GINGER

– THE SAZERAC –

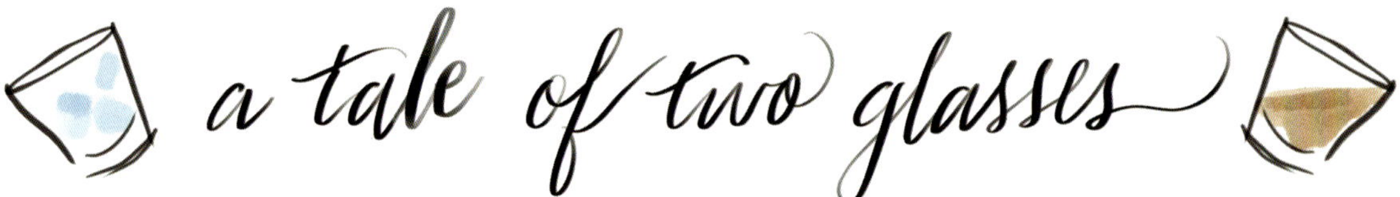

- GRAB 2 OLD FASHIONED GLASSES.
- PACK 1st GLASS WITH ICE
- IN 2ND GLASS, ADD SUGAR CUBE & BITTERS, MUDDLE, THEN ADD WHISKEY.
- DISCARD ICE FROM 1st GLASS COAT GLASS WITH ABSINTHE, SWIRL & DISCARD.
- POUR THE SUGAR, BITTERS & WHISKEY FROM THE 1st GLASS INTO THE 2ND GLASS.
- TWIST A PEEL OF LEMON INTO THE GLASS TO RELEASE THE OILS & RUB THE PEEL ON THE RIM OF THE GLASS.
- FLOAT THE LEMON PEEL, AS A GARNISH!

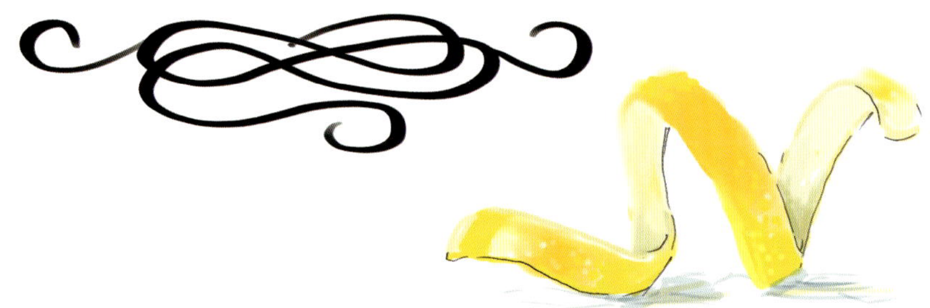

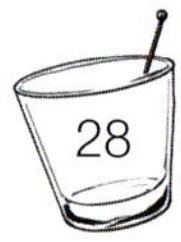

The Sazerac

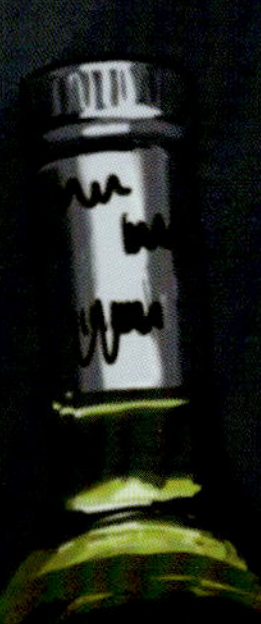

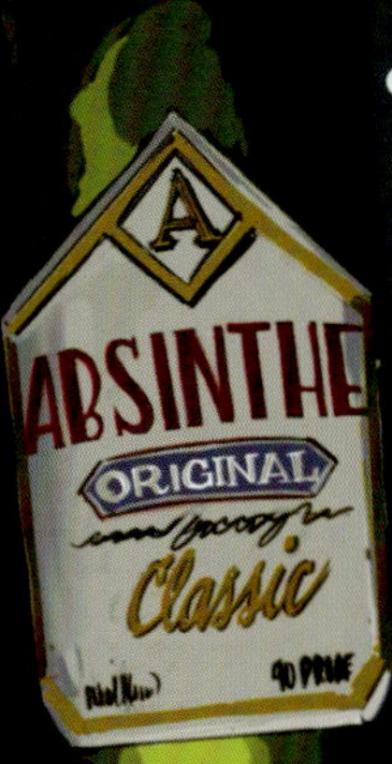

- 1/4 oz. Absinthe

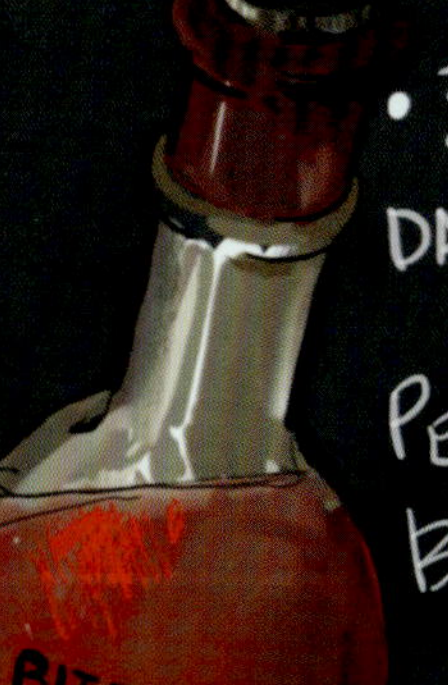

- 3 dashes of Peychaud's Bitters

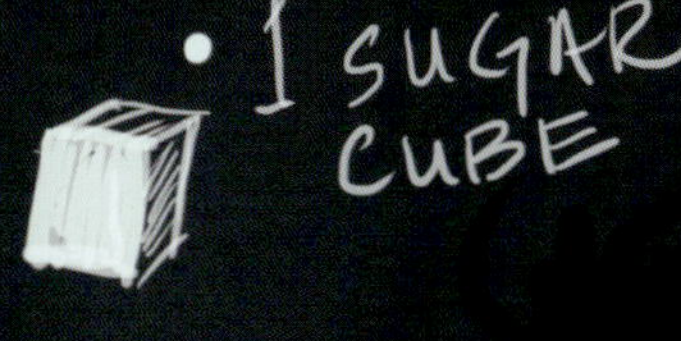

- 1 sugar cube

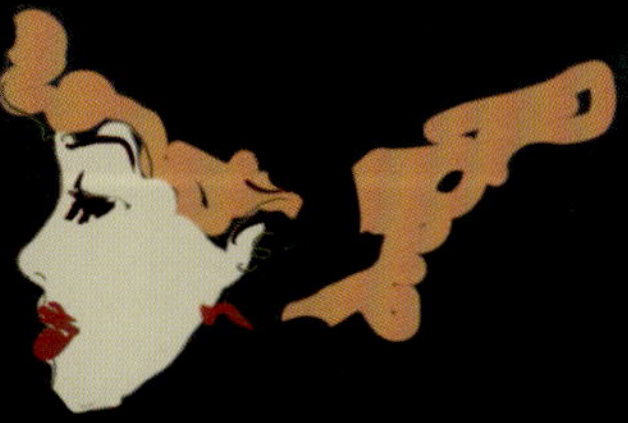

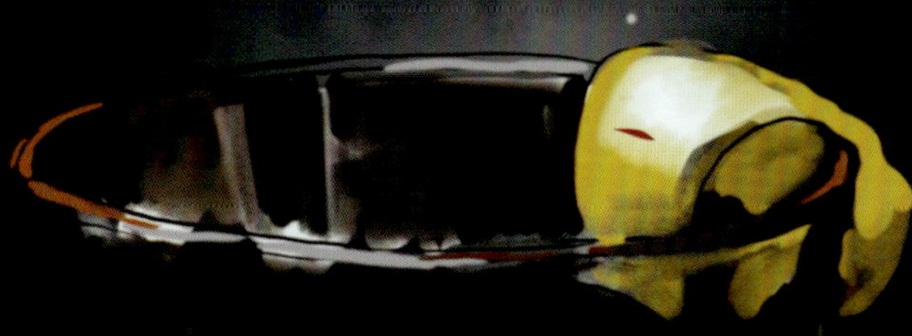

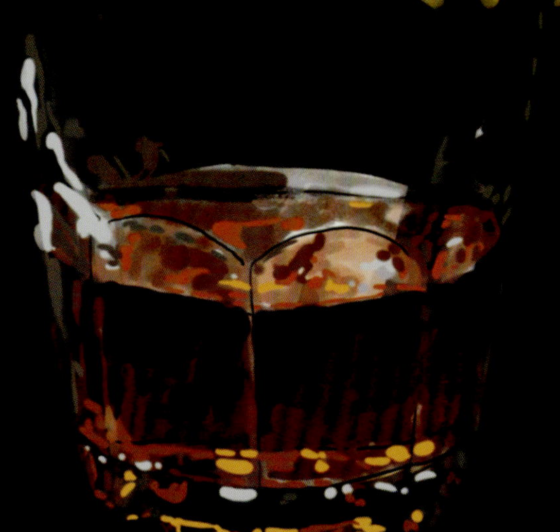

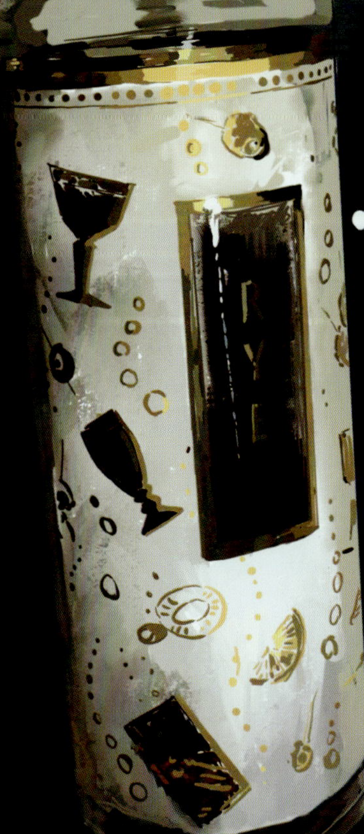

- 1 3/4 oz Rye Whiskey

Whiskey Sour

When I drink a Whiskey Sour I feel like I should be sitting a little bit straighter, that my hair needs to be perfectly coiffed and that I should be wearing pearls. And smoking – or at least holding – a cigarette. In other words, I should be *Mad Men's* Betty Draper. Like Betty, a Whiskey Sour is refreshment with a "kick". And for an extra kick, add an egg white to your shaker with the other ingredients. The results are well worth it.

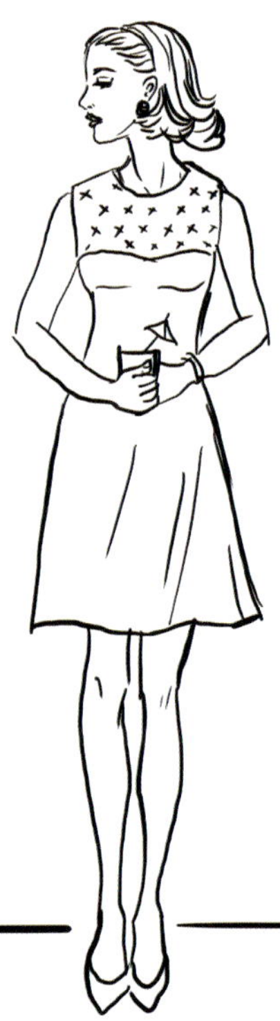

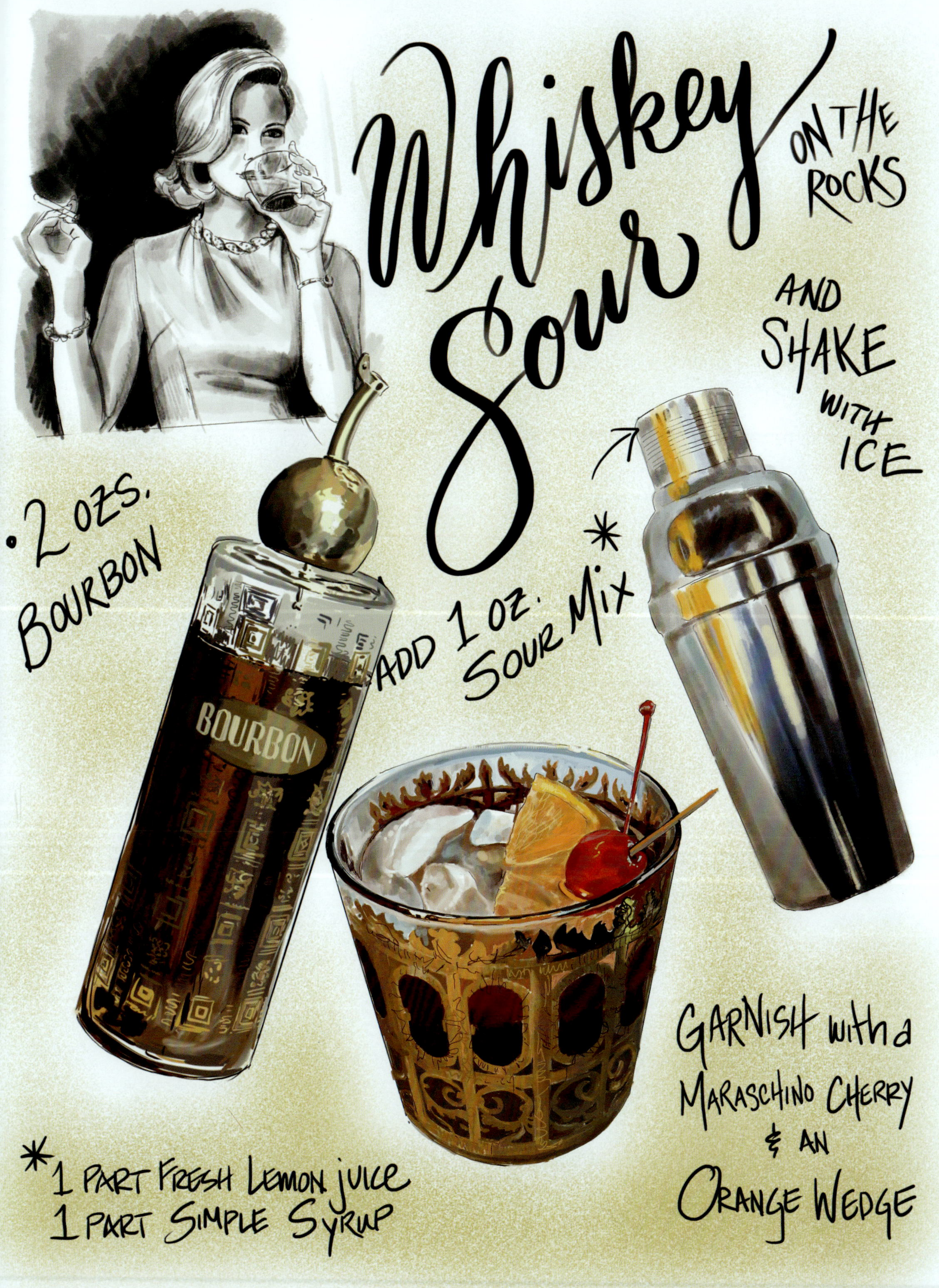
Whiskey Sour
ON THE ROCKS
•2 OZS.
BOURBON
BOURBON
ADD 1 OZ.
SOUR MIX
*
AND
SHAKE
WITH
ICE
GARNISH with a
MARASCHINO CHERRY
& AN
ORANGE WEDGE
* 1 PART FRESH LEMON JUICE
1 PART SIMPLE SYRUP

"The only time I ever enjoyed ironing was the day I accidentally got gin in the steam iron."

—Phyllis DIller

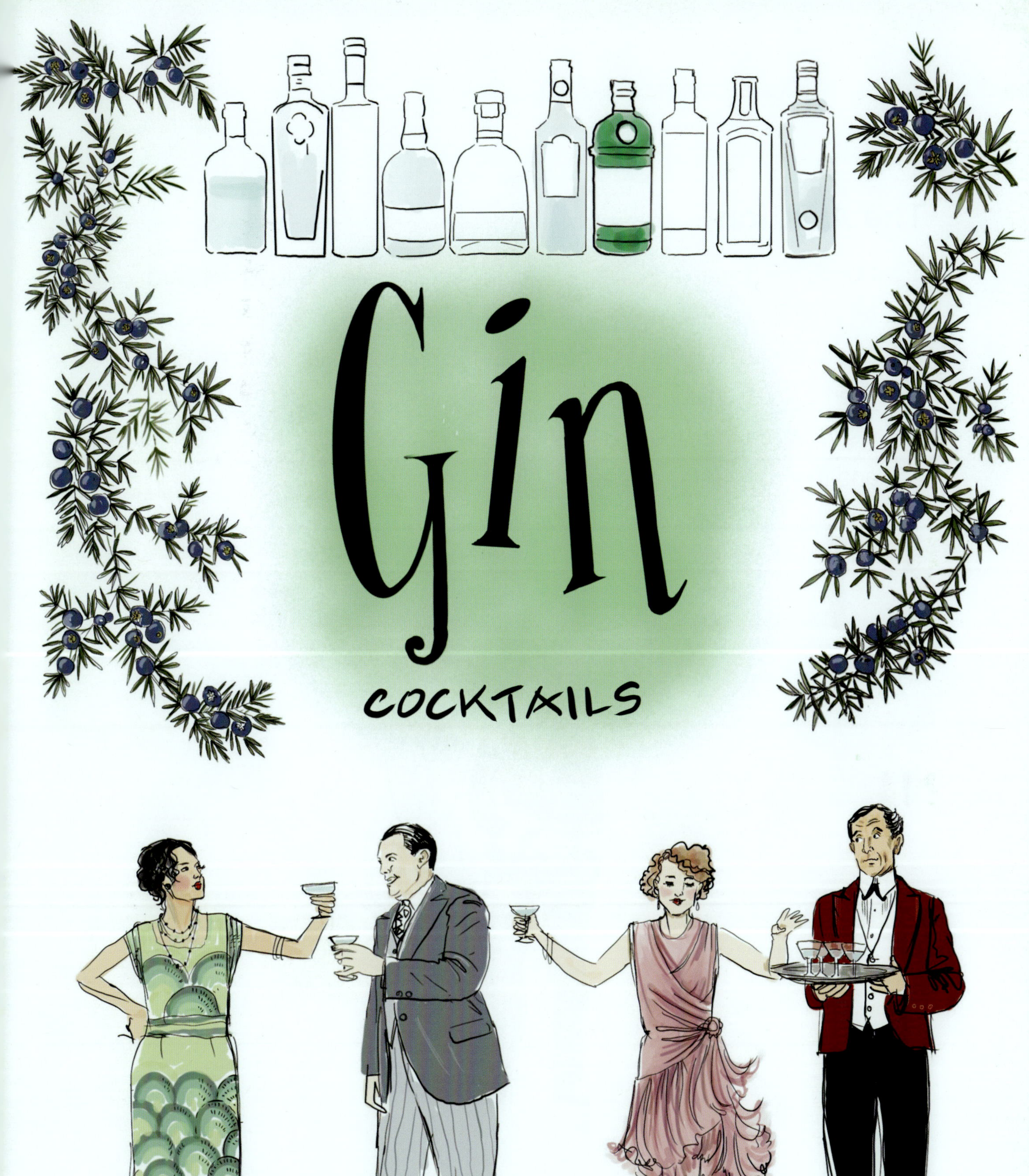
Gin
COCKTAILS

The Aviation

During the golden age of air travel, the service and the food onboard an airplane were as good as in any fine restaurant. A flight attendant could mix any cocktail you could want. Except for the Aviation Cocktail. Crème de Violette was difficult to obtain, and by the 1960's had all but disappeared from the U.S. market. That all changed in the 21st century and this cocktail (as well as the gin that is named for it) is once again popular. But a warning, not too heavy on the purple liqueur or your drink will taste soapy.

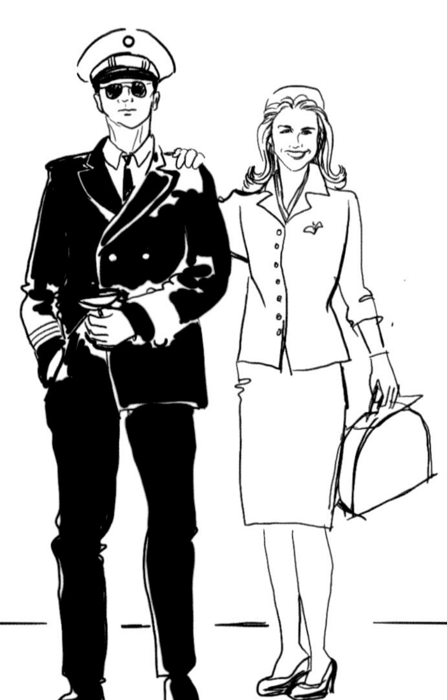

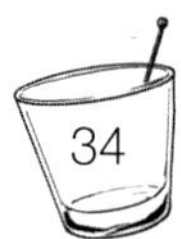

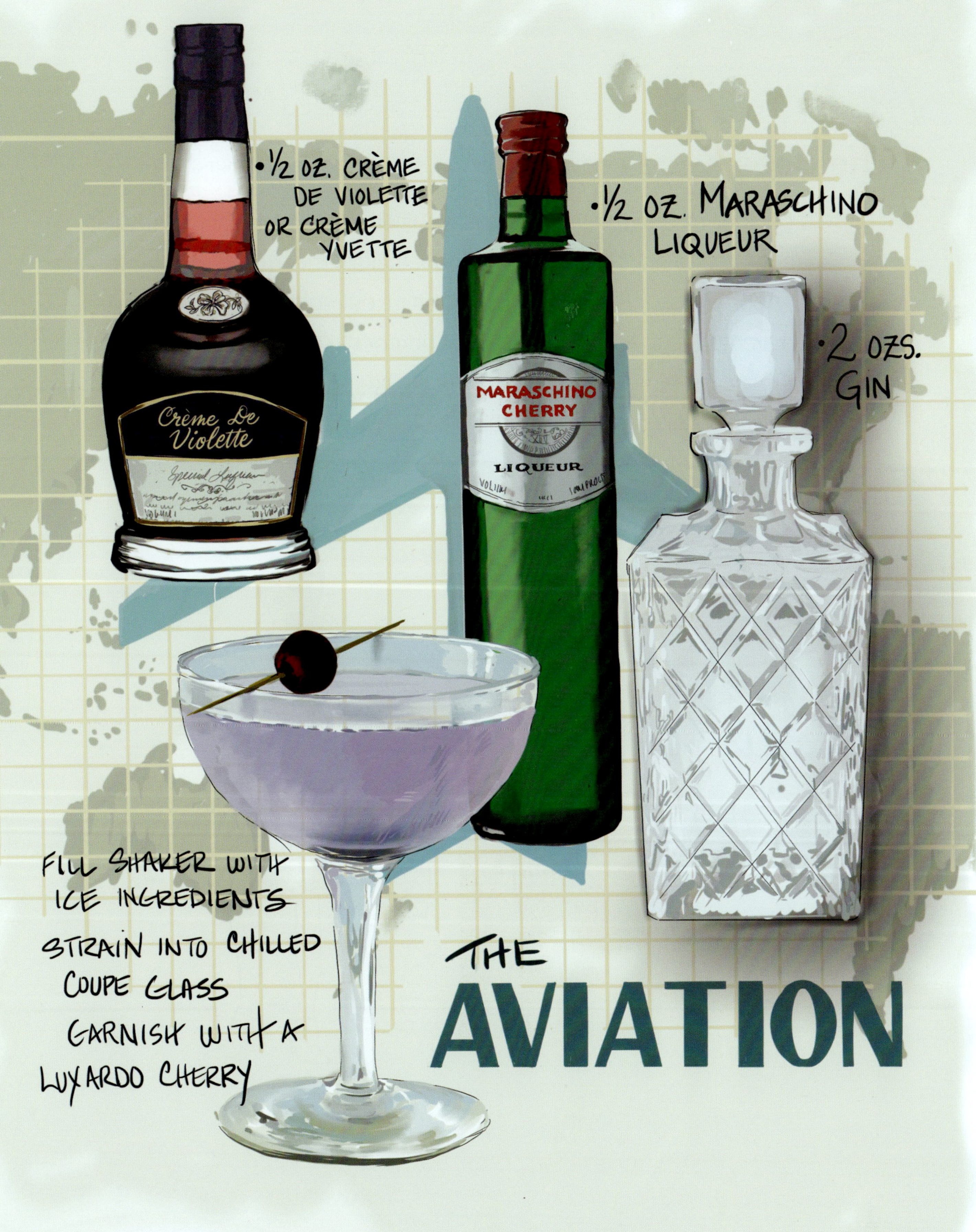

•½ OZ. CRÈME DE VIOLETTE OR CRÈME YVETTE
•½ OZ. MARASCHINO LIQUEUR
•2 OZS. GIN
Crème De Violette
MARASCHINO CHERRY
LIQUEUR
FILL SHAKER WITH ICE INGREDIENTS
STRAIN INTO CHILLED COUPE GLASS
GARNISH WITH A LUXARDO CHERRY
THE AVIATION

The Bees Knees

This cocktail makes me think of speakeasies and prohibition. "Bathtub" Gin (homemade spirits made using industrial alcohol mixed with water and juniper berry juice for flavoring) was plentiful during the era, and cocktails were invented to mask the bad taste and poor quality of the spirits. This cocktail made with gin and lemon was all the rage, but what makes this drink so special is the simple syrup made from honey instead of sugar.

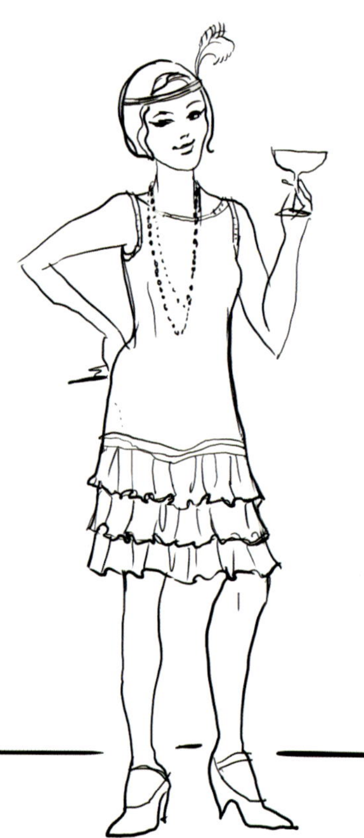

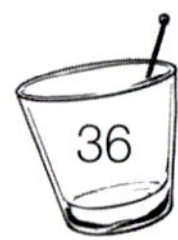

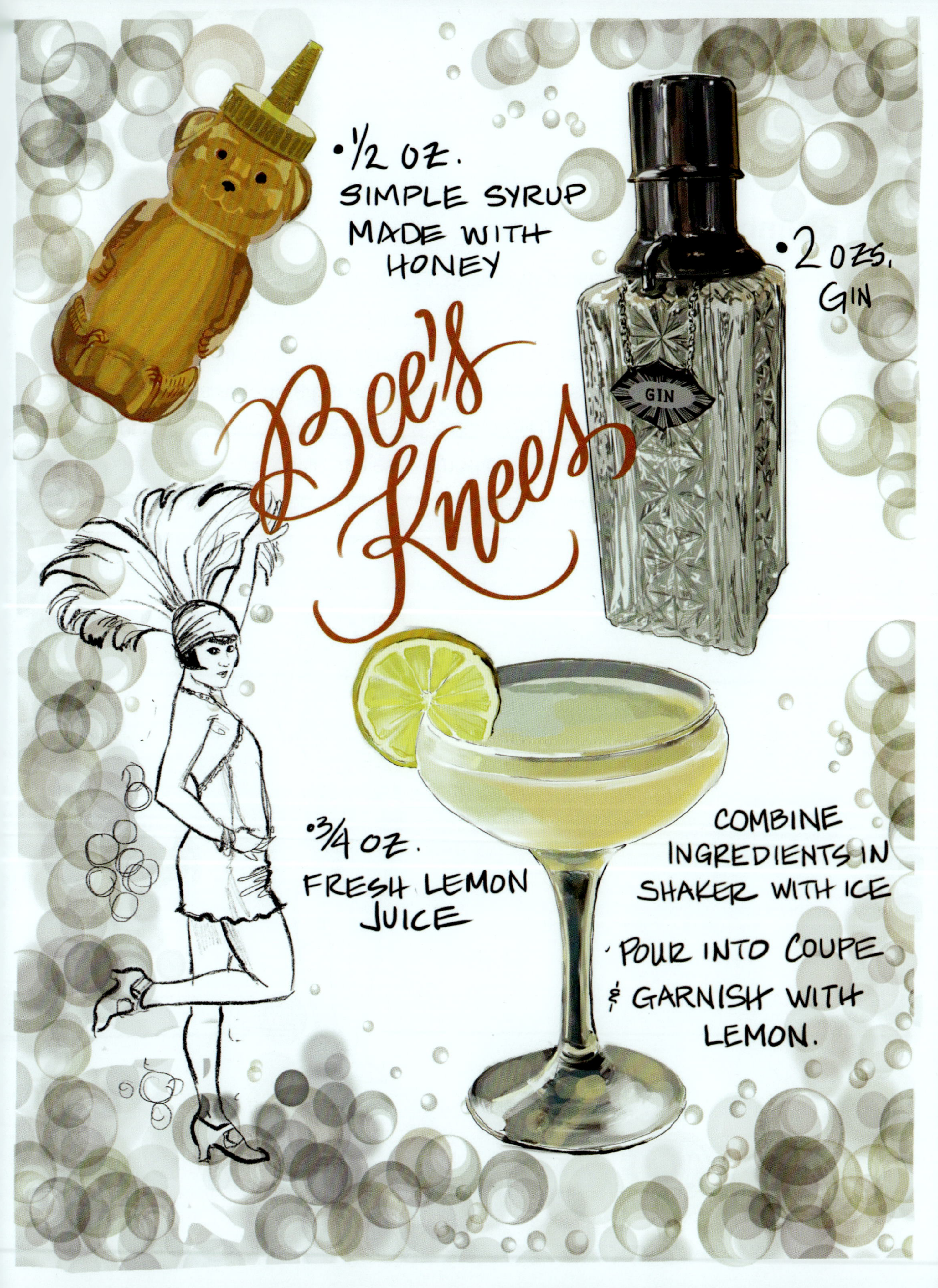
•1/2 OZ.
SIMPLE SYRUP
MADE WITH
HONEY
•2 OZS.
GIN
GIN
Bee's Knees
•3/4 OZ.
FRESH LEMON
JUICE
COMBINE
INGREDIENTS IN
SHAKER WITH ICE
· POUR INTO COUPE
& GARNISH WITH
LEMON.

Bramble

July in Missouri is blackberry season. For as long as I can remember, I have taken my daughters to our pick-your-own orchard to pick blackberries. We harvest so many and always have plans to bake them and make jellies, but usually we just end up eating them fresh. Fresh berries are great in so many cocktails, but the Bramble uses blackberry liqueur, which really takes it up a notch. Use lots of ice and garnish this refreshing drink with fresh berries and you will not be disappointed.

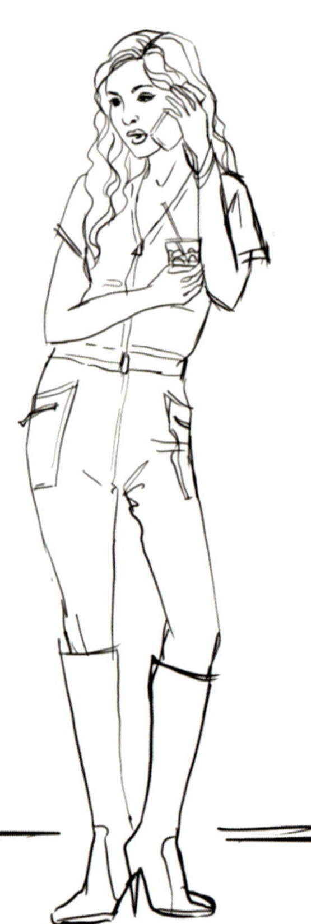

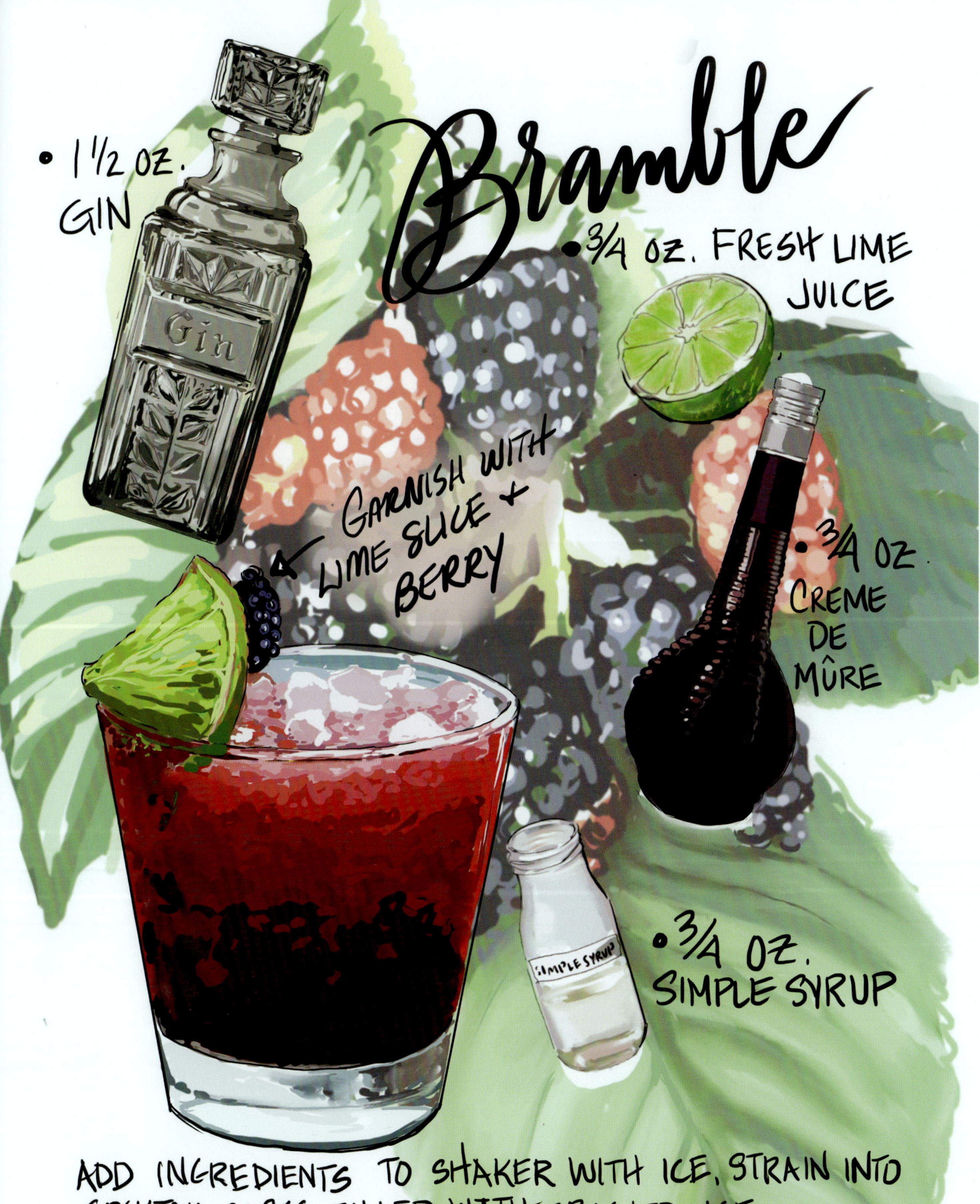

ADD INGREDIENTS TO SHAKER WITH ICE, STRAIN INTO COCKTAIL GLASS FILLED WITH CRUSHED ICE.

Clover Club

Raspberry season? You have got to try this drink. I know making the Raspberry syrup is a bit of a fuss, but it's worth the effort. Plus, this raspberry sauce is divine on vanilla ice cream, just saying. This drink is also pretty, and it is pink. That is a bonus!

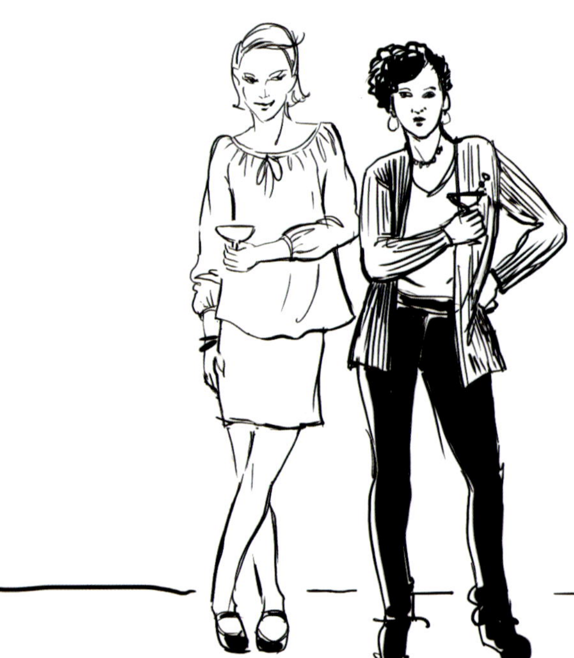

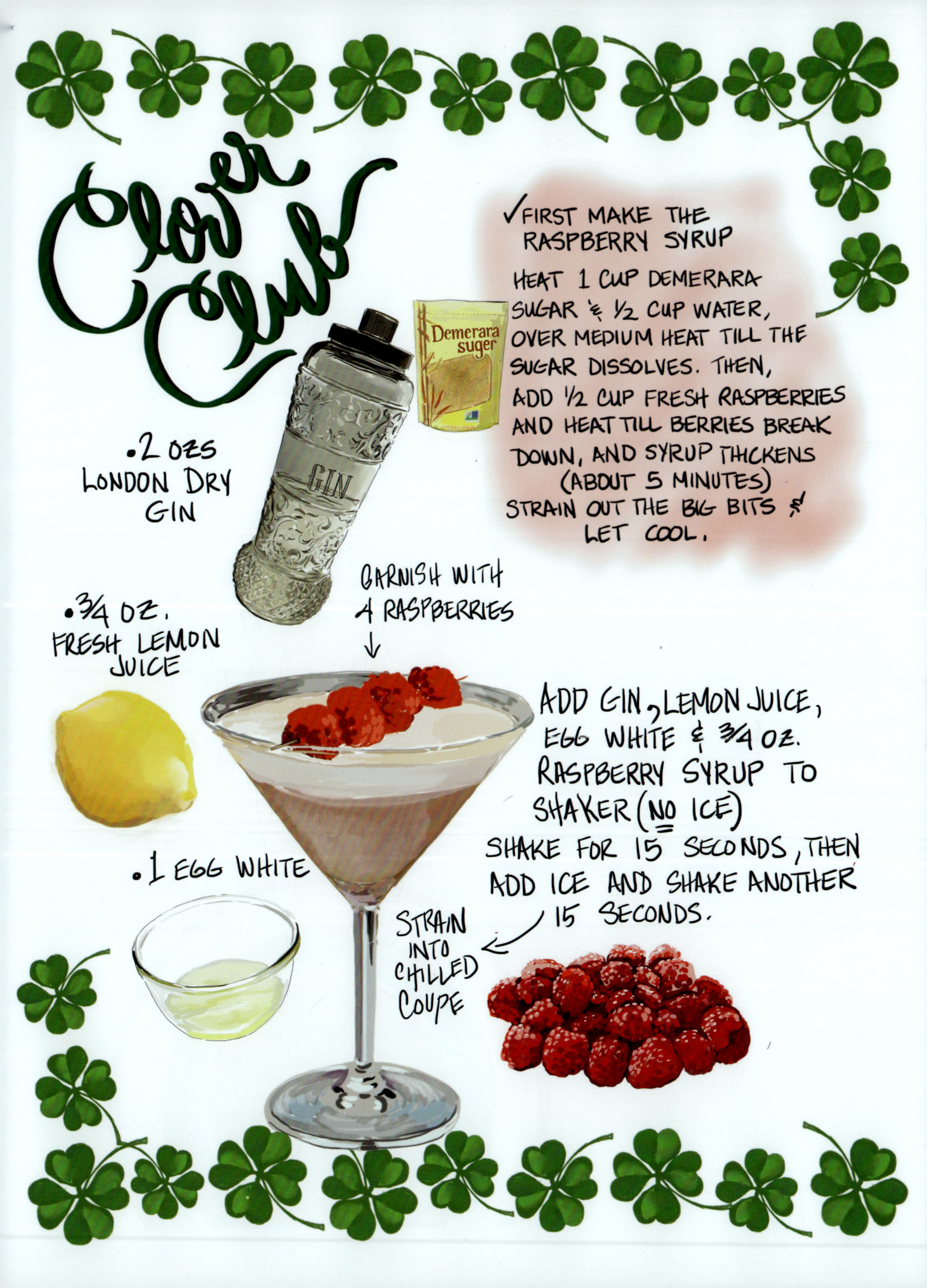
Clover Club
✓FIRST MAKE THE RASPBERRY SYRUP
HEAT 1 CUP DEMERARA SUGAR & 1/2 CUP WATER, OVER MEDIUM HEAT TILL THE SUGAR DISSOLVES. THEN, ADD 1/2 CUP FRESH RASPBERRIES AND HEAT TILL BERRIES BREAK DOWN, AND SYRUP THICKENS (ABOUT 5 MINUTES)
STRAIN OUT THE BIG BITS & LET COOL.
Demerara suger
GIN
•2 OZS LONDON DRY GIN
GARNISH WITH 4 RASPBERRIES
•3/4 OZ. FRESH LEMON JUICE
ADD GIN, LEMON JUICE, EGG WHITE & 3/4 OZ. RASPBERRY SYRUP TO SHAKER (NO ICE)
SHAKE FOR 15 SECONDS, THEN ADD ICE AND SHAKE ANOTHER 15 SECONDS.
•1 EGG WHITE
STRAIN INTO CHILLED COUPE

The Eye Candy

The best part of writing a cookbook of any kind is getting to try the recipes. Especially the more obscure recipes, like this one, which hails from the Touché Miami, a now-shuttered bar in downtown Miami. The combination of ginger and mint give it a zing, but what really sets this drink apart is the Elderflower taste of the St. Germain liquor. Definitely worth the fuss.

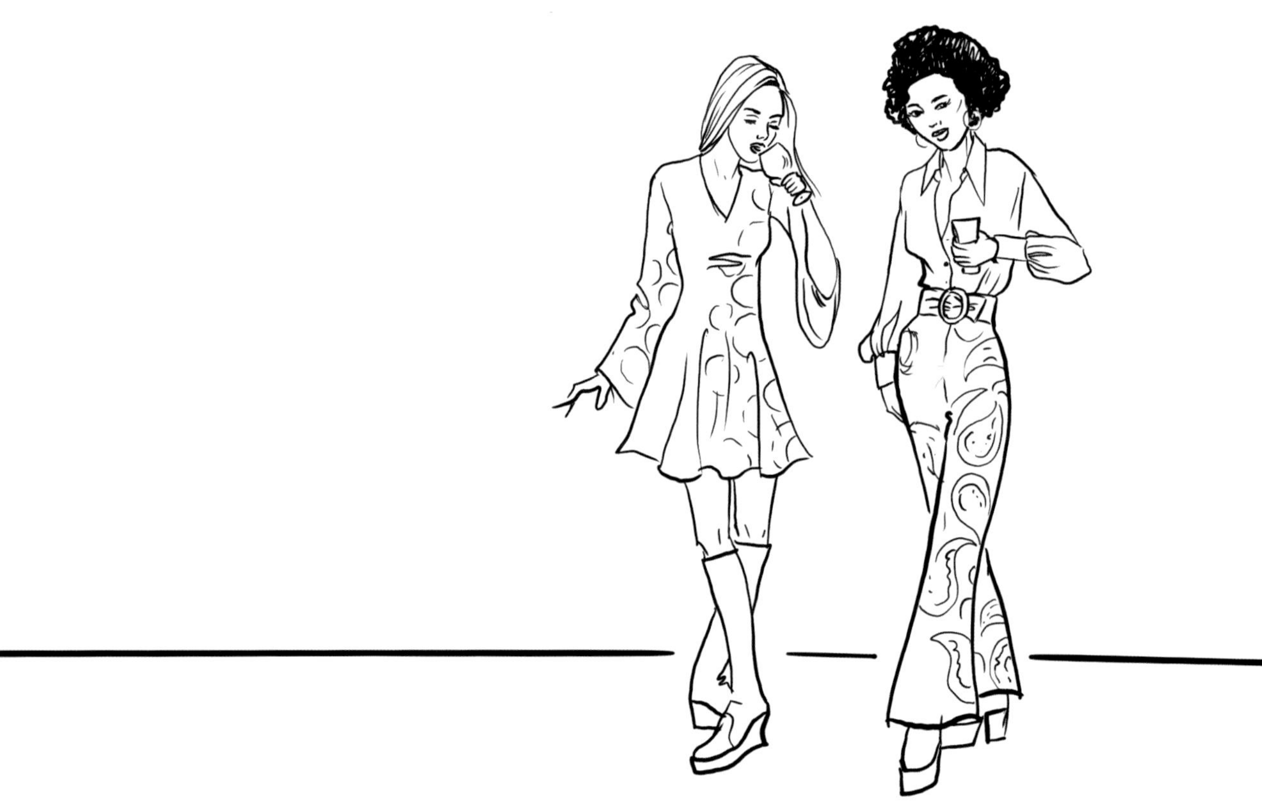

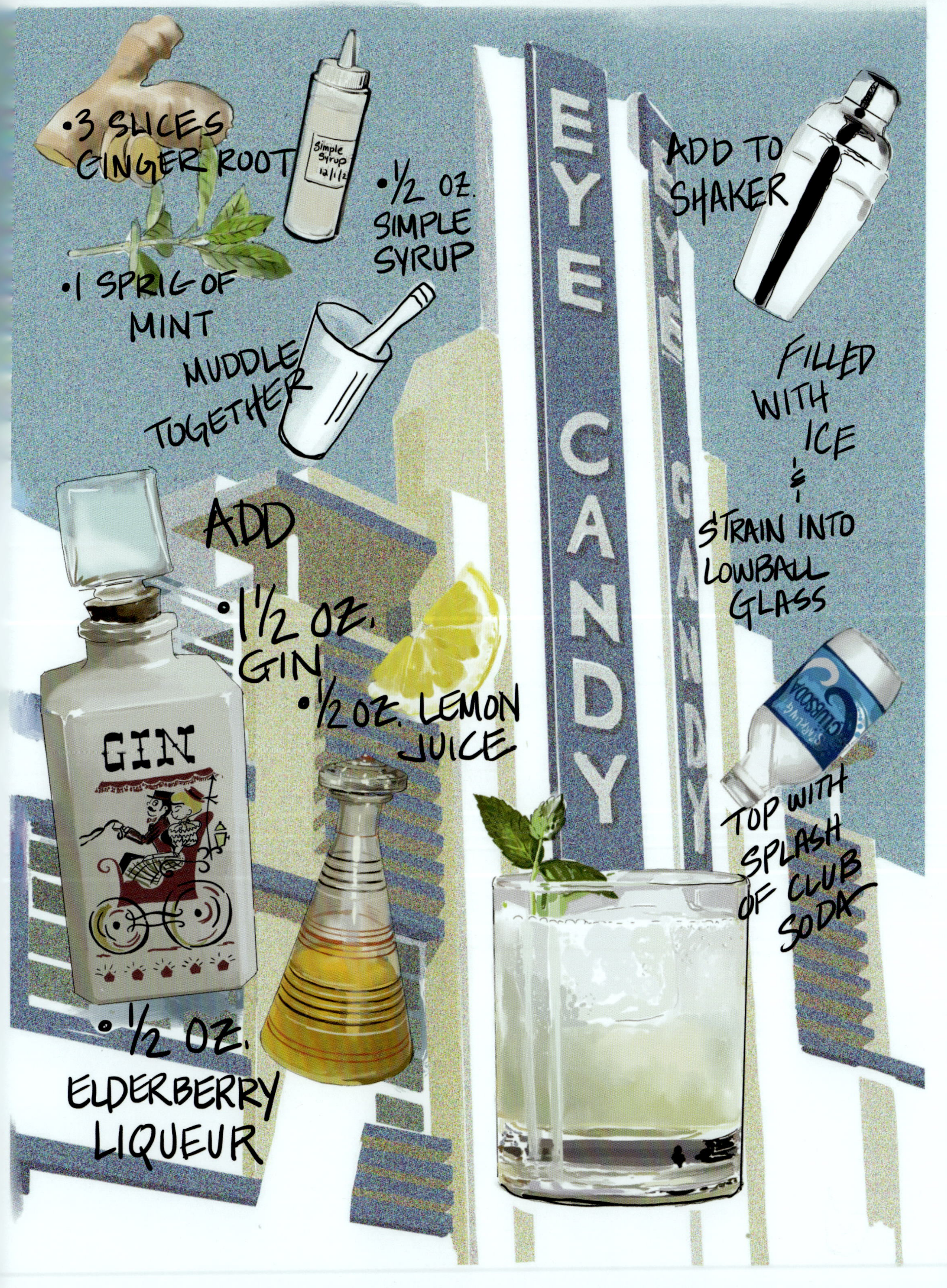
•3 SLICES GINGER ROOT
Simple Syrup 12/1/12
•½ OZ. SIMPLE SYRUP
•1 SPRIG OF MINT
MUDDLE TOGETHER
EYE CANDY
ADD TO SHAKER
FILLED WITH ICE
&
STRAIN INTO LOWBALL GLASS
ADD
•1½ OZ. GIN
•½ OZ. LEMON JUICE
GIN
•½ OZ. ELDERBERRY LIQUEUR
TOP WITH SPLASH OF CLUB SODA

The French 75

I never thought that in researching this book I would learn history from cocktails. I was wrong. Take the French 75, for instance. Invented by French and British troops during World War I using the readily available ingredients of (English) Gin and (French) Champagne, the cocktail was named for the 75mm Howitzer field gun used in World War I. Why? Because the French 75 is said to have a kick that felt like being hit by a Howitzer.

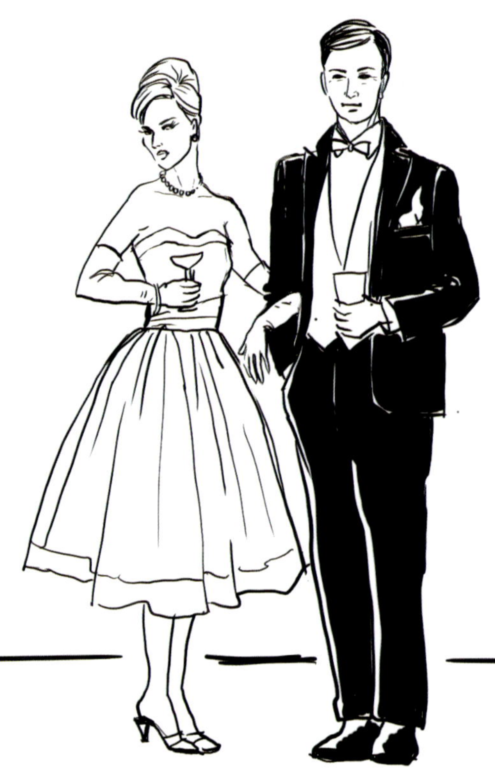

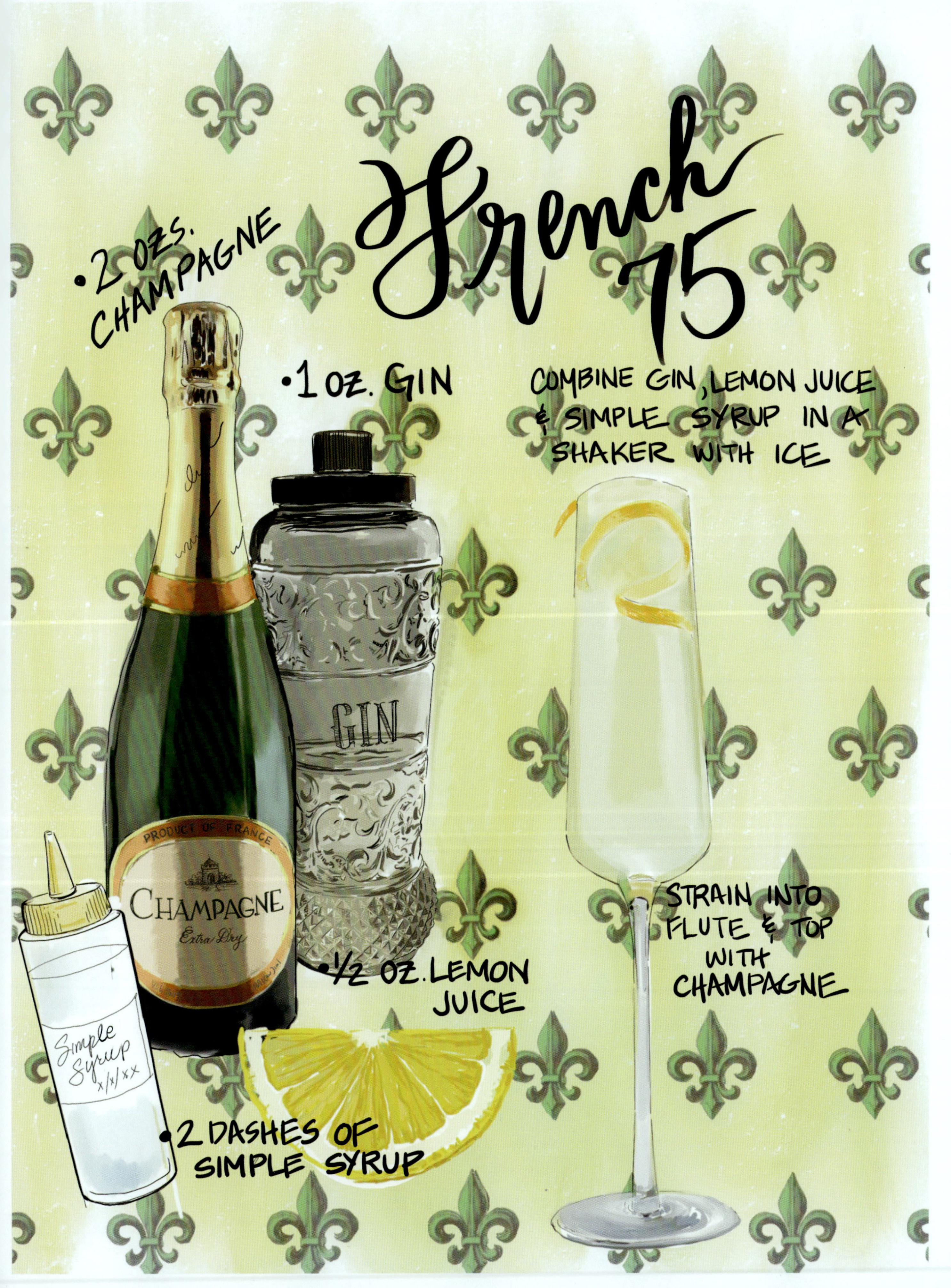
French 75
•2 OZS. CHAMPAGNE
•1 OZ. GIN
COMBINE GIN, LEMON JUICE & SIMPLE SYRUP IN A SHAKER WITH ICE
GIN
PRODUCT OF FRANCE
CHAMPAGNE
Extra Dry
•1/2 OZ. LEMON JUICE
STRAIN INTO FLUTE & TOP WITH CHAMPAGNE
Simple Syrup
x/x/xx
•2 DASHES OF SIMPLE SYRUP

The Gin & Tonic

Invented in 18th century by a British officer in India, the G & T is a perfect example of creative problem solving. The problem was malaria and the quinine that was used to treat it. The solution? Quinine was made into a tonic by dissolving it in water and sweetening it with sugar. It still tasted awful and compliance with daily malaria treatment was not what it needed to be. Then some enterprising British soldier decided to add his daily Gin ration to the mix. The new creation was not just palatable, but actually tasted good… and a national drink (of Britain) was born.

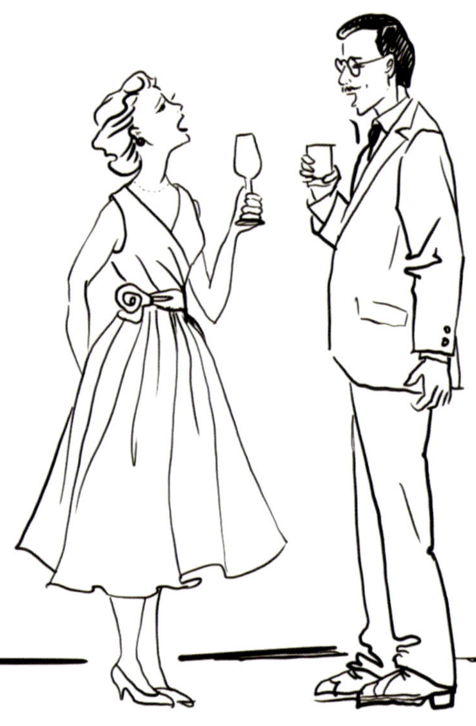

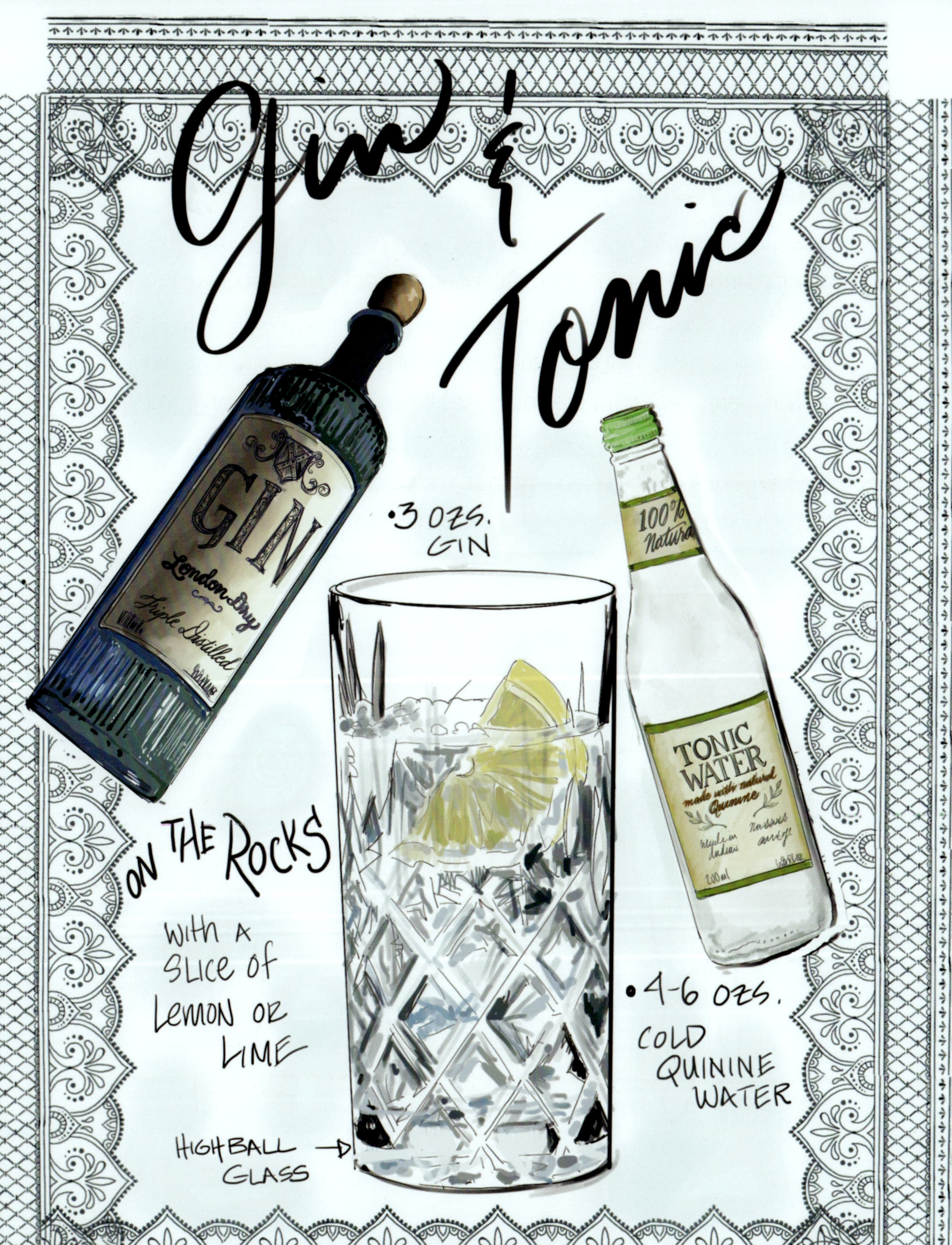
Gin & Tonic
GIN
London Dry
Triple Distilled
•3 OZS.
GIN
100%
Natural
TONIC WATER
made with natural Quinine
ON THE ROCKS
WITH A
SLICE OF
LEMON OR
LIME
•4-6 OZS.
COLD
QUININE
WATER
HIGHBALL
GLASS

The Last Word

There are a few things we can agree upon about Chartreuse. It's a really beautiful color, and it has a distinct flavor. Described as both sweet and pungent, this liqueur has an herbal flavor with notes of citrus, cinnamon, clove, and rosemary. It is made by Carthusian monks in France, from a centuries-old secret recipe. So secret, in fact, there are only two monks in the world who know the recipe. which just adds to the mystique.

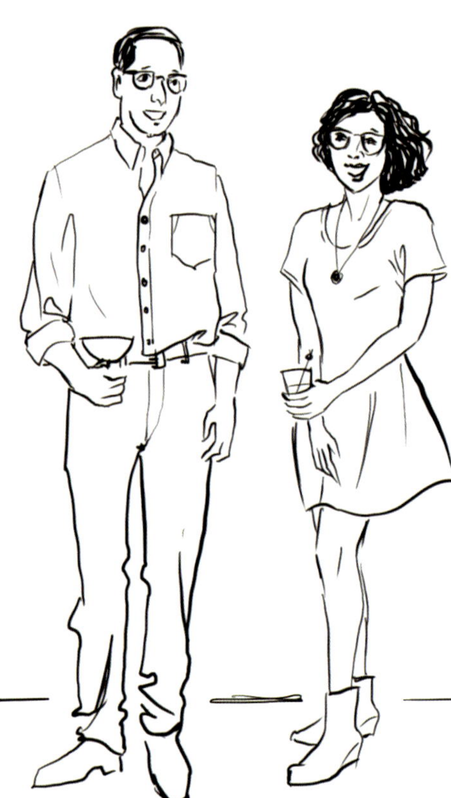

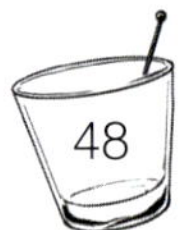

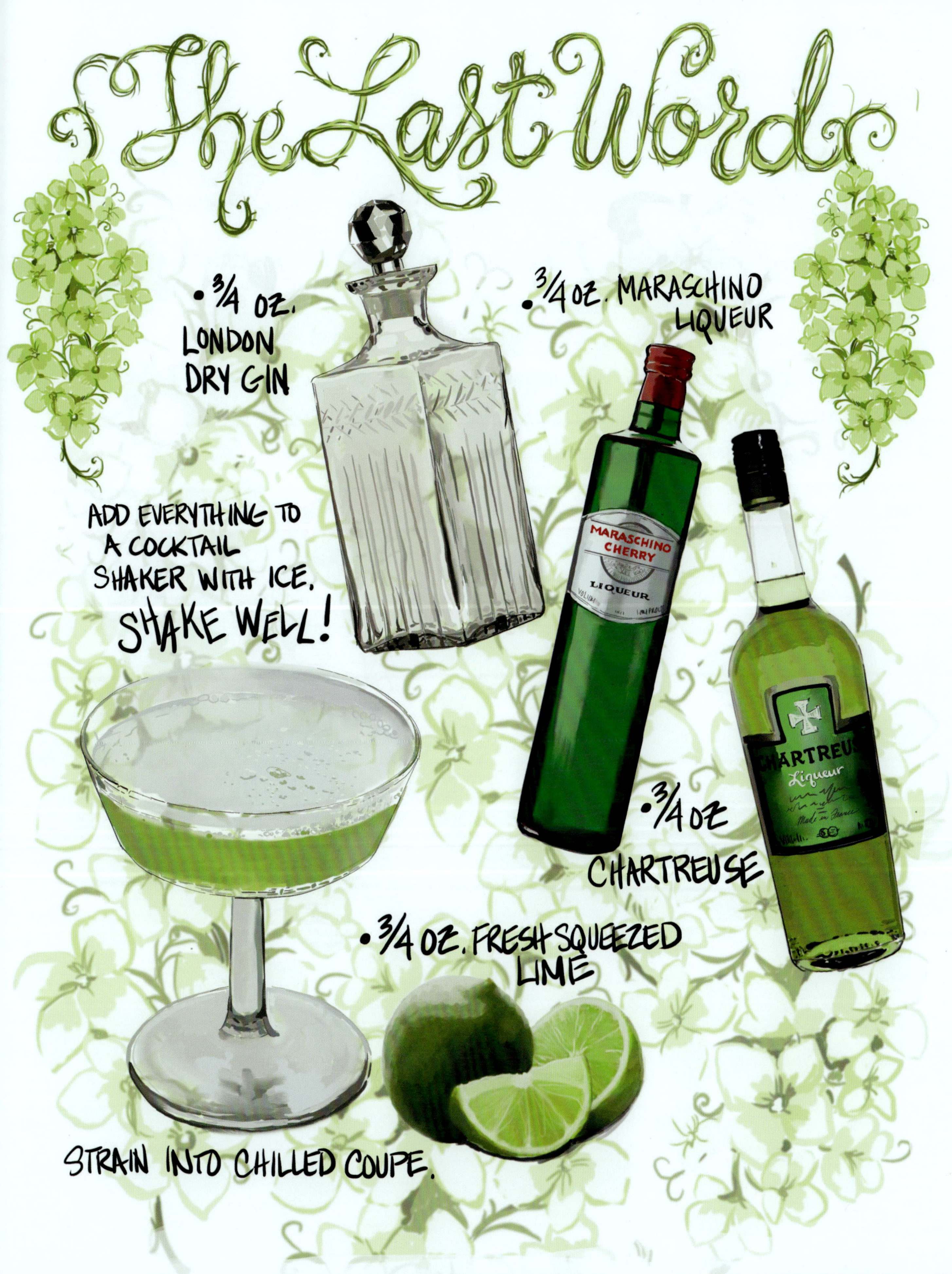
The Last Word
• 3/4 OZ. LONDON DRY GIN
• 3/4 OZ. MARASCHINO LIQUEUR
MARASCHINO CHERRY
LIQUEUR
ADD EVERYTHING TO A COCKTAIL SHAKER WITH ICE. SHAKE WELL!
CHARTREUS
Liqueur
• 3/4 OZ CHARTREUSE
• 3/4 OZ. FRESH SQUEEZED LIME
STRAIN INTO CHILLED COUPE.

The Negroni

One of the most popular cocktails in the world, this cocktail was created in Florence, Italy, in 1919. My first sip of a Negroni was when I was visiting my Aunt and Uncle who lived in Florence. I was 12 and did NOT like it! But… now I know that the Campari makes it bitter, and the gin and vermouth make it sweet and refreshing. My palate has matured.

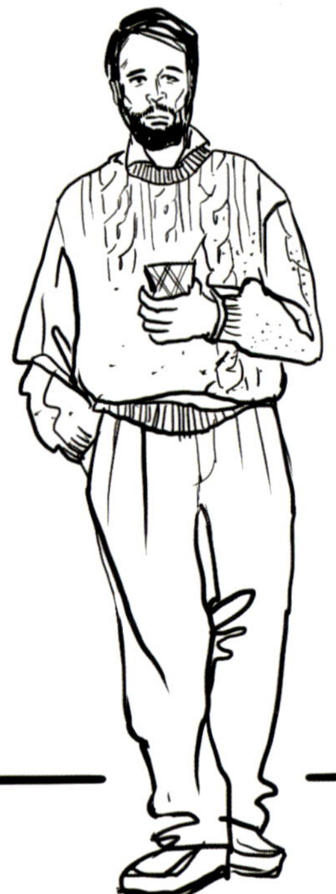

ADD INGREDIENTS TO A 6 OZ. GLASS, WITH 2 ICE CUBES

• 1½ OZ. CAMPARI

TWIST & ADD LEMON PEEL

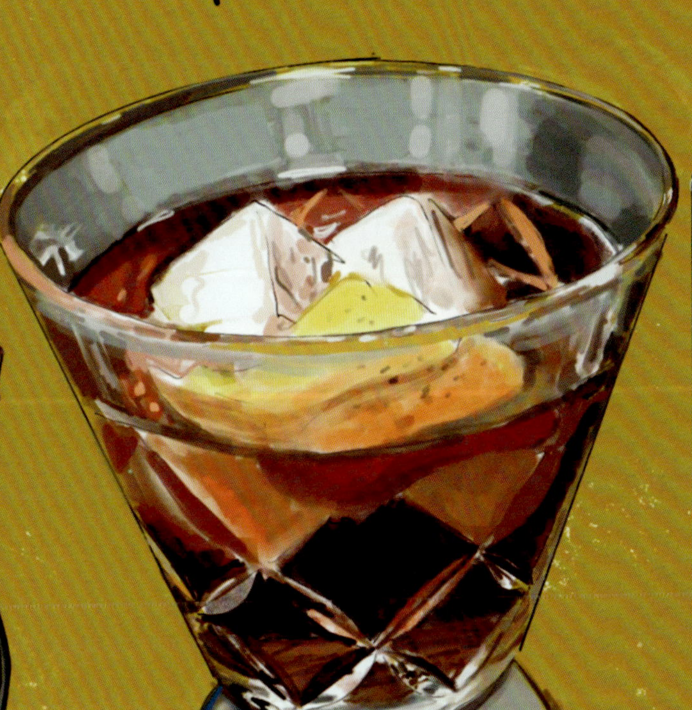

• 1½ OZ. SWEET VERMOUTH

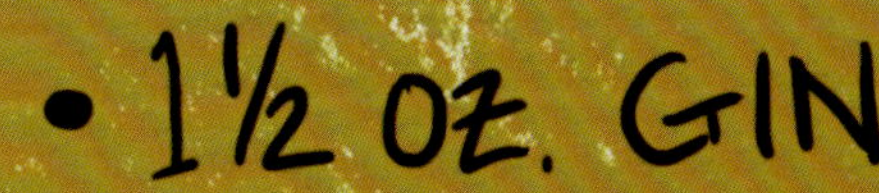

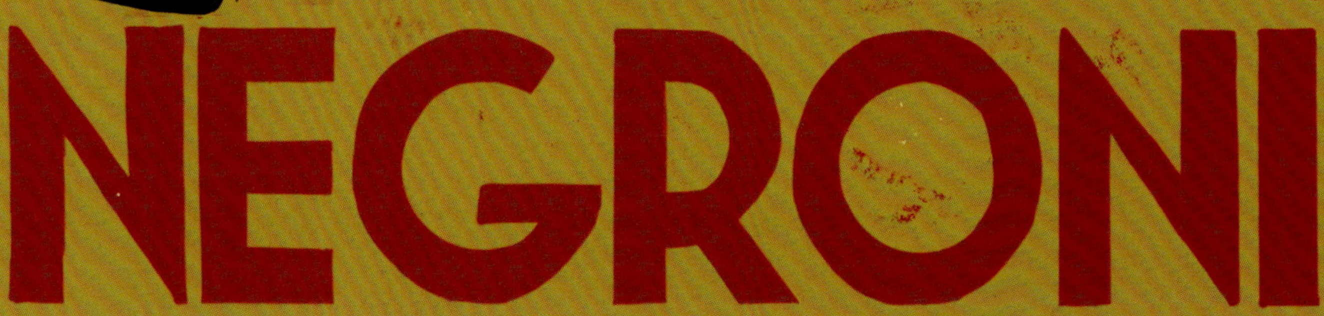

Singapore Sling

There are many world class hotels in Singapore, but Raffles is old school elegance. The Singapore Sling is said to have been invented there, and you can still order one today at the hotel's Long Bar. The bar is like stepping back in time. The décor is English Colonial, with teak wood paneling, wicker furniture and ceiling fans that cool the air. This drink pairs well with "monkey nuts" (the British term for peanuts in the shell) which they also serve at the Long Bar. You are encouraged to drop the shells on the bar floor. I'll leave that up to you.

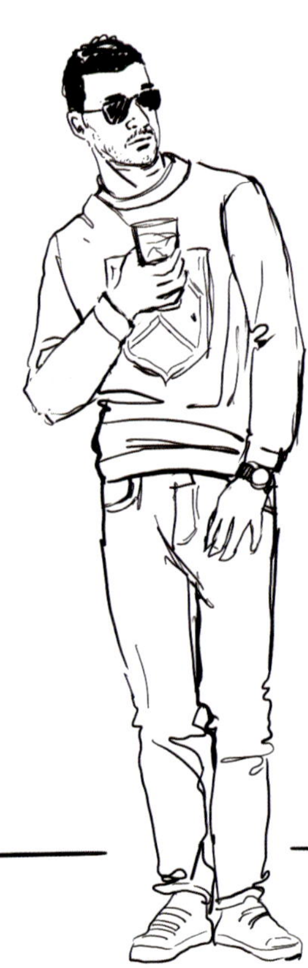

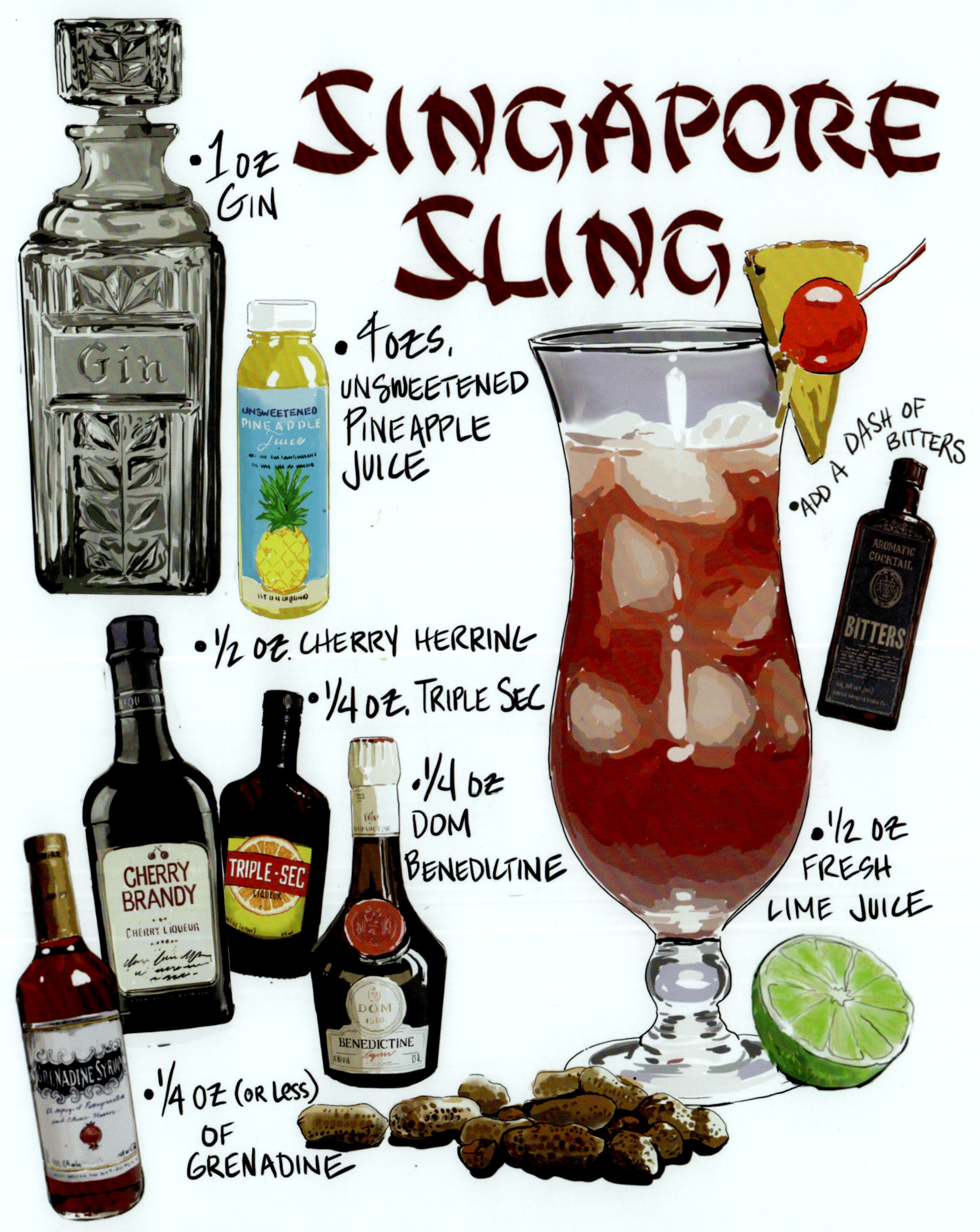

·POUR INGREDIENTS INTO SHAKER WITH ICE, SHAKE HARD FOR 30 SECONDS, STRAIN INTO HURRICANE GLASS FILLED WITH ICE. GARNISH WITH A CHERRY & PINEAPPLE WEDGE.

Southside

The Southside is a sweet-and-sour concoction with a sprig of fresh mint. The cocktail gets its name from the southside of some place, many claim Chicago, where the gin was rougher during prohibition and so the sweet was added. I like to rim this drink using raw turbinado sugar.

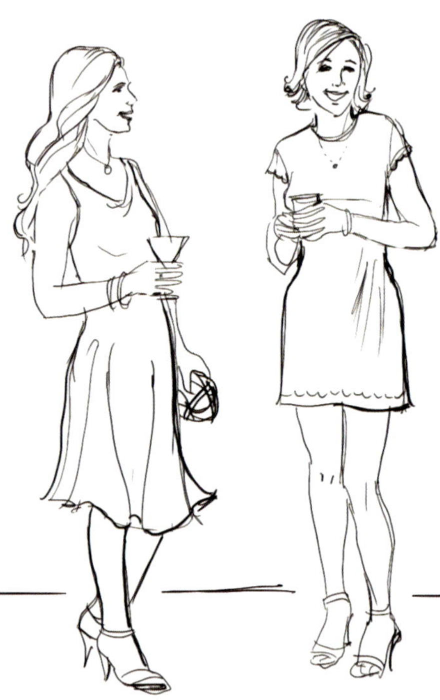

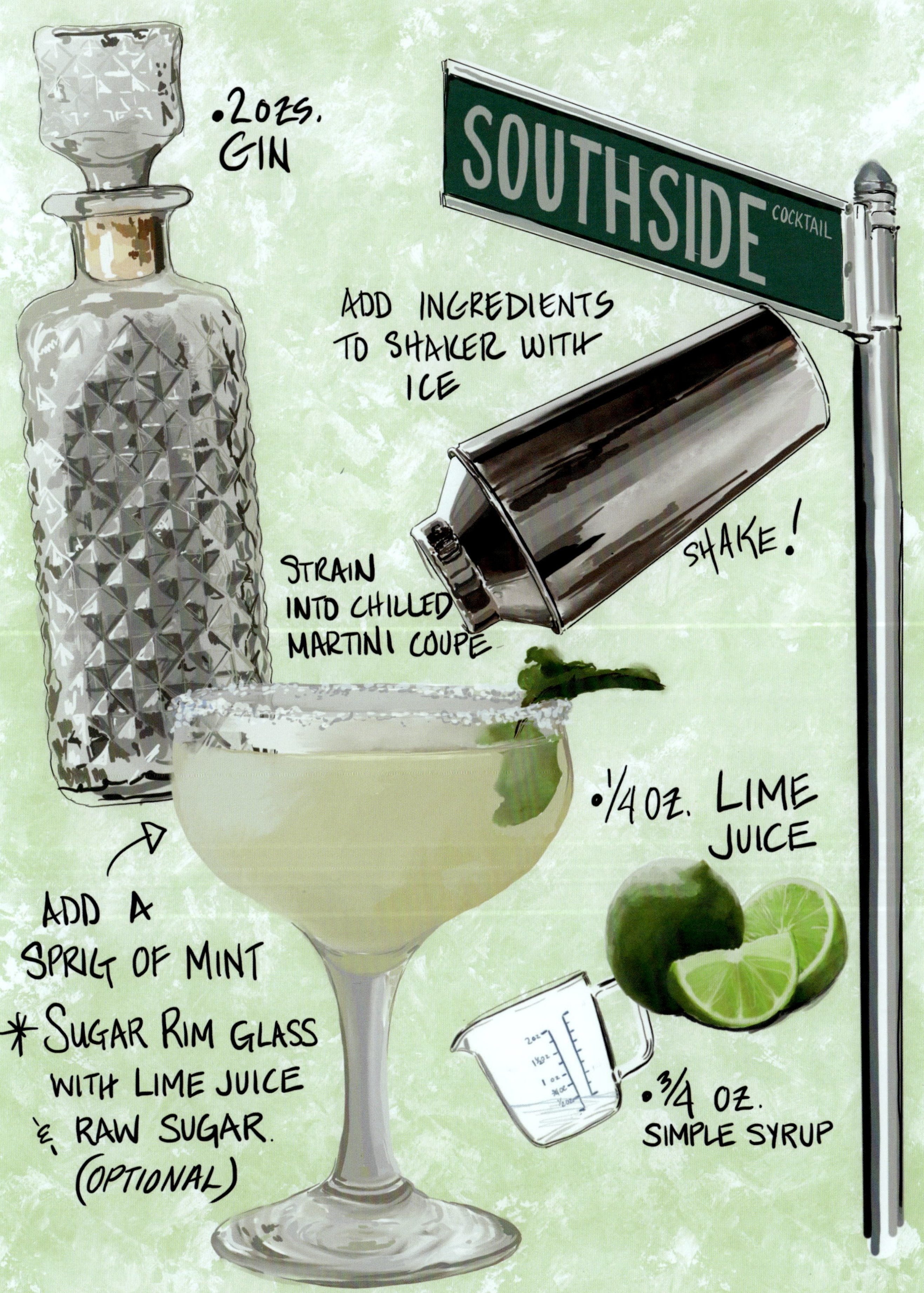
SOUTHSIDE
COCKTAIL
•2ozs. GIN
ADD INGREDIENTS TO SHAKER WITH ICE
SHAKE!
STRAIN INTO CHILLED MARTINI COUPE
•¼ OZ. LIME JUICE
ADD A SPRIG OF MINT
* SUGAR RIM GLASS WITH LIME JUICE & RAW SUGAR. (OPTIONAL)
•¾ OZ. SIMPLE SYRUP

Tom Collins

"Have you seen Tom Collins?" was the question being asked in bars around the country in 1874. The answer would be, predictably, "I don't know a Tom Collins," to which the questioner would reply "Well, I just heard him talking about you at…" (pick one: the bar down the street; around the corner; etc.). Great hilarity would ensue when the object of the joke would walk into a bar asking to speak to "Tom Collins." Newspapers began printing stories about "Tom Collins sightings," songs were written about the hoax, and, well… it was a simpler time.

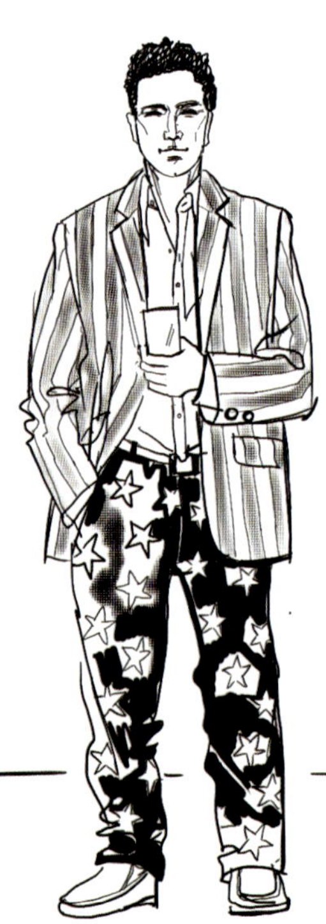

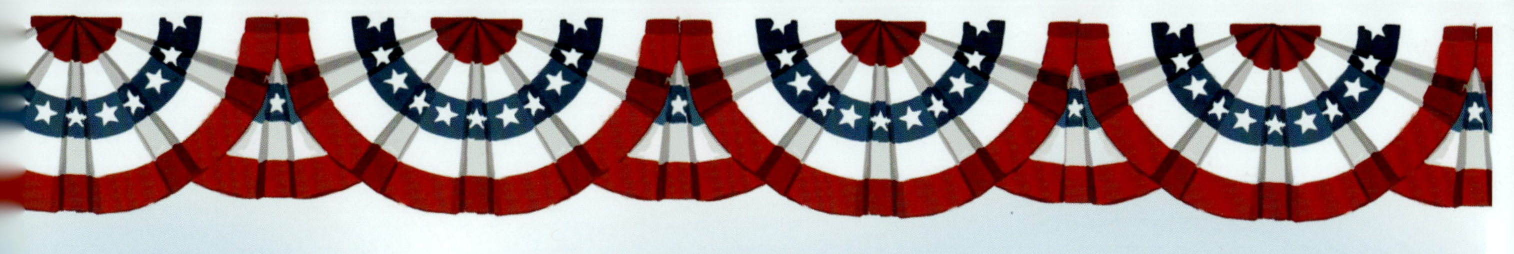

MIX INGREDIENTS TOGETHER ON ICE. GARNISH WITH AN ORANGE WHEEL & CHERRY.

- 2 OZS. GIN
- 1 OZ. SIMPLE SYRUP
- 3/4 OZ. LEMON JUICE

TOP WITH SELTZER

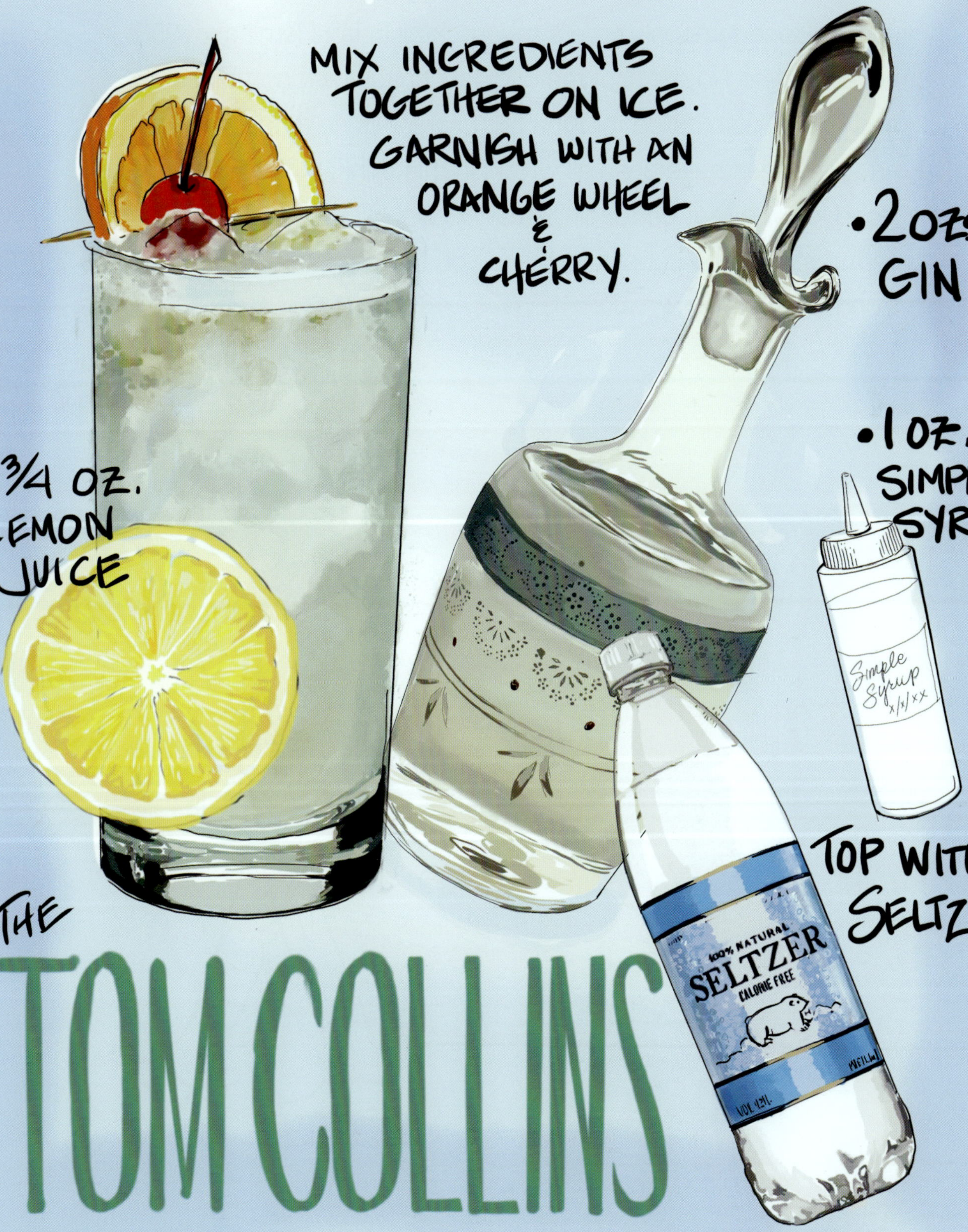

THE

TOM COLLINS

Vesper

James Bond famously orders this cocktail in Ian Fleming's 1953 novel, *Casino Royale*. But the original drink, which combines gin and vodka, also called for Kina Lillet, which is no longer available and may even have been all wrong in this drink, what does James Bond know about bartending, really? Lillet Blanc or any quality dry vermouth may be substituted, and you too can channel your inner Bond, James Bond.

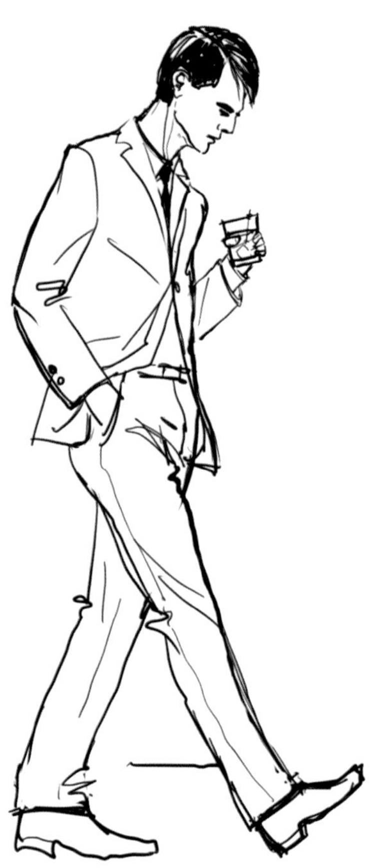

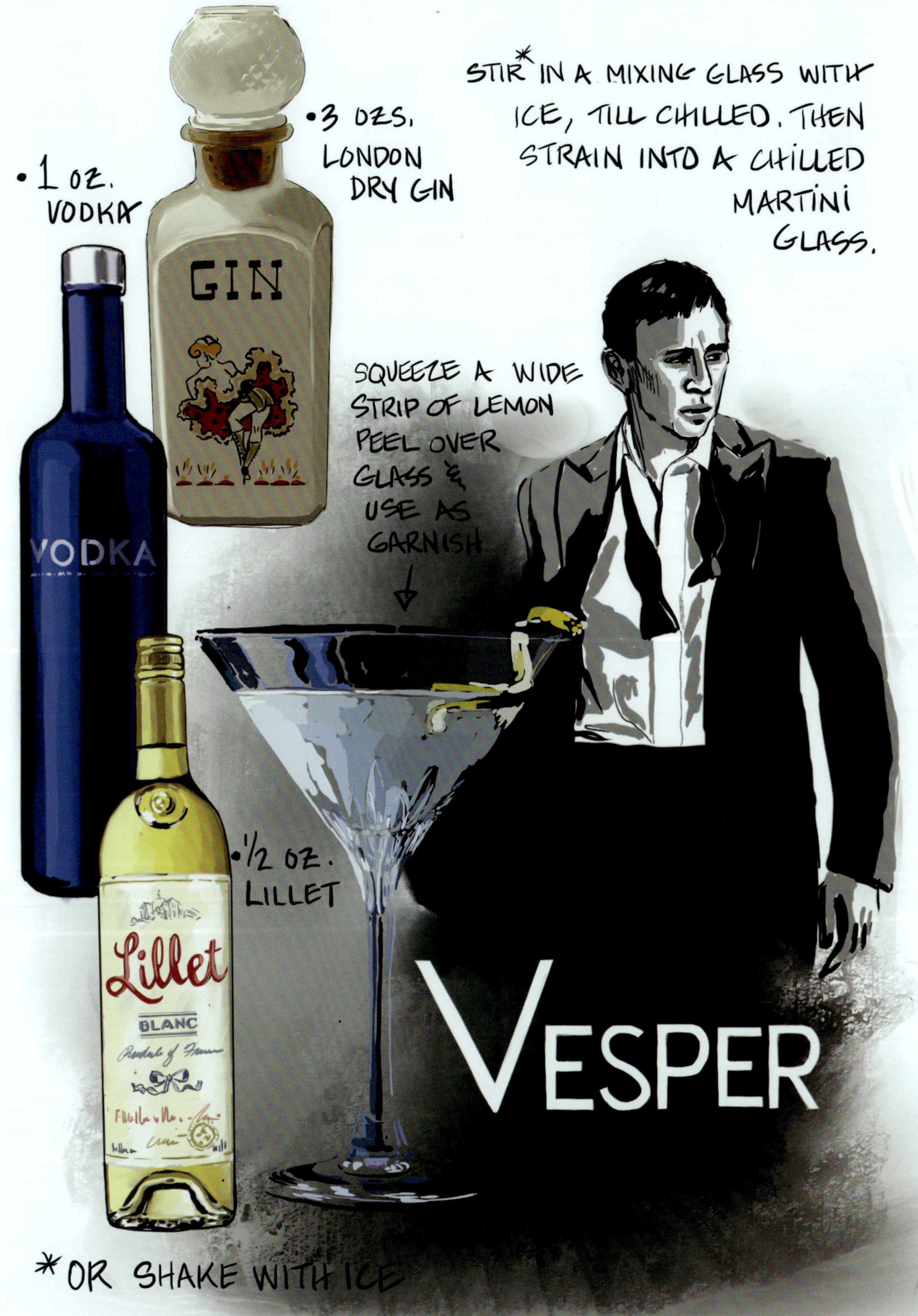
STIR* IN A MIXING GLASS WITH ICE, TILL CHILLED. THEN STRAIN INTO A CHILLED MARTINI GLASS.
•3 OZS. LONDON DRY GIN
•1 OZ. VODKA
GIN
VODKA
SQUEEZE A WIDE STRIP OF LEMON PEEL OVER GLASS & USE AS GARNISH
•1/2 OZ. LILLET
Lillet
BLANC
VESPER
*OR SHAKE WITH ICE

"It doesn't matter if the glass is half empty or half full. There is clearly room for more vodka."

—Unknown

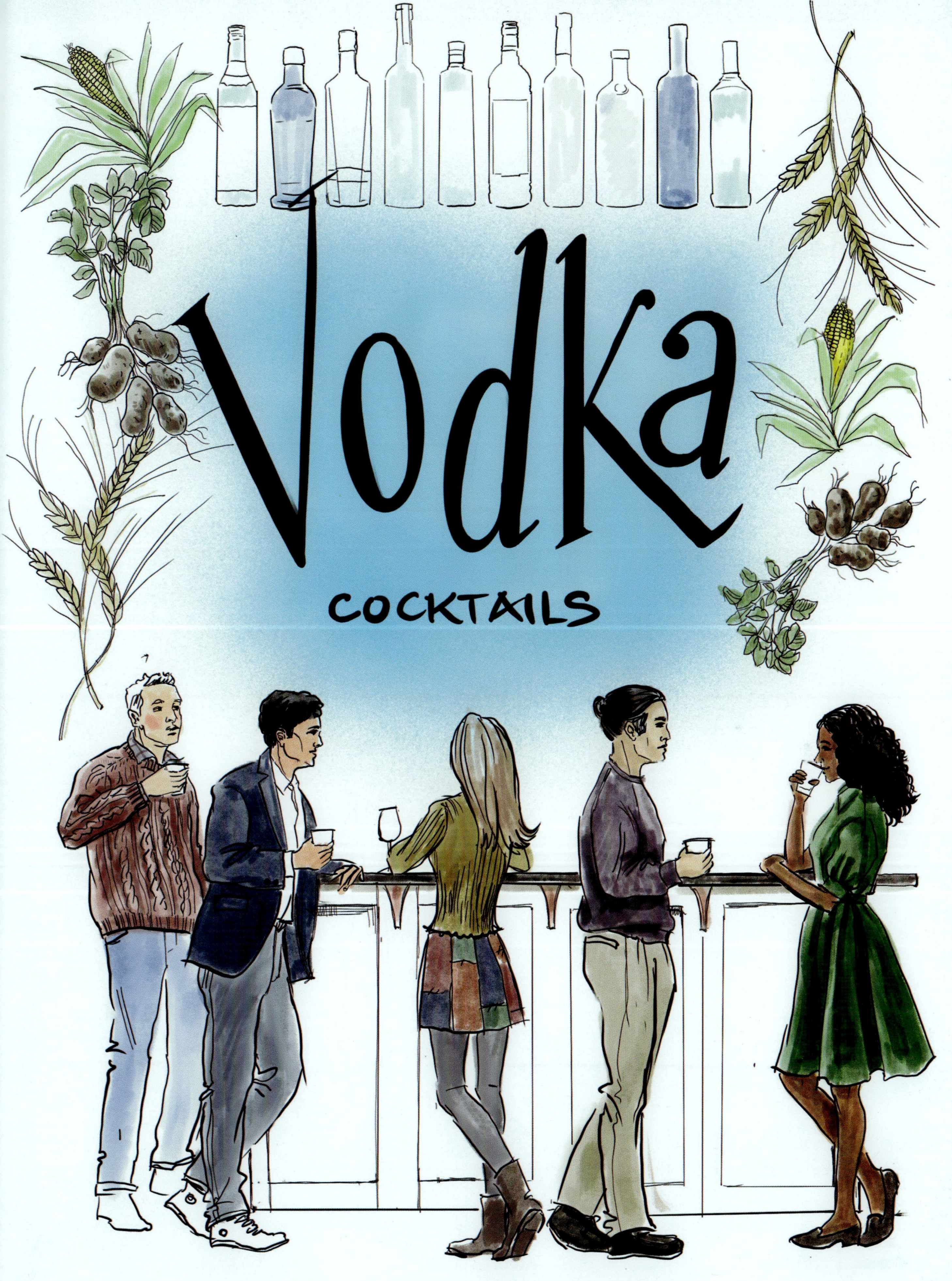

Vodka
COCKTAILS

The Bloody Mary

What would brunch be without a Bloody Mary? The slightly-salty-and-savory drink not only pairs well with breakfast food, but because of its combination of a vegetable base, salt and alcohol, it is considered a “cure” for too much partying the night before. While there are some outstanding mixes available, here is a standard recipe that you can make and adapt to your own tastes. Traditional garnishes include celery sticks and pickle spears (good for stirring); or go wild and add shrimp or mini sliders or whatever strikes your fancy to make this cocktail more like a meal.

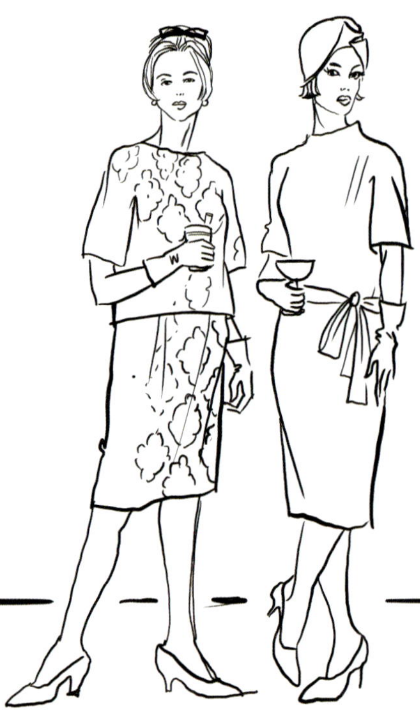

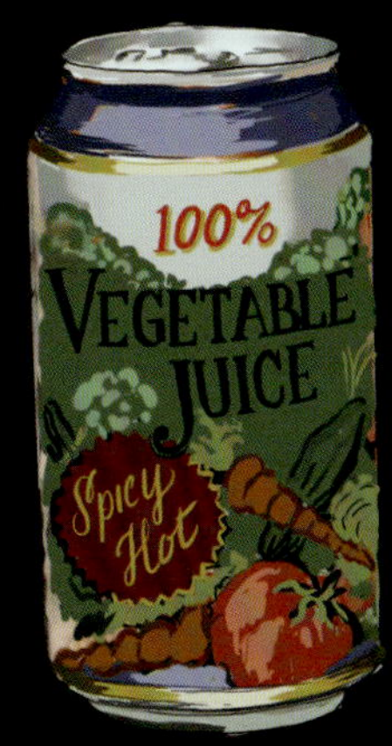

• 4 OZS. V8
SPICY HOT

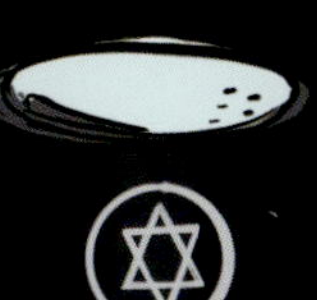
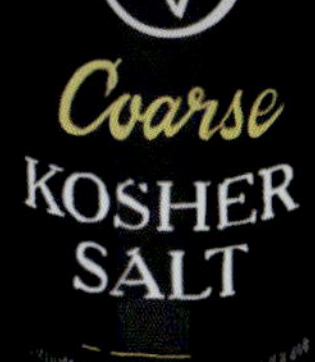

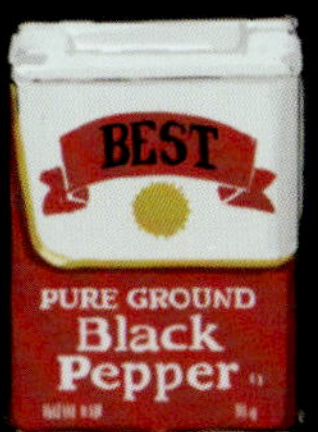

• 1 PINCH
OF PEPPER

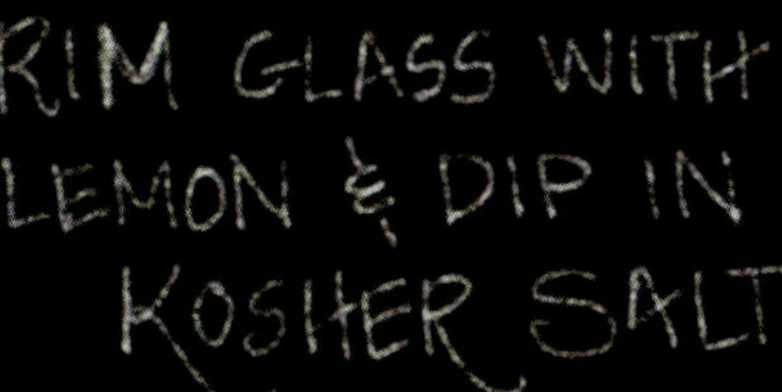

RIM GLASS WITH
LEMON & DIP IN
KOSHER SALT

• 1½ OZ.
VODKA

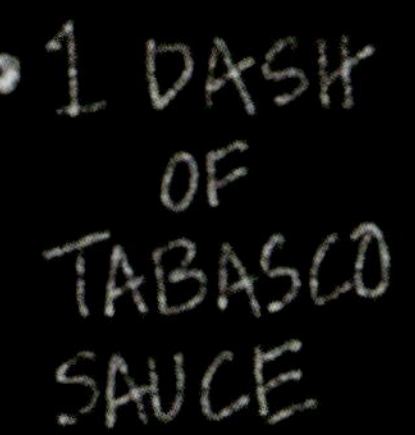

• 1 DASH
OF
TABASCO
SAUCE

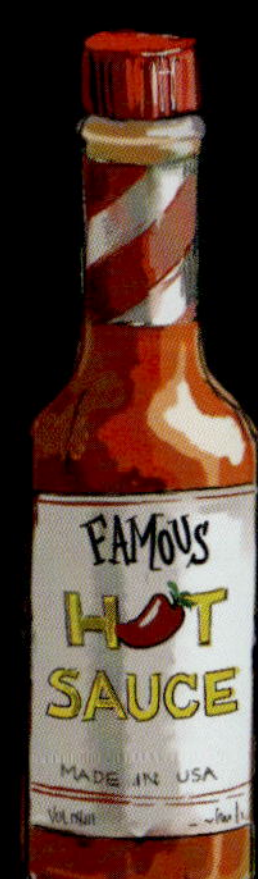
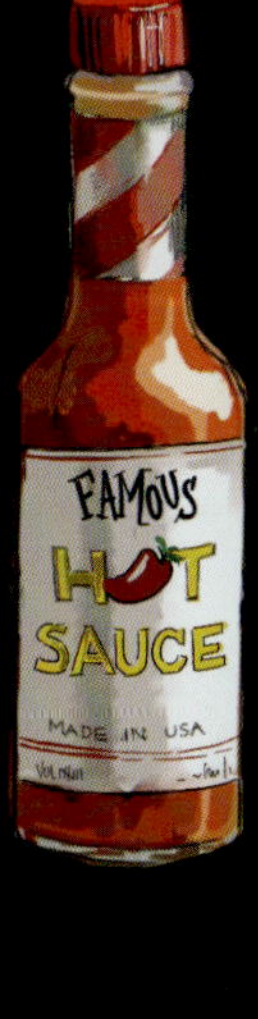

• 2 DASHES OF
WORCESTERSHIRE
SAUCE

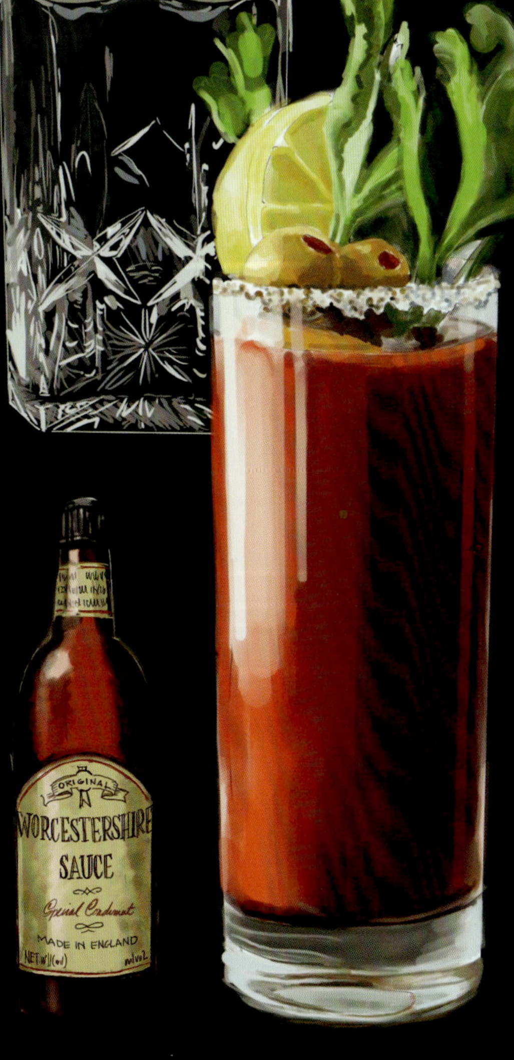

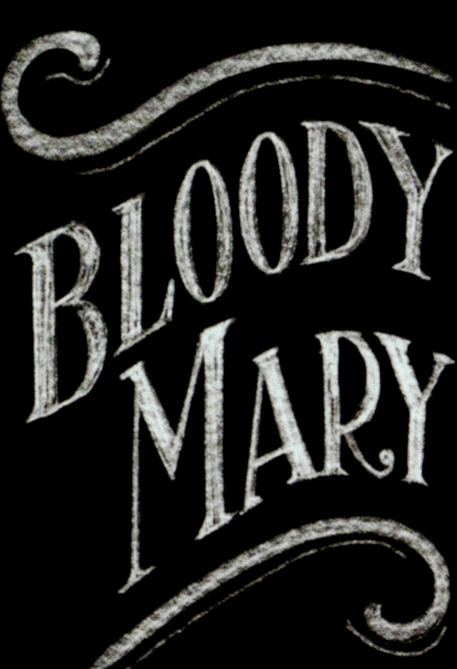

BLOODY MARY

MIX TOGETHER & GARNISH WITH CELERY, OLIVES & LEMON.

The Cosmopolitan

Imagine… you and three friends are at an outrageously fabulous café sipping "Cosmos" and arguing over which one of you is Carrie, Charlotte, Miranda or Samantha. You are making the case that you are Carrie when you look down at your shoes. You are about to concede that maybe you are Miranda, but then you decide that if you can't have Carrie's shoes, you can at least drink her drink! So yes, you ARE Carrie Bradshaw! And you can make the Cosmopolitan to prove it.

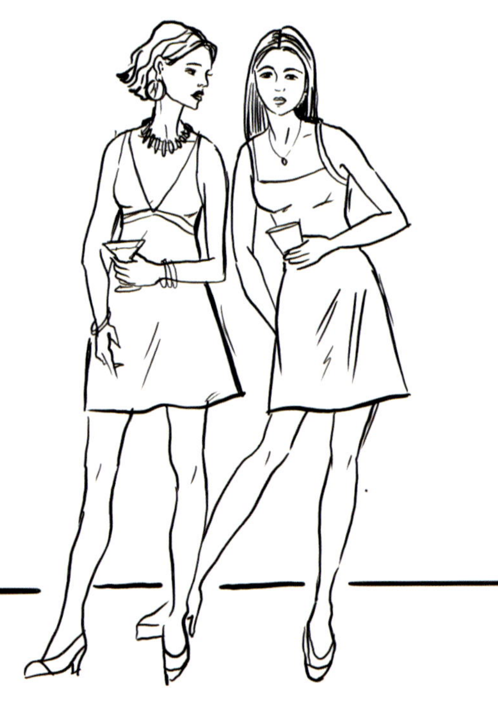

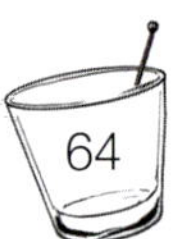

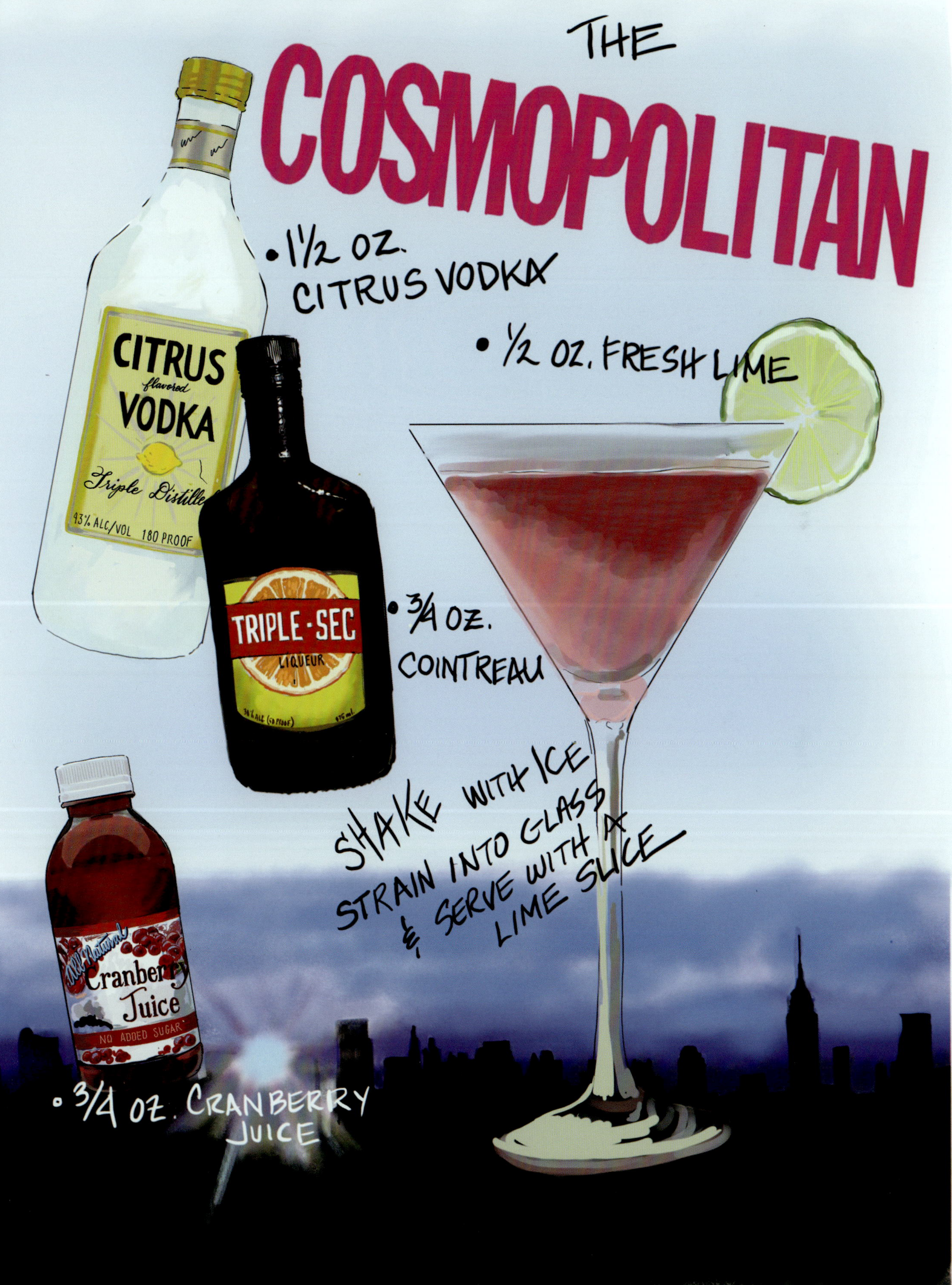
THE
COSMOPOLITAN
• 1½ OZ. CITRUS VODKA
• ½ OZ. FRESH LIME
• ¾ OZ. COINTREAU
• ¾ OZ. CRANBERRY JUICE
SHAKE WITH ICE
STRAIN INTO GLASS
& SERVE WITH A LIME SLICE
CITRUS
flavored
VODKA
Triple Distilled
43% ALC/VOL 180 PROOF
TRIPLE-SEC
LIQUEUR
All Natural
Cranberry
Juice
NO ADDED SUGAR

The "Diet" Cocktail

Sometimes you just want a drink. But you've been eating healthy and don't want to lose your momentum. This refreshing cocktail clocks in at just 100 calories and zero carbs — if you make this drink with standard 80 proof vodka. There are lower calorie vodkas, but the downside is these are only 60 proof. Fewer calories equals less buzz. If you choose a 60 proof version here is a tip, use the refrigerator instead of the freezer to chill, or it will ice up.

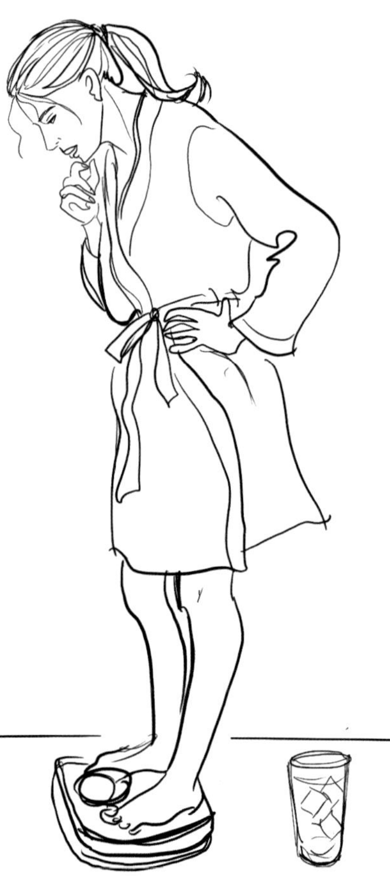

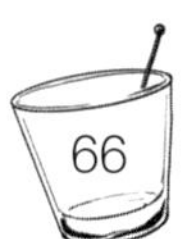

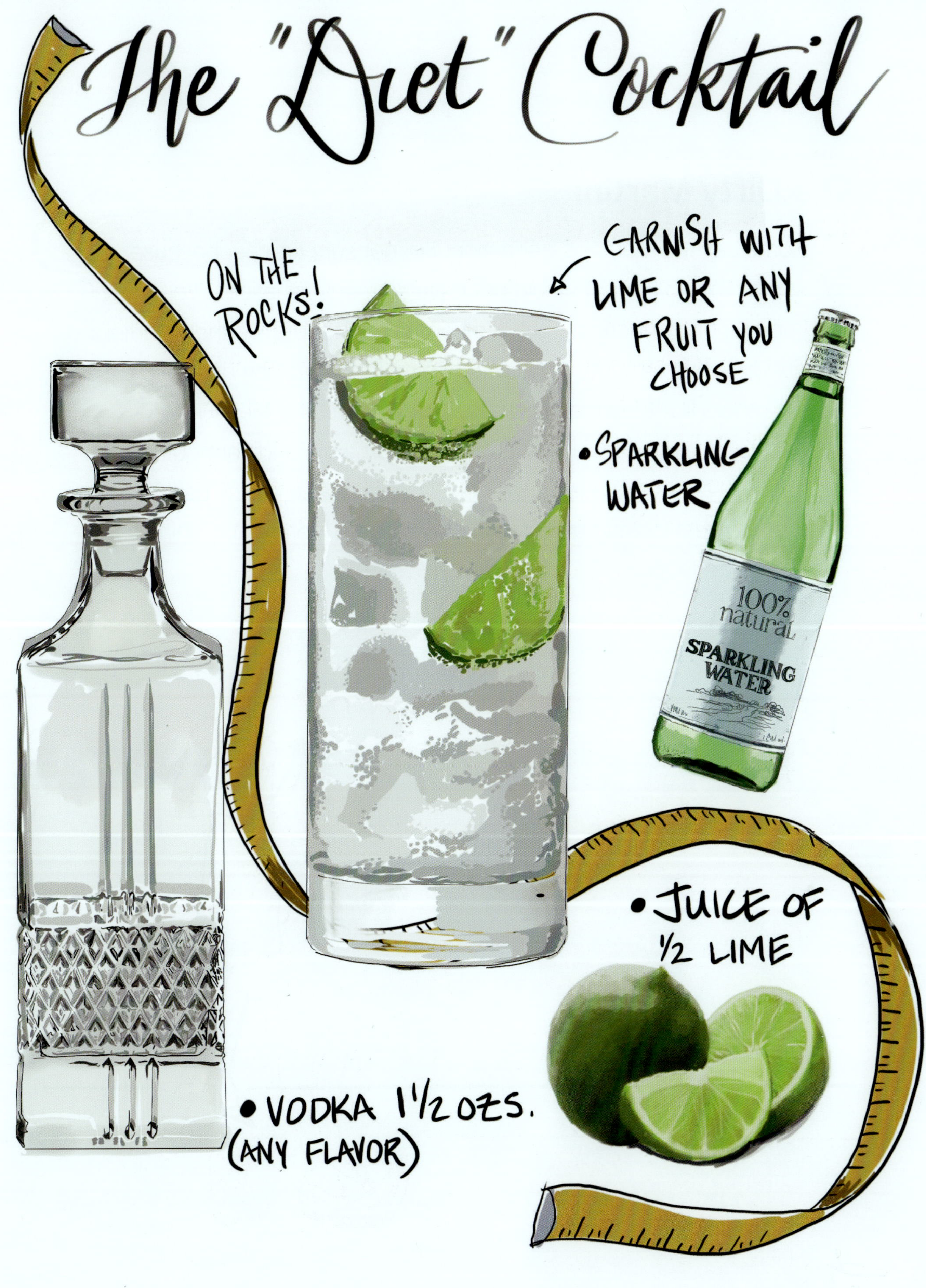
The "Diet" Cocktail
ON THE ROCKS!
GARNISH WITH LIME OR ANY FRUIT YOU CHOOSE
• SPARKLING WATER
100% natural
SPARKLING WATER
• JUICE OF ½ LIME
• VODKA 1½ OZS. (ANY FLAVOR)

The Dirty Martini

Some say the martini is perfection. I'm not sure I agree, because something so perfect would not have so many variations. You can't improve on perfection, right? I mean, some people like their martini's dry (gin and vermouth only), others dirty (add a splash of olive brine), still others like their martinis made with vodka, etc. Me? Find me a cocktail shaker, a lovely antique glass, some gin and vermouth, a beautiful summer's evening, a comfortable chaise on my patio and a really great looking guy working on my yard - preferably shirtless. That is perfection.

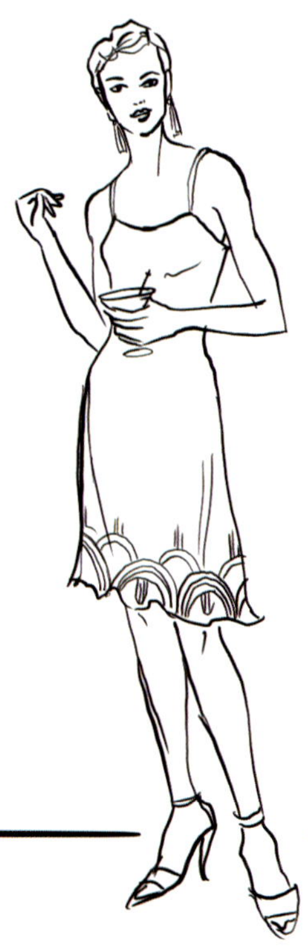

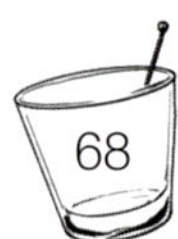

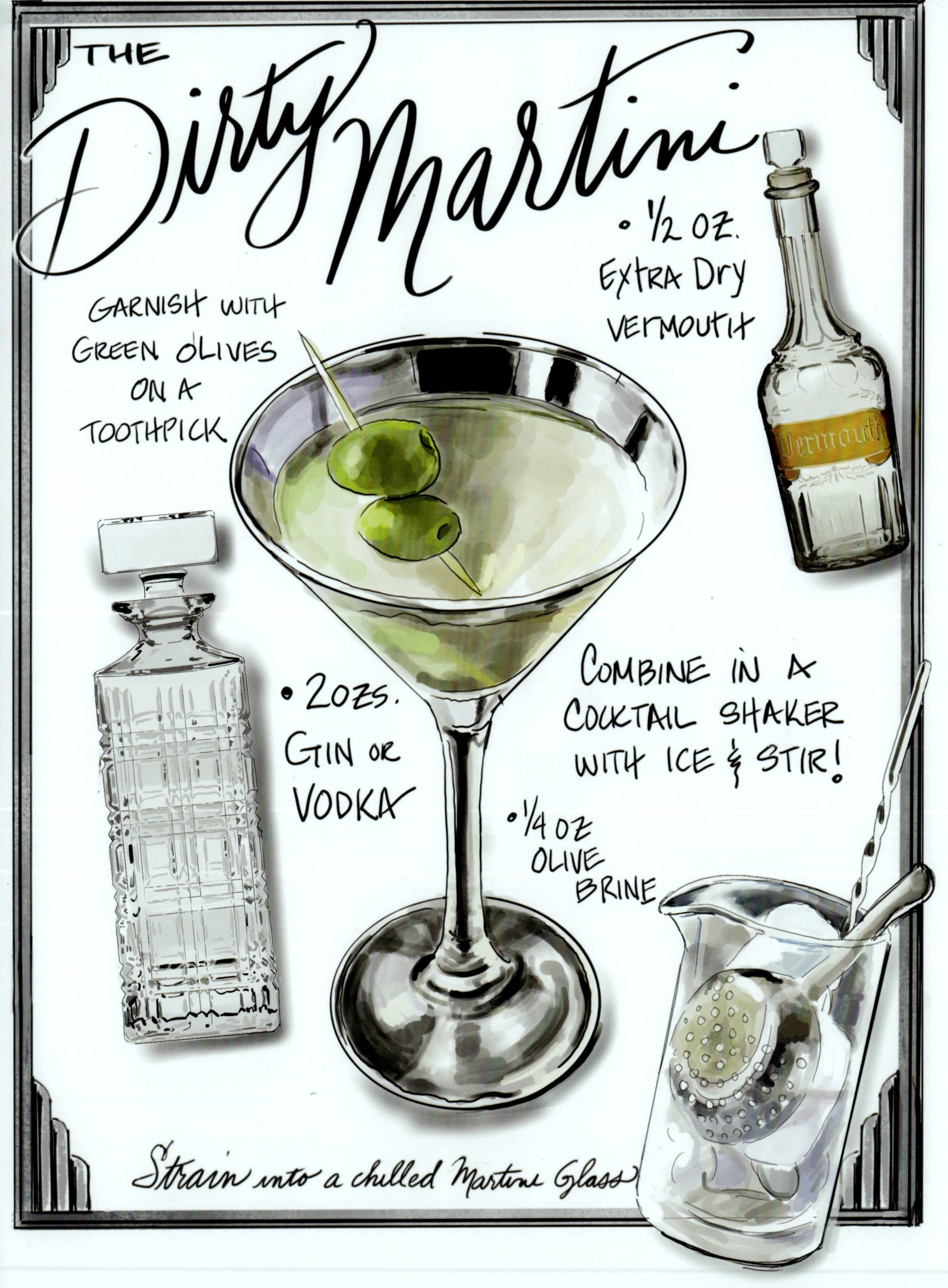
THE
Dirty Martini
• 1/2 OZ.
Extra Dry
VERMOUTH
GARNISH WITH
GREEN OLIVES
ON A
TOOTHPICK
Vermouth
• 2OZS.
GIN OR
VODKA
COMBINE IN A
COCKTAIL SHAKER
WITH ICE & STIR!
• 1/4 OZ
OLIVE
BRINE
Strain into a chilled Martini Glass

Espresso Martini

Legend has it that this cocktail was created in London in 1983, when a young woman — a future supermodel (check out the drawing for pose ideas) — asked a bartender to make something that would "Wake me up, then fuck me up!" The Bartender added some expresso to a Black Russian and the Espresso Martini was born.

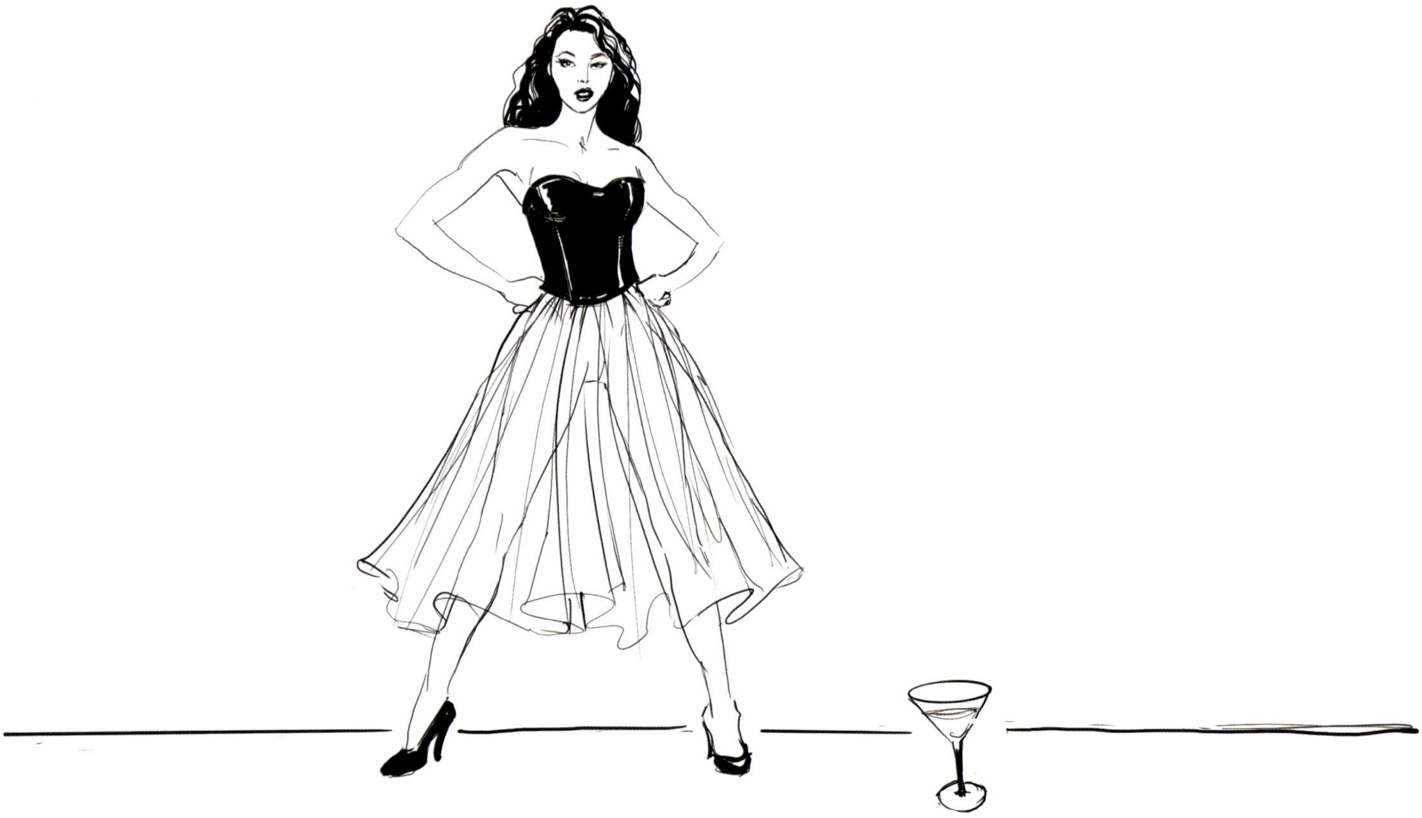

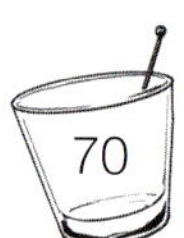

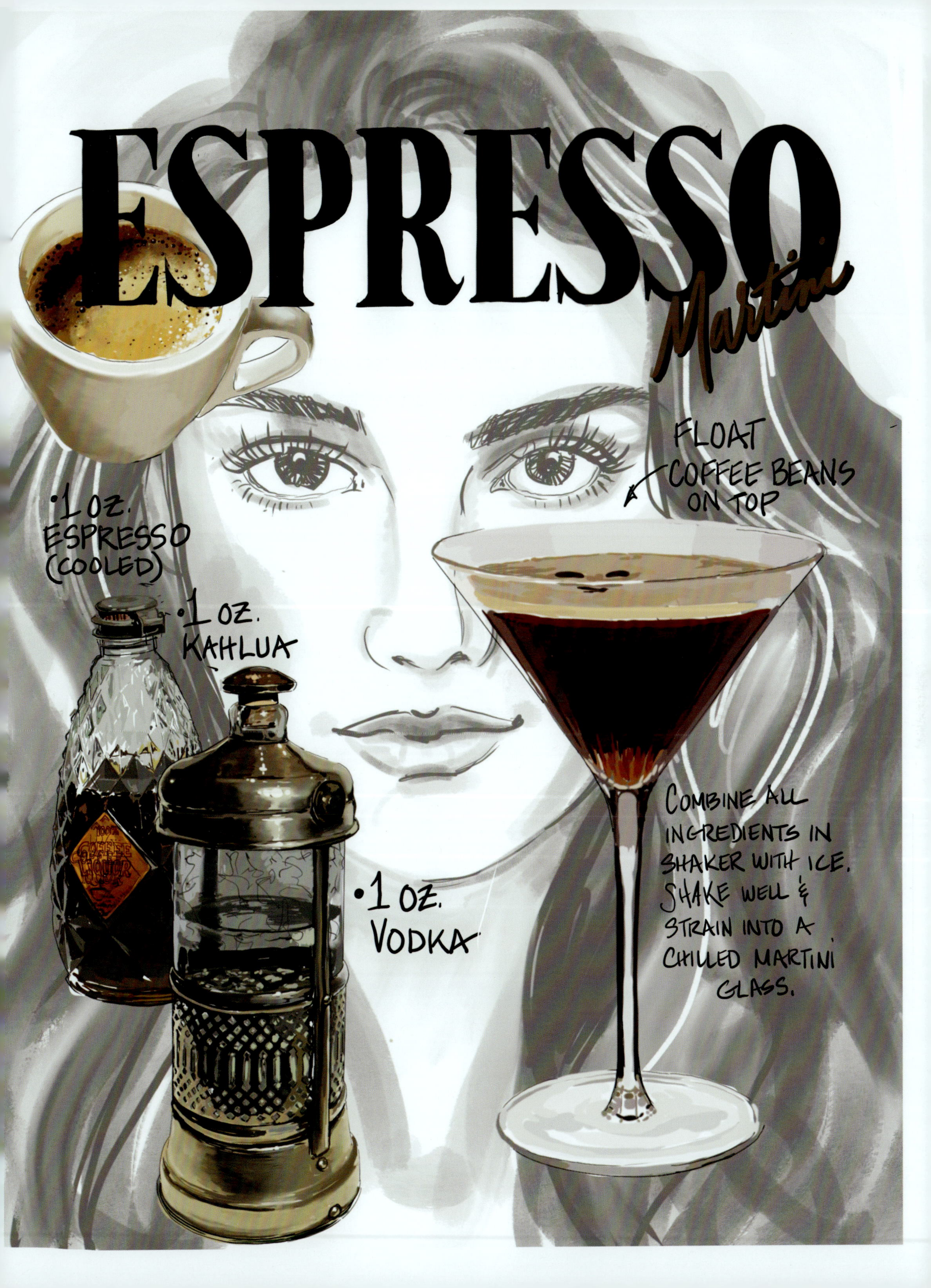

ESPRESSO
Martini

- 1 oz. ESPRESSO (COOLED)
- 1 oz. KAHLUA
- 1 oz. VODKA

FLOAT COFFEE BEANS ON TOP

COMBINE ALL INGREDIENTS IN SHAKER WITH ICE. SHAKE WELL & STRAIN INTO A CHILLED MARTINI GLASS.

Gimlet

My first "real" boyfriend drank Vodka Gimlets. I thought that was very sophisticated. A Gimlet is a simple drink, tart with a touch of sweet. The Rose's Lime Juice makes all the difference; this is one time that fresh is not best.

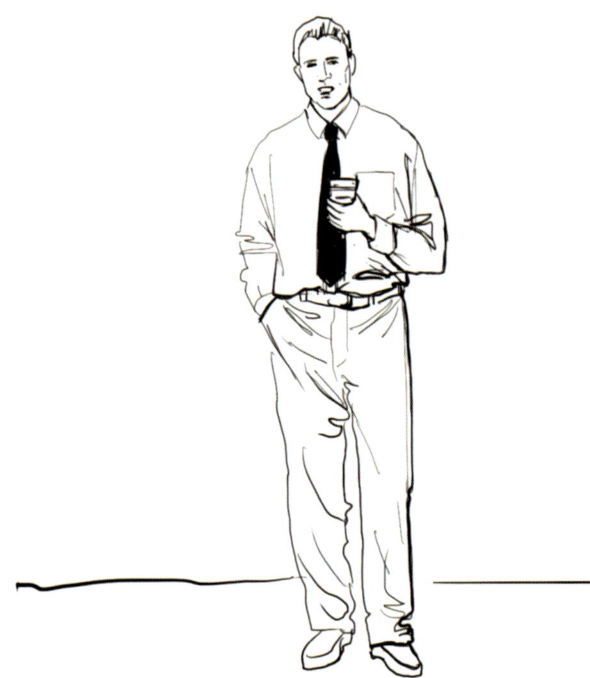

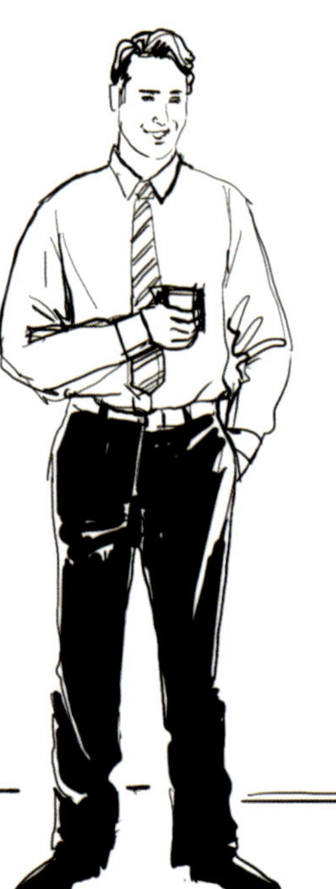

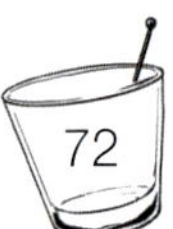

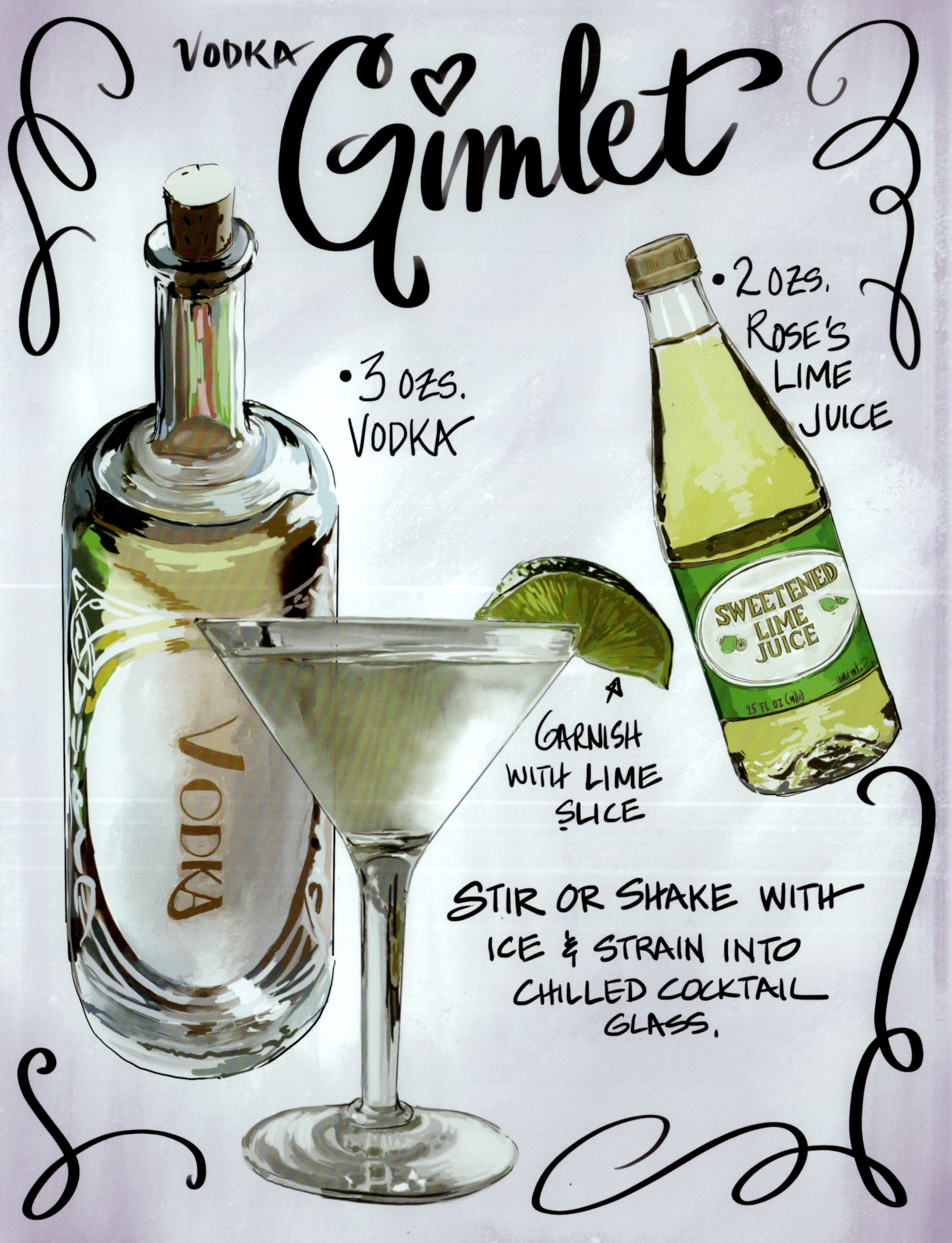

VODKA
Gimlet
•3 OZS. VODKA
•2 OZS. ROSE'S LIME JUICE
VODKA
SWEETENED LIME JUICE
GARNISH WITH LIME SLICE
STIR OR SHAKE WITH ICE & STRAIN INTO CHILLED COCKTAIL GLASS.

The Moscow Mule

First, let's say what this cocktail isn't — it is not from Russia. Nor does it have anything to do with Mules. Now, for what this cocktail is — it's delicious. Created in 1939, it was great way for bars to use up extra inventory of ginger beer and vodka, and a way to sell the copper mugs in which Mules are traditionally served. The mug keeps the cocktail extra cold and refreshing.

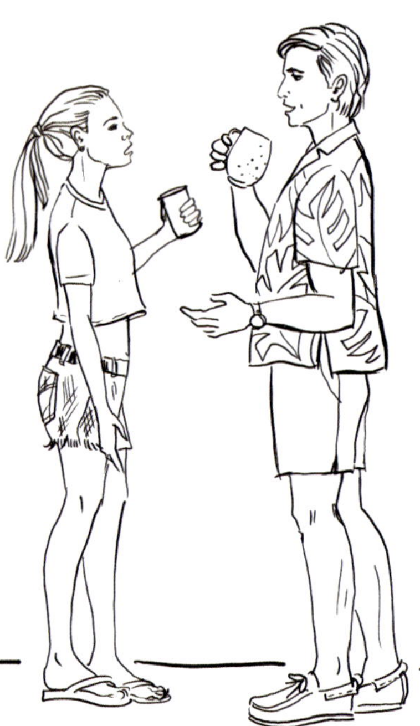

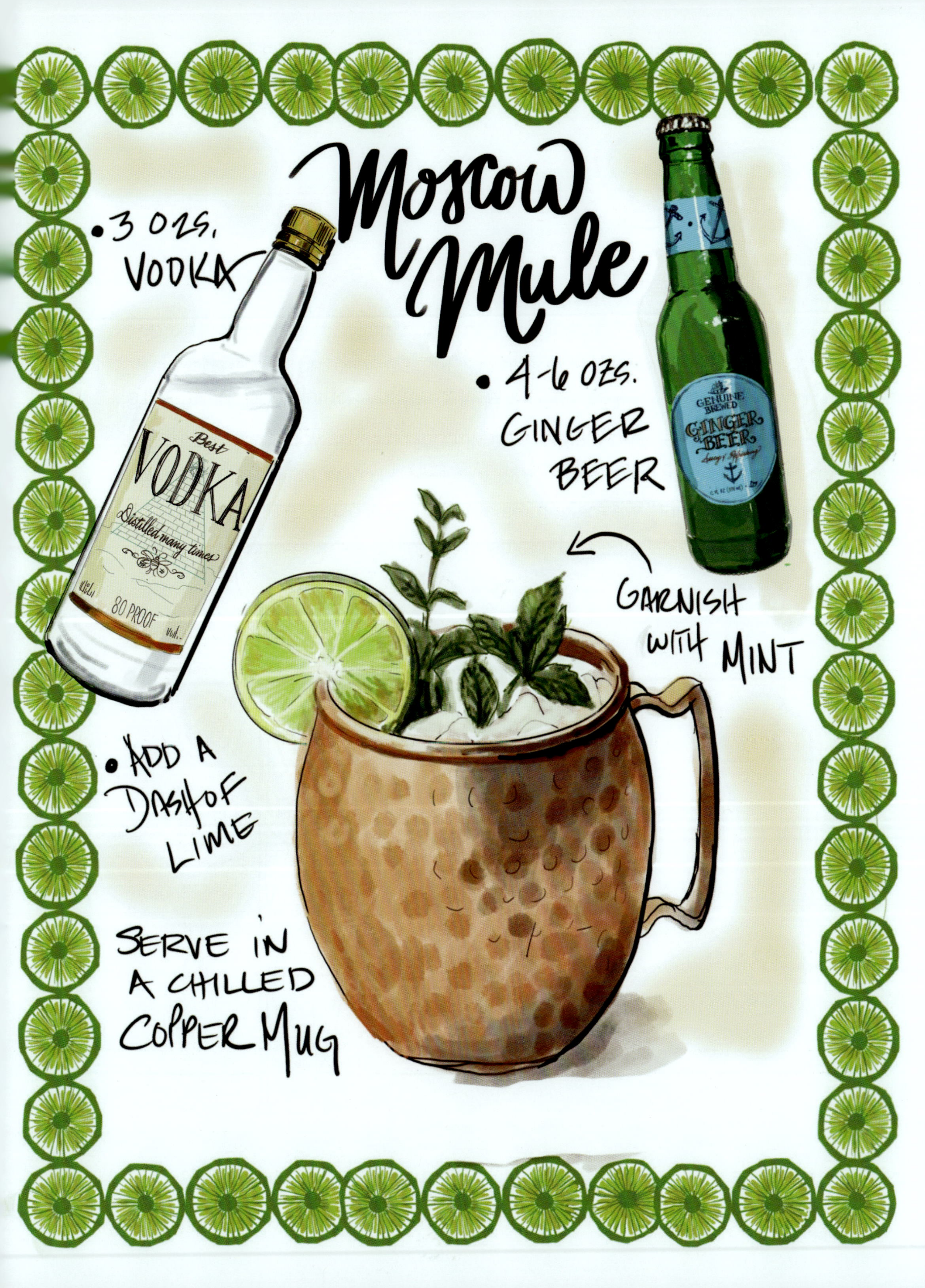
Moscow Mule
• 3 OZS. VODKA
Best
VODKA
Distilled many times
80 PROOF
• 4-6 OZS. GINGER BEER
GENUINE BREWED
GINGER BEER
GARNISH WITH MINT
• ADD A DASH OF LIME
SERVE IN A CHILLED COPPER MUG

Porn Star Martini

What's in a name? Actually, not as much as you might think. This drink, which was invented in London in 1999, has nothing at all to do with porn stars. The name is just a provocative one, which you undoubtedly will remember, and therefore order again. Unless you are more like me and would be mortified to order this delicious concoction at a bar. I know that's silly, but I will make mine at home. The glass of Prosecco is a nice, sweet balance and makes this cocktail extra special.

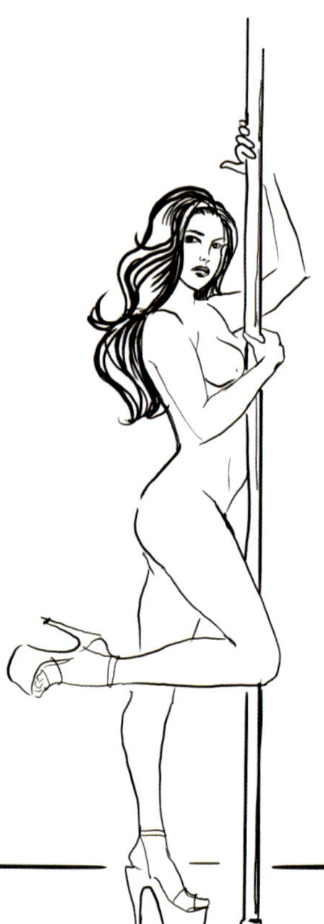

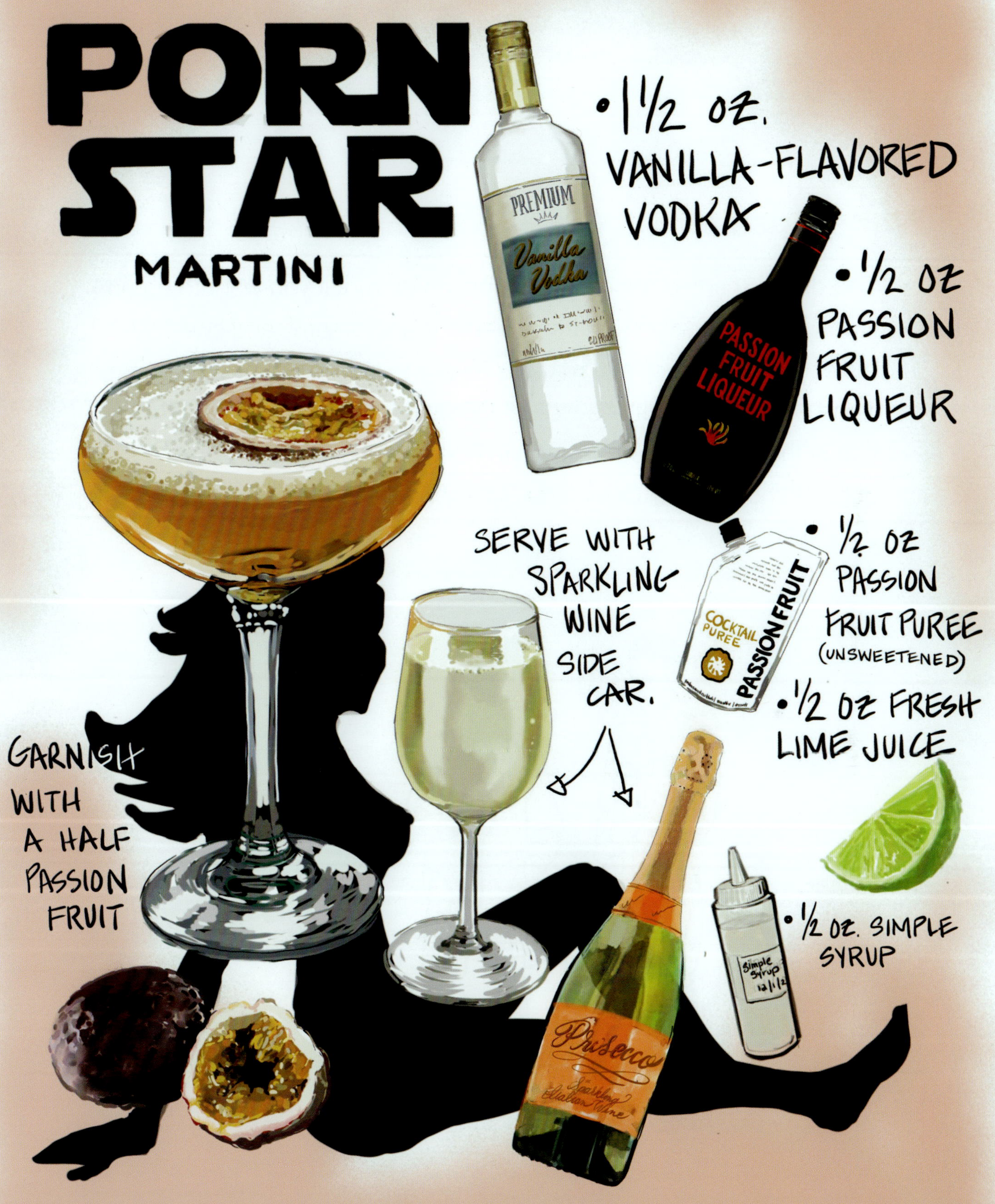

ADD VODKA, LIQUEUR, PUREE, LIME & SYRUP TO SHAKER WITH ICE. STRAIN INTO CHILLED COUPE.

White Russian

This drink is named "white" for the cream (or milk if you want to dumb it down) and "Russian" for the vodka. It is also creamy and sweet and tastes a lot like chocolate milk. It is meant to be drank slowly, savored, if you will, which is not easy to do. Drink too many and you will not be happy the next morning. The White Russian was the title character's drink of choice in the movie *The Big Lebowski*. Love that movie, and the cocktail too.

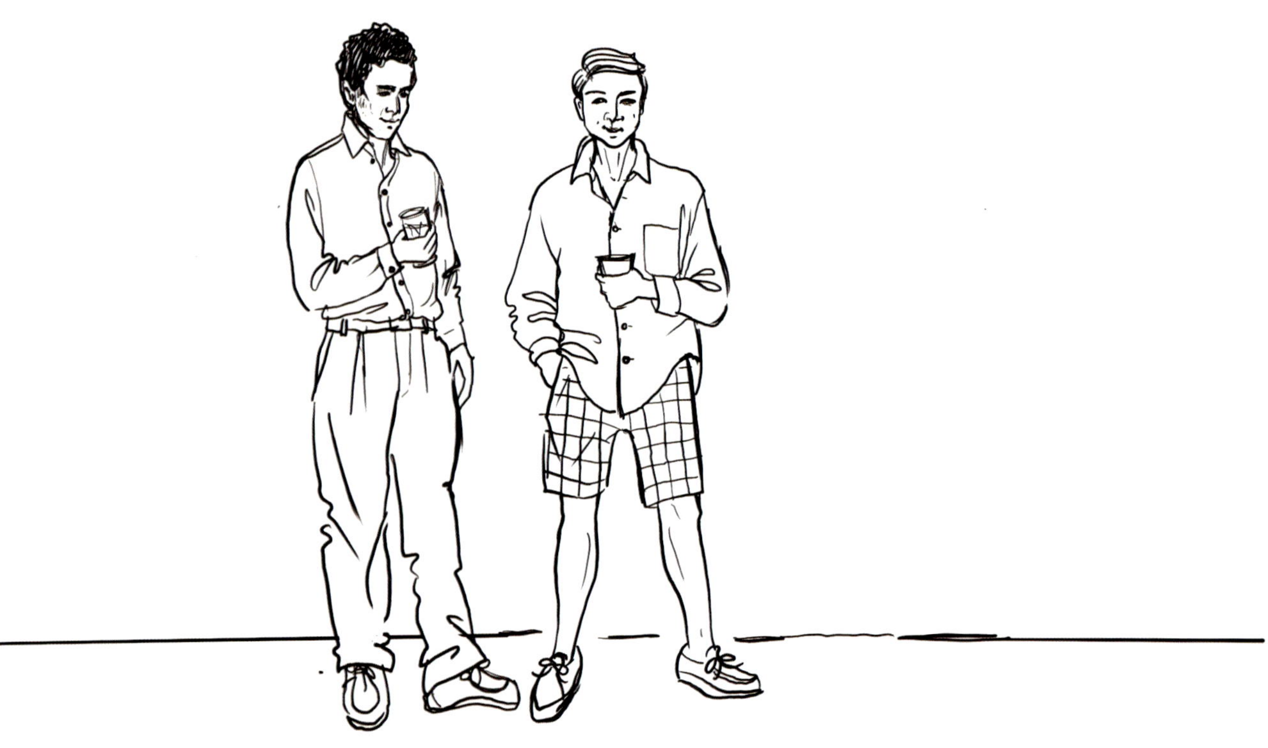

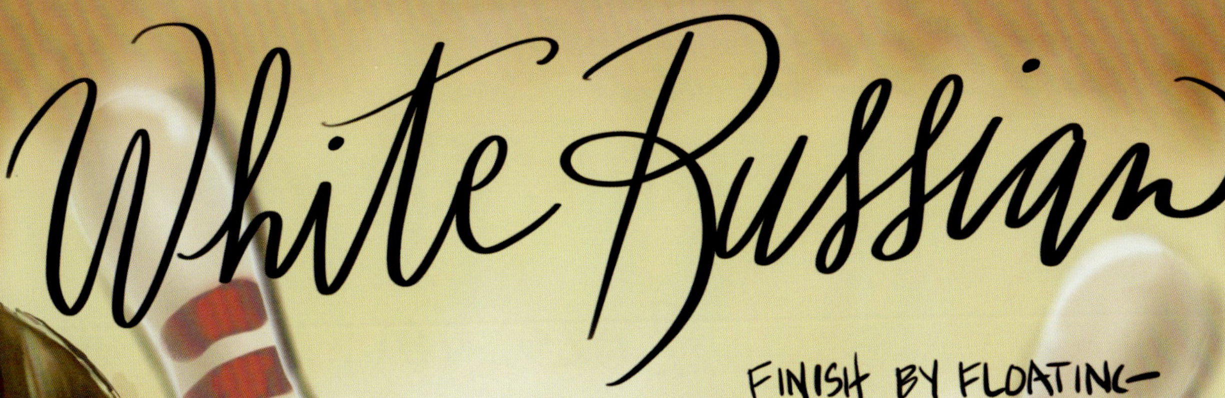

FINISH BY FLOATING

• 1 PART CREAM

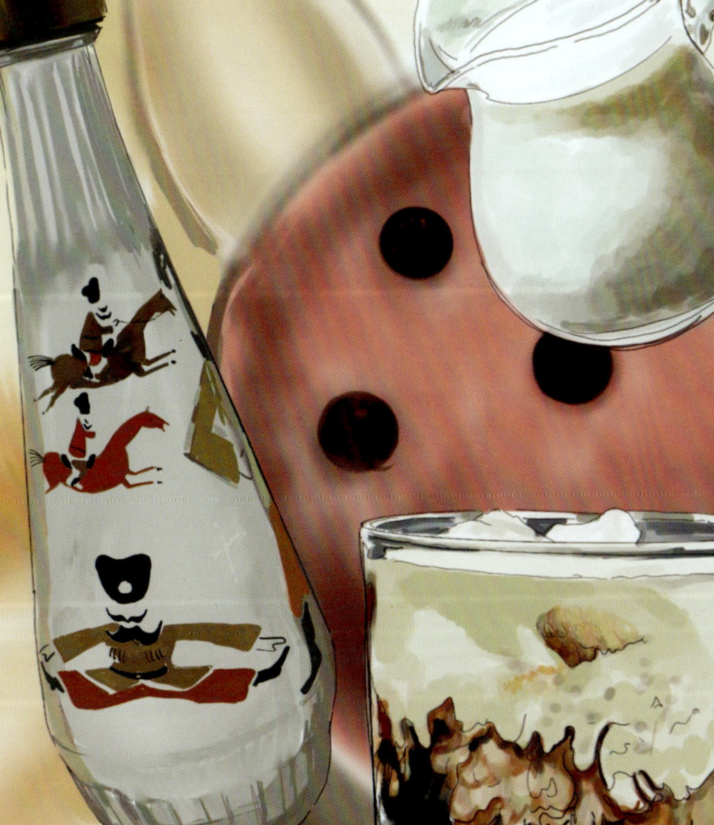

• 1 PART KAHLUA

• 2 PARTS VODKA

ON THE ROCKS

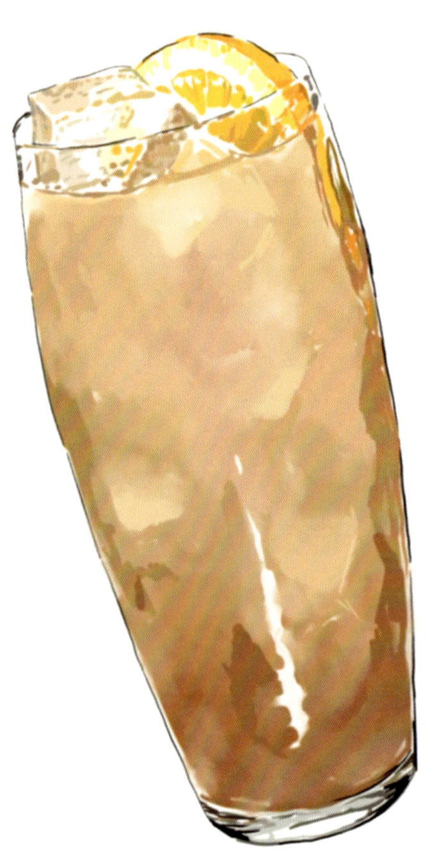

The Greyhound

2 ozs. vodka or gin
4 ozs. grapefruit juice

VODKA

The Sea Breeze

1½ ozs. vodka
2 ozs. cranberry juice
4 oz. grapefruit juice

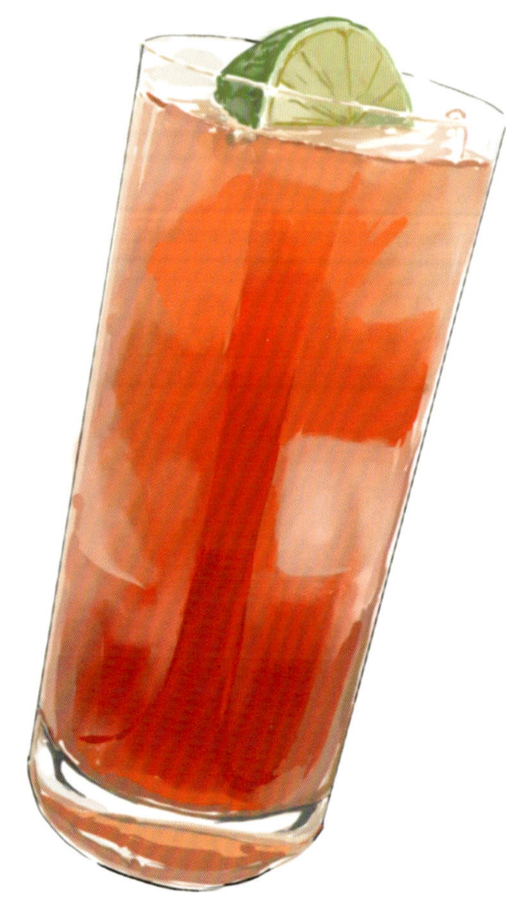

THE MADRAS

1½ OZ. VODKA

3 OZS. CRANBERRY JUICE

1 OZ. ORANGE JUICE

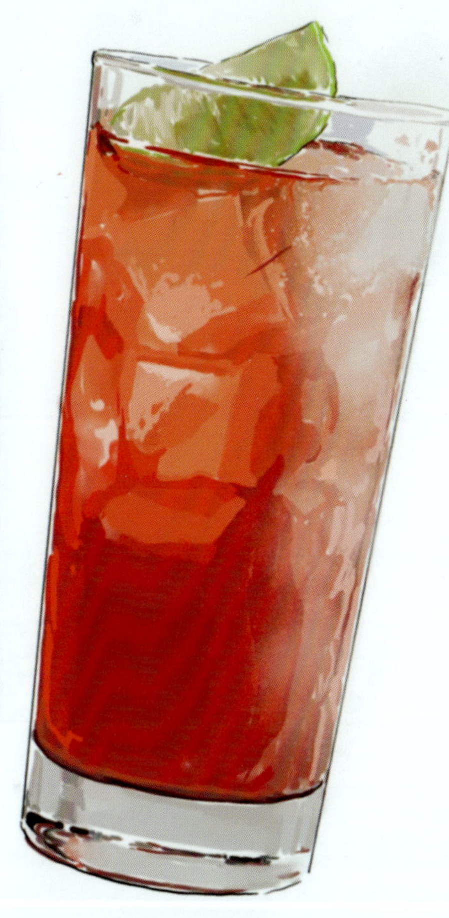

DRINKS

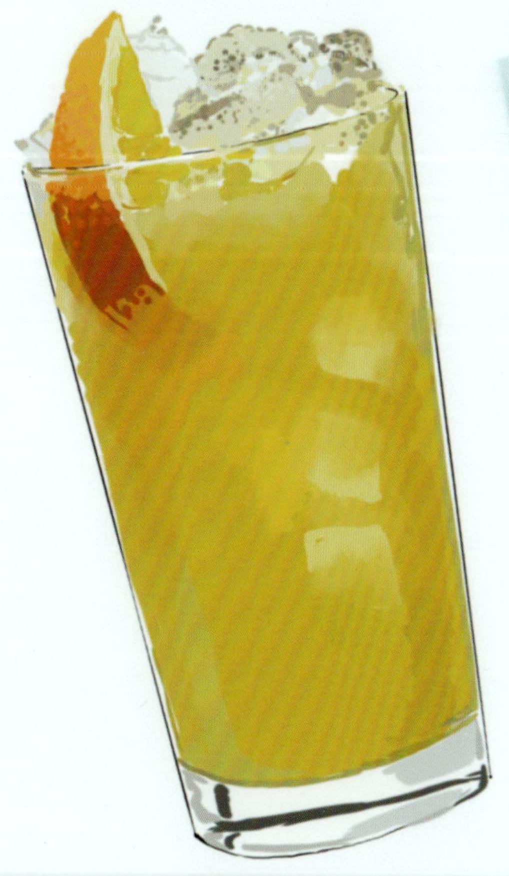

THE SCREW DRIVER

2 OZ. VODKA

4 OZ. ORANGE JUICE

“One tequila, two tequila, three tequila, floor..”

—George Carlin

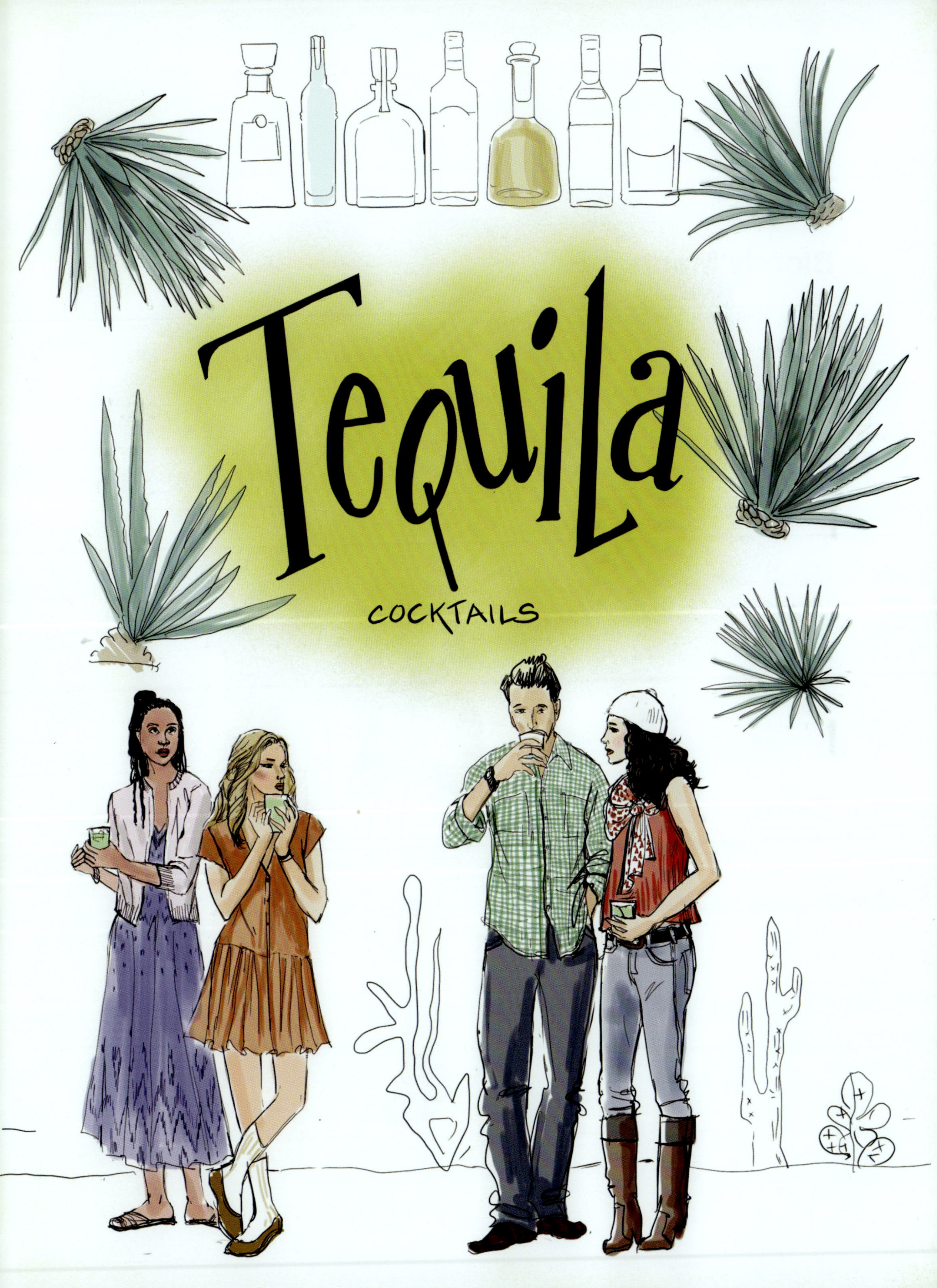
Tequila
COCKTAILS

Bloody Maria

Is this just a Bloody Mary made with Tequila instead of Vodka? Not exactly. This recipe contains more citrus, and that pairs well with Tequila's depth. I think that people who favor a brunchtime "Bloody" might like the tequila version even more than the classic vodka version. I know I do.

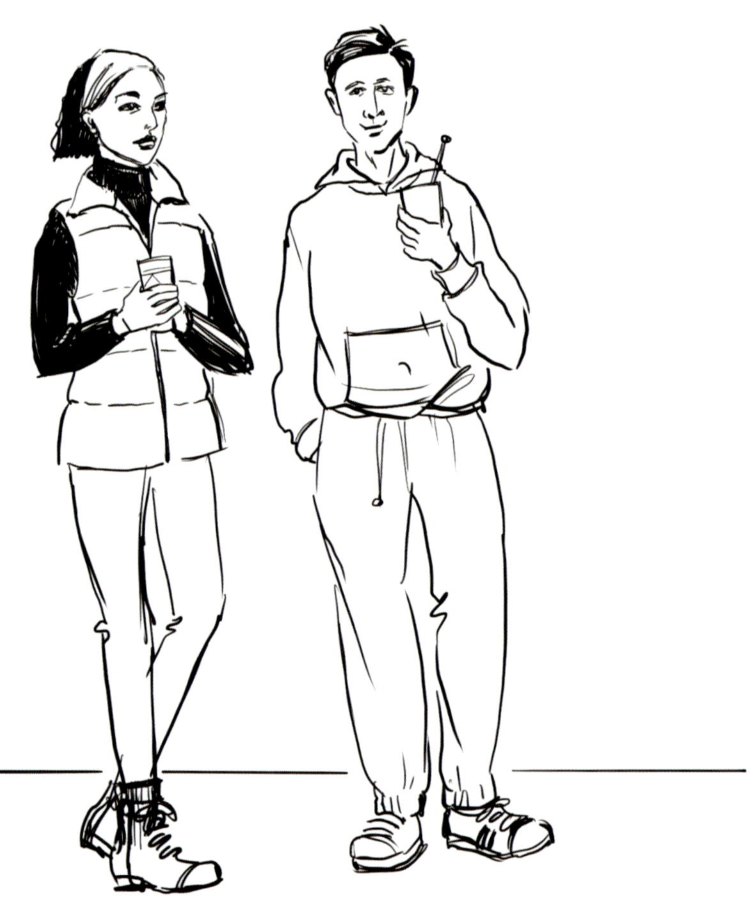

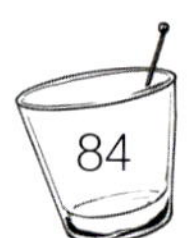

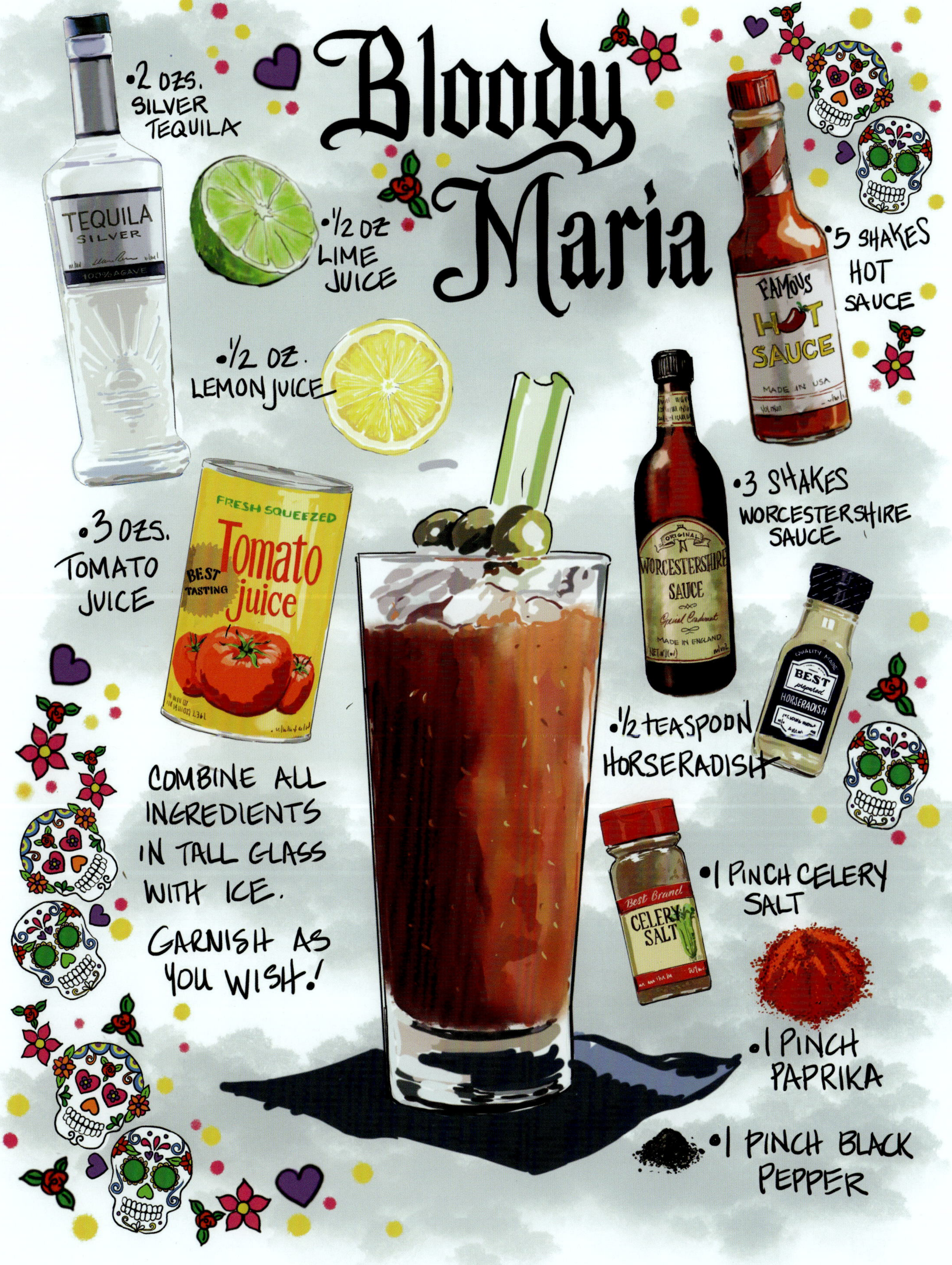

Bloody Maria
•2 OZS. SILVER TEQUILA
•1/2 OZ LIME JUICE
•1/2 OZ. LEMON JUICE
•3 OZS. TOMATO JUICE
COMBINE ALL INGREDIENTS IN TALL GLASS WITH ICE.
GARNISH AS YOU WISH!
•5 SHAKES HOT SAUCE
•3 SHAKES WORCESTERSHIRE SAUCE
•1/2 TEASPOON HORSERADISH
•1 PINCH CELERY SALT
•1 PINCH PAPRIKA
•1 PINCH BLACK PEPPER
TEQUILA SILVER
100% AGAVE
FRESH SQUEEZED
BEST TASTING
Tomato juice
FAMOUS HOT SAUCE
MADE IN USA
ORIGINAL
WORCESTERSHIRE SAUCE
MADE IN ENGLAND
BEST
HORSERADISH
Best Brand
CELERY SALT

Dardar

This is not a classic cocktail. The recipe is my own, or like most drinks, a combination of many recipes. I was looking for cocktail recipes for this book and I shouted out to my Facebook and Instagram friends for some help. This recipe (not a recipe, but a list of ingredients) came from Israel. So, I measured and tweaked and came up with this cocktail. Orgeat (almond syrup), pineapple and passion fruit paired with Tequila and Vodka are amazing, but the pinch of chili and the Tajin rim, which is spicy not salty, make this drink tasty and complex. I do not know if this tastes anything like the Dardar on the menu that was sent to me, but it tastes damn good.

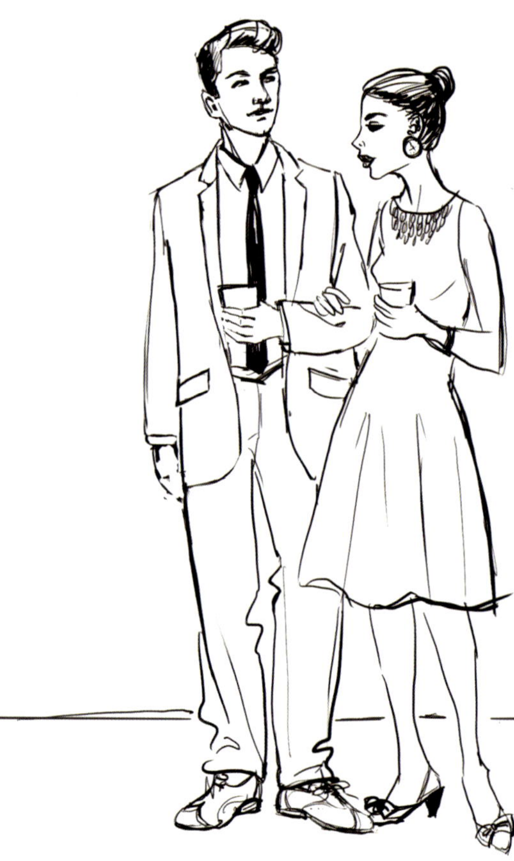

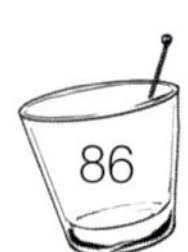

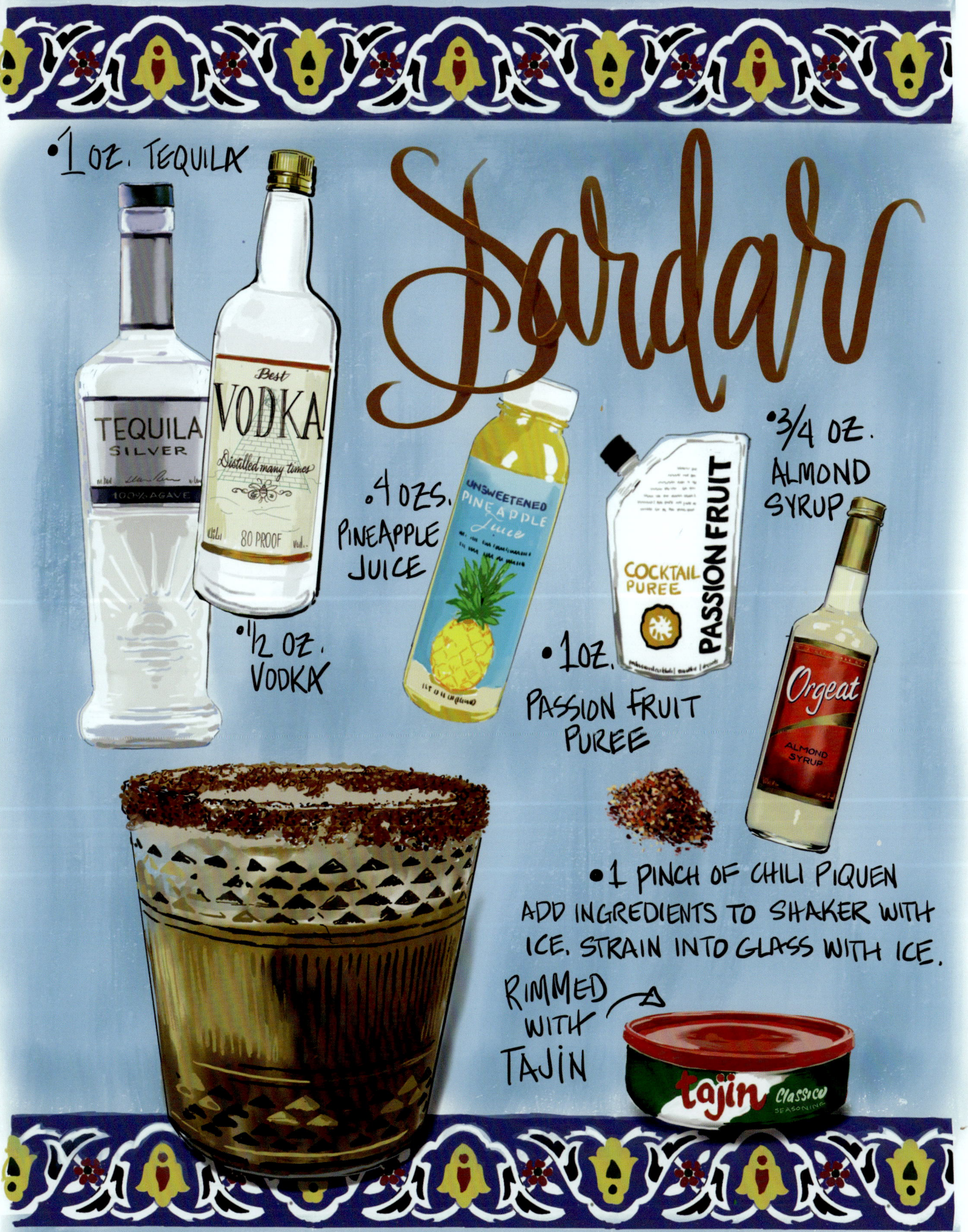

Sardar

- 1 oz. Tequila
- ½ oz. Vodka
- 4 ozs. Pineapple Juice
- 1 oz. Passion Fruit Puree
- ¾ oz. Almond Syrup
- 1 pinch of Chili Piquen

Add ingredients to shaker with ice. Strain into glass with ice.

Rimmed with Tajin

Margarita

A Margarita is one of the easiest drinks to make from scratch. All you need is Tequila, some fresh limes, and something to cut the tartness of the lime. The "something" that cuts the tartness can be liquor based (like Cointreau orange liqueur), another juice (like orange juice) or a sweetener such as sugar or agave. As for the amount to add – it's a matter of personal taste. And be sure to taste often.

I am telling you this to dissuade you from buying those bottled mixes. They taste OK, but even those without preservatives aren't 'fresh" and the taste of your cocktail will suffer. And once opened they only last from a few days to two weeks, which mean you must use them up really quickly. And now I have to ask myself why this last point is a bad thing.

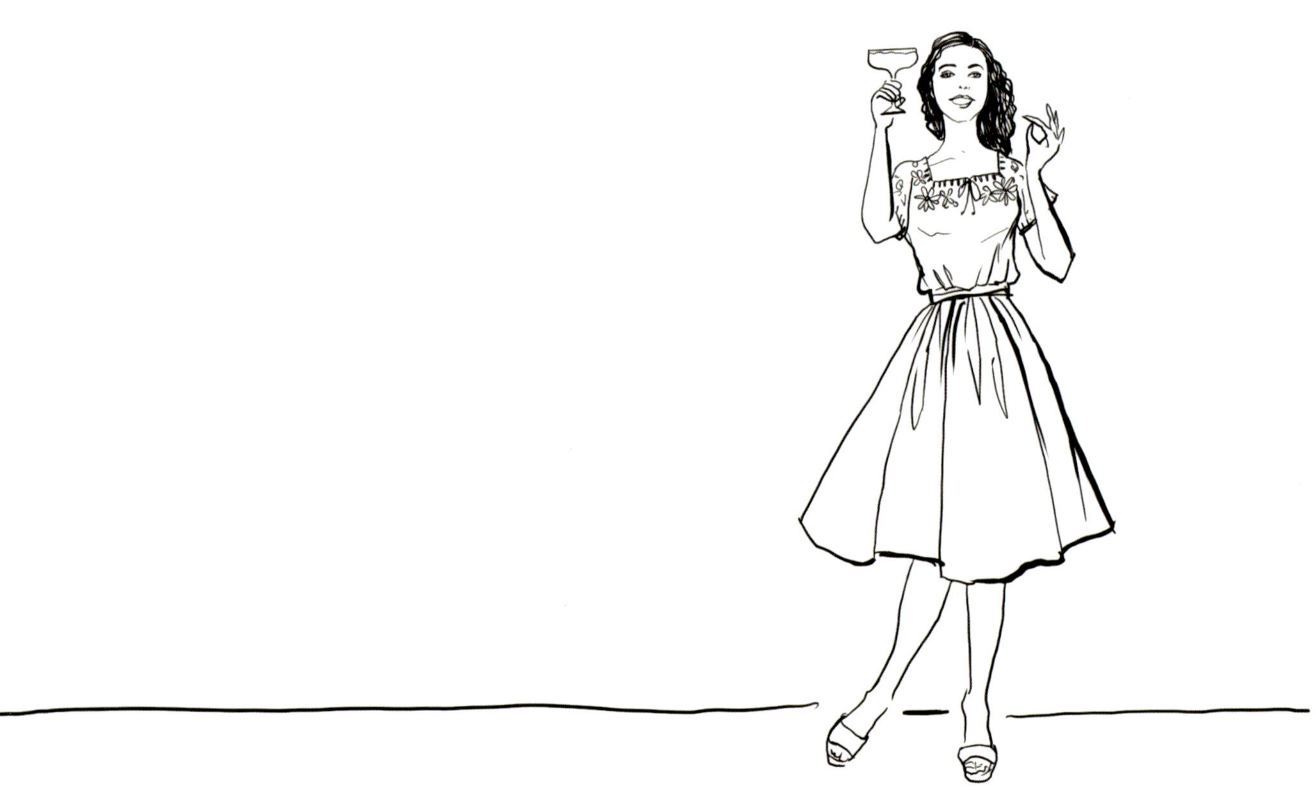

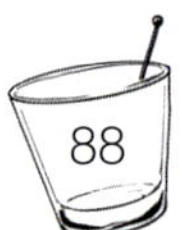

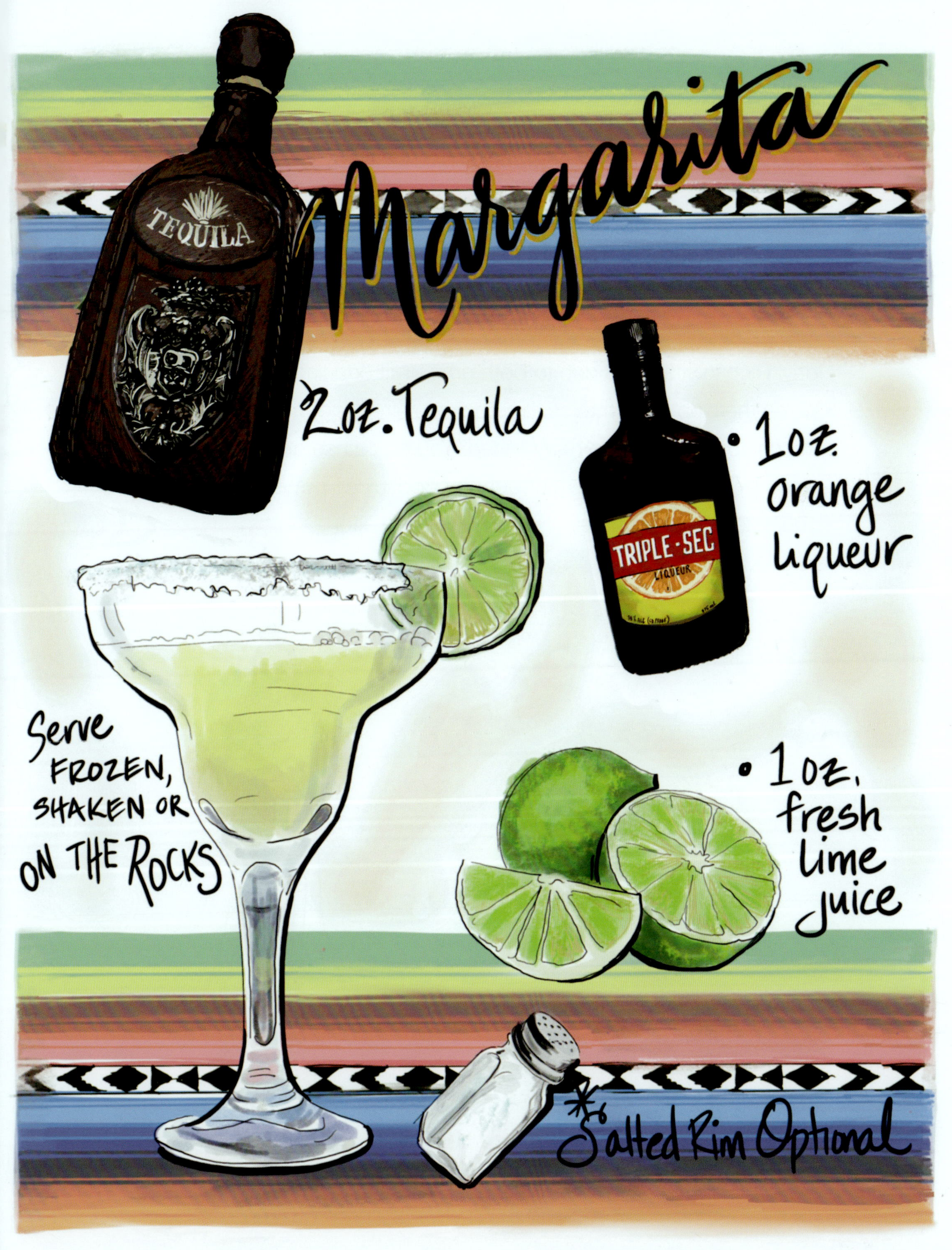
Margarita
TEQUILA
2oz. Tequila
• 1oz. orange liqueur
TRIPLE-SEC
LIQUEUR
Serve FROZEN, SHAKEN OR ON THE ROCKS
• 1oz. fresh lime juice
*Salted Rim Optional

The Paloma

The most popular drink in Mexico, the Paloma is perfect for hot summer's day. Rich in vitamin C due to both grapefruit and lime juices (no scurvy here!) the club soda makes this cocktail refreshing, and the salted rim keeps you from getting dehydrated. You could use grapefruit soda, but since by now you will have bought a good juicer, put it to good use and squeeze the fruit yourself. It's well worth the effort.

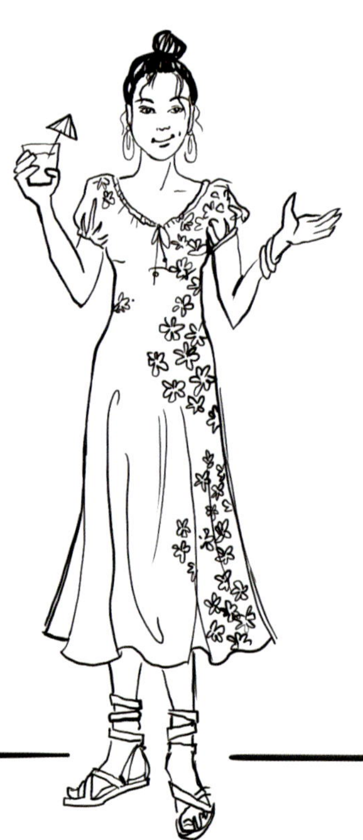

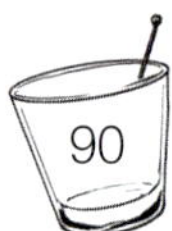

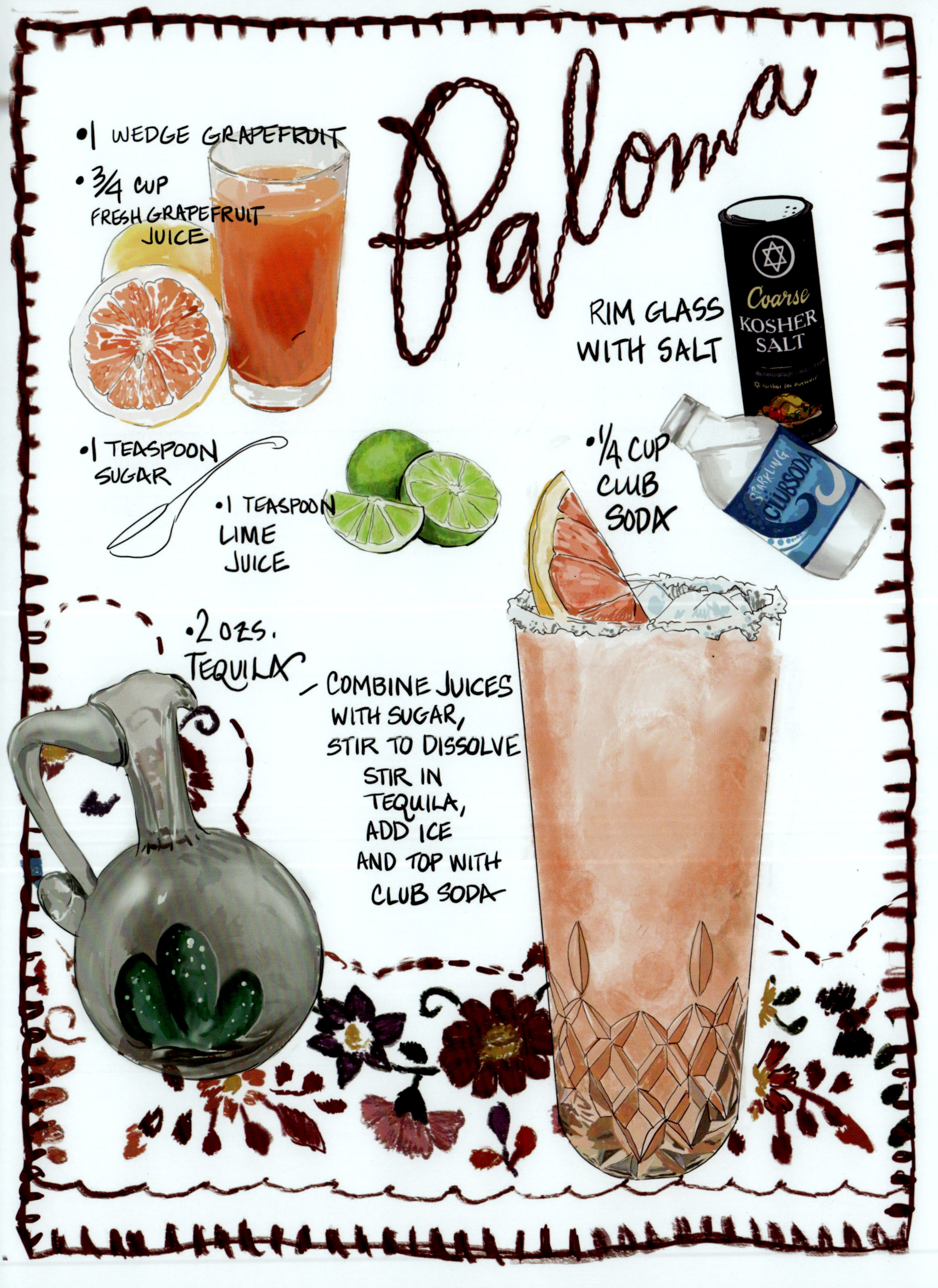

Paloma
•1 WEDGE GRAPEFRUIT
•3/4 CUP
FRESH GRAPEFRUIT
JUICE
RIM GLASS
WITH SALT
Coarse
KOSHER
SALT
•1 TEASPOON
SUGAR
•1 TEASPOON
LIME
JUICE
•1/4 CUP
CLUB
SODA
SPARKLING
CLUBSODA
•2 OZS.
TEQUILA
COMBINE JUICES
WITH SUGAR,
STIR TO DISSOLVE
STIR IN
TEQUILA,
ADD ICE
AND TOP WITH
CLUB SODA

Ranch Water

The secret to a great glass of ranch water is Top-O-Chico. Everyone will tell you that there is no substituting this brand of sparkling water in this cocktail. The Mexican mineral water has a smooth mouth feel and bubbliness that is rated at the top of the lists from people who make the lists of the top sparkling waters. There is also the need for limes, lots of them, and lemons too if you want. I am going to spare you the story arguing if this drink was invented in Austin or Marfa, just know that it is refreshing on a hot day in Texas, or anywhere else.

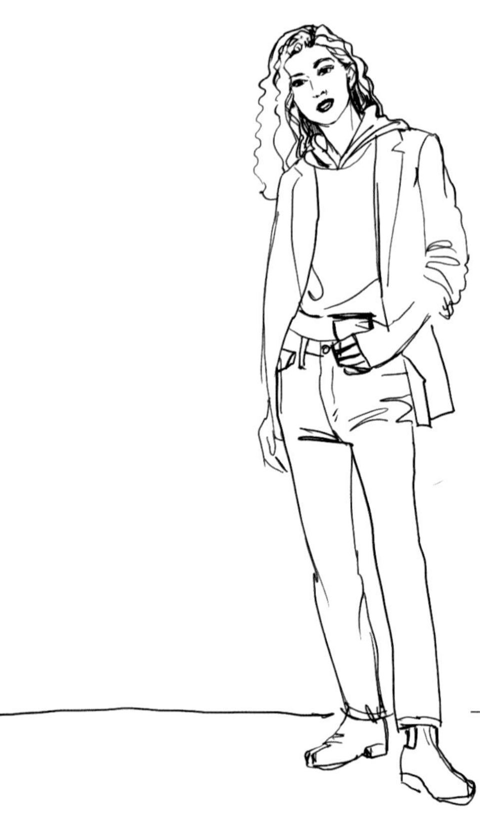

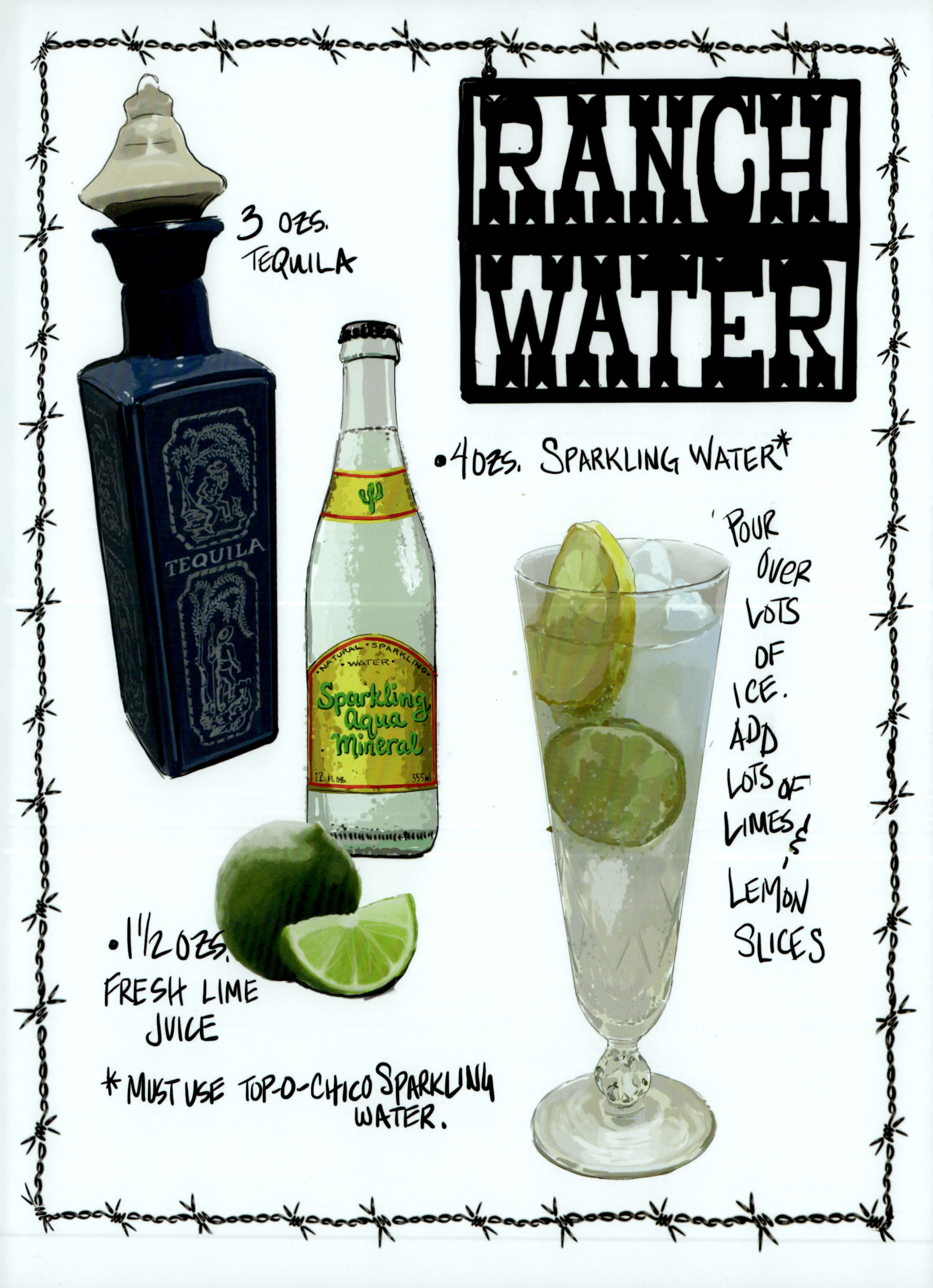
RANCH
WATER
3 OZS.
TEQUILA
TEQUILA
•4OZS. SPARKLING WATER*
NATURAL · SPARKLING · WATER
Sparkling Aqua Mineral
12 FL.OZ.
355ml
POUR OVER LOTS OF ICE. ADD LOTS OF LIMES & LEMON SLICES
•1½ OZS.
FRESH LIME JUICE
* MUST USE TOP-O-CHICO SPARKLING WATER.

Tequila Sunrise

"It's another Tequila Sunrise, starin' slowly 'cross the sky" (Henley & Frey, 1973, Track 4) as the Eagle's song says so well. In yet another music connection, the Rolling Stones favored the drink and dubbed their 1972 tour the "*Cocaine and Tequila Sunrise Tour*". So put on your bright blue and fuchsia polyester bellbottom jumpsuit, take the oversized rollers out of your feathered hair, and enjoy the taste of 70's deliciousness.

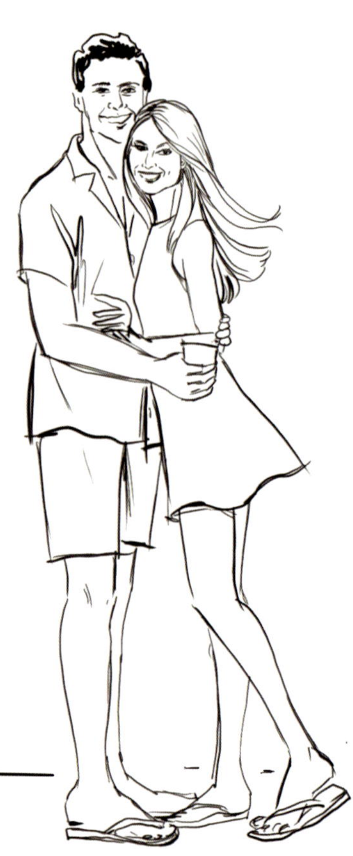

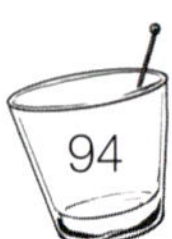

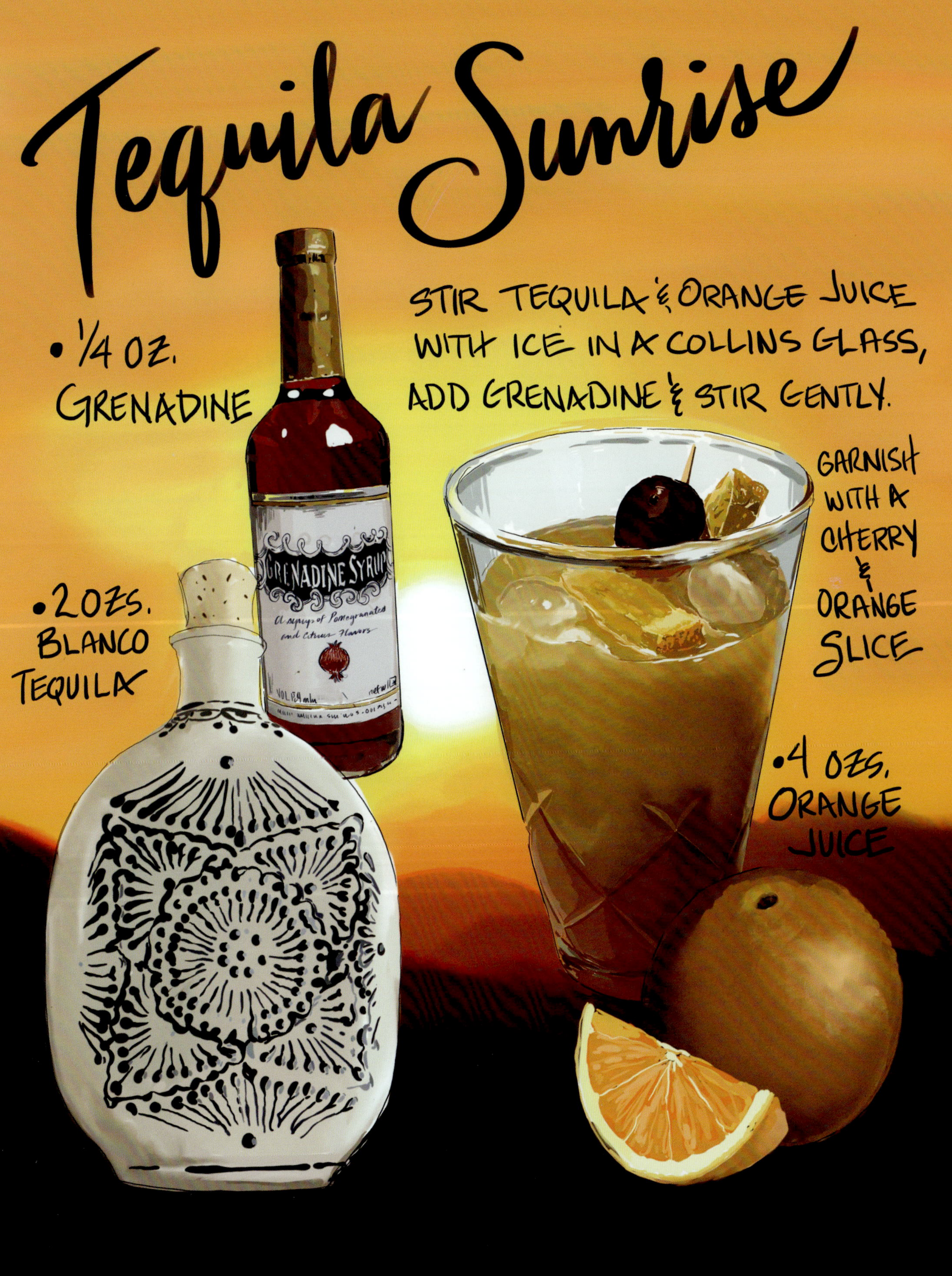
Tequila Sunrise
• 1/4 OZ. GRENADINE
STIR TEQUILA & ORANGE JUICE WITH ICE IN A COLLINS GLASS, ADD GRENADINE & STIR GENTLY.
GARNISH WITH A CHERRY & ORANGE SLICE
GRENADINE SYRUP
• 2 OZS. BLANCO TEQUILA
• 4 OZS. ORANGE JUICE

"I want someone to look at me the way I look at rum."

—Unknown

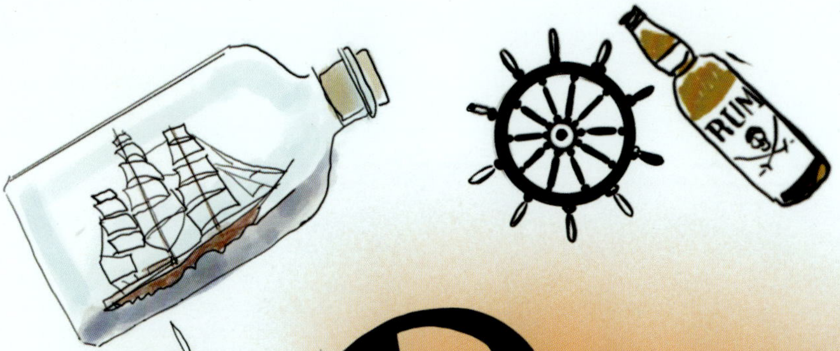

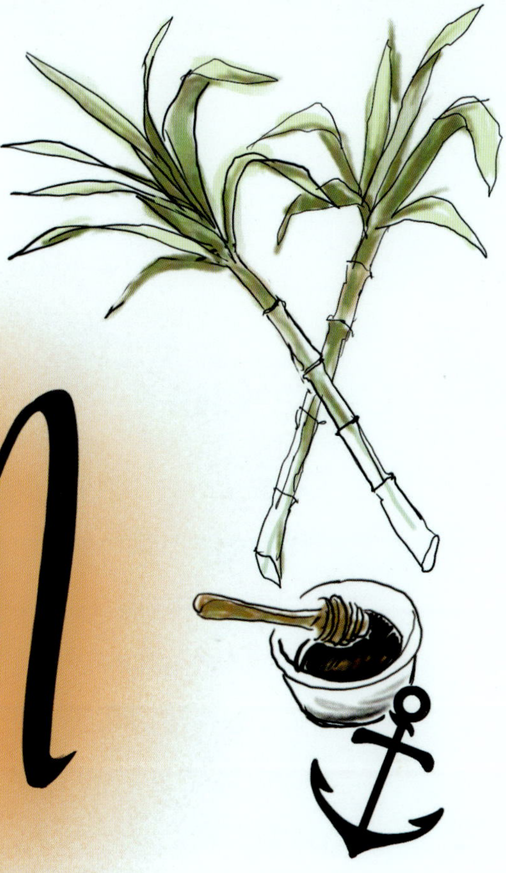

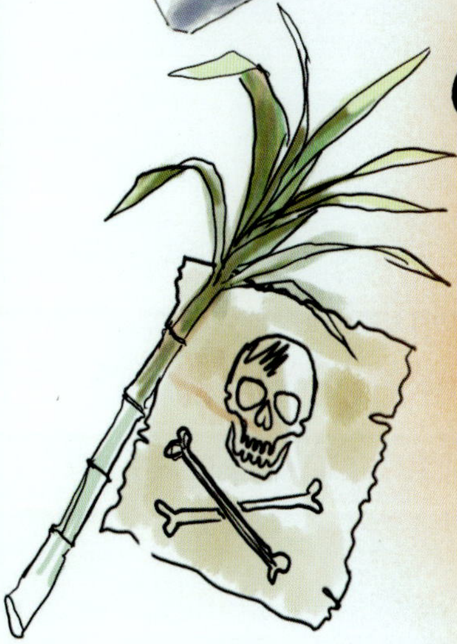

Rum

COCKTAILS

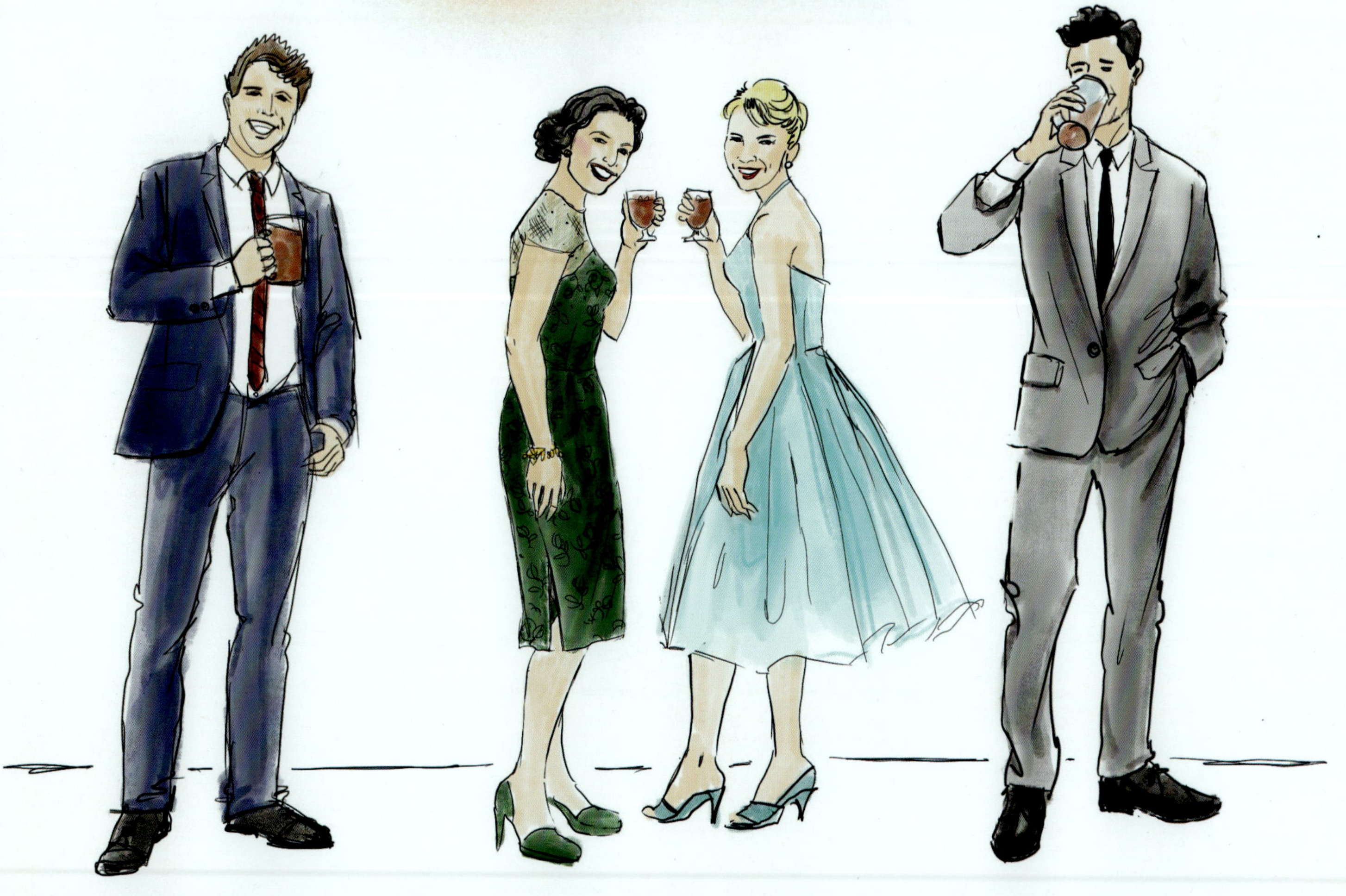

Cuba Libre

Cuba Libre is a fancy name for a very basic drink, a rum and coke. This is traditionally prepared with Coca-Cola, even more commonly Diet Coke. When I think of this drink, I am reminded of football parties in high school in suburban St Louis. The boys drank beer, and the girls favored the Rum and Coke. Even though this cocktail is a perfect pairing of two ingredients, I will forever equate this cocktail to those awkward teenage parties.

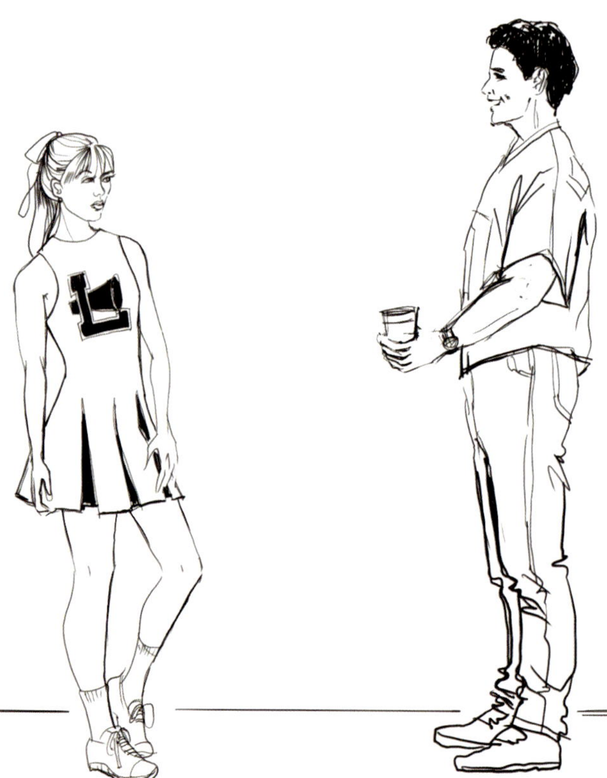

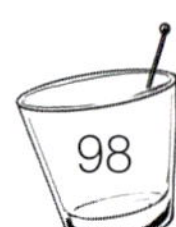

Cuba Libre

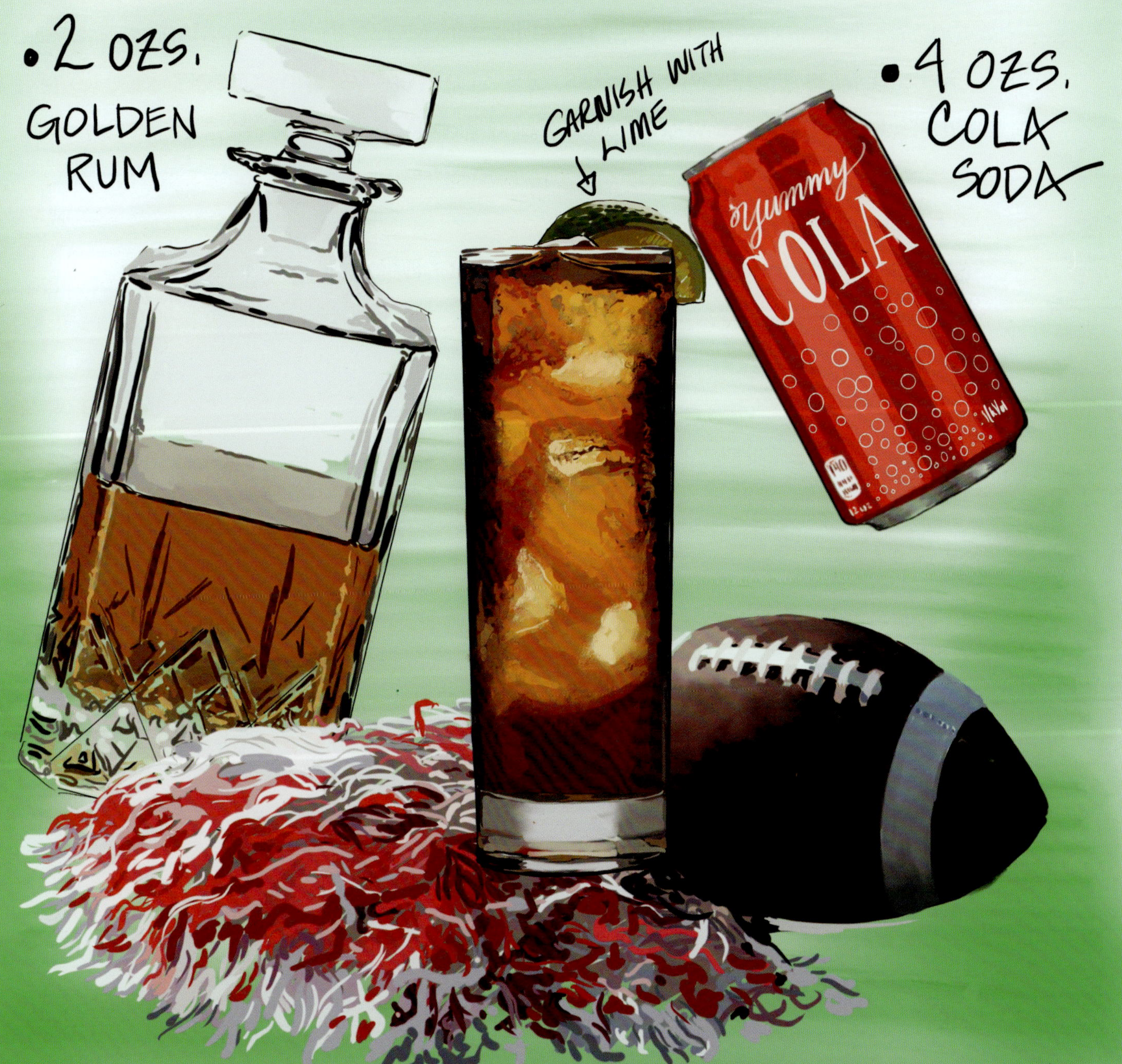

ADD INGREDIENTS TO TALL GLASS OVER ICE. SQUEEZE IN A LIME (OR TWO).

The Daiquiri

In the 1930's Ernest Hemmingway drank Daiquiris in Cuba. In ninth grade in St. Louis in the 1970's we had to read *The Old Man and the Sea* (Hemingway, 1952). Ernest Hemingway's third wife, Martha Gelhorn, was also from St. Louis, and she went to high school near where I live, so there you have it… and in only five degrees.

1. Daiquiri invented in Cuba
2. Ernest Hemmingway develops a taste for Daiquiris and introduces them to the U.S.
3. Hemmingway marries Martha Gelhorn
4. I read The Old Man and the Sea.
5. I re-read The Old Man and the Sea while sipping a Frozen Daiquiri.

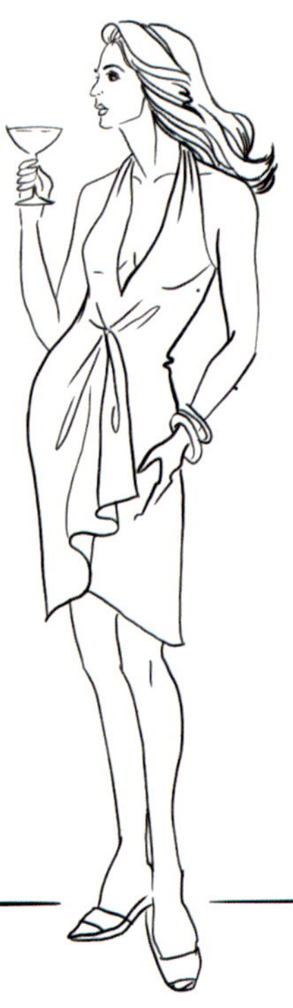

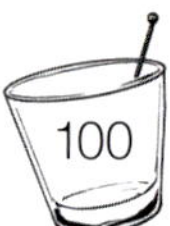

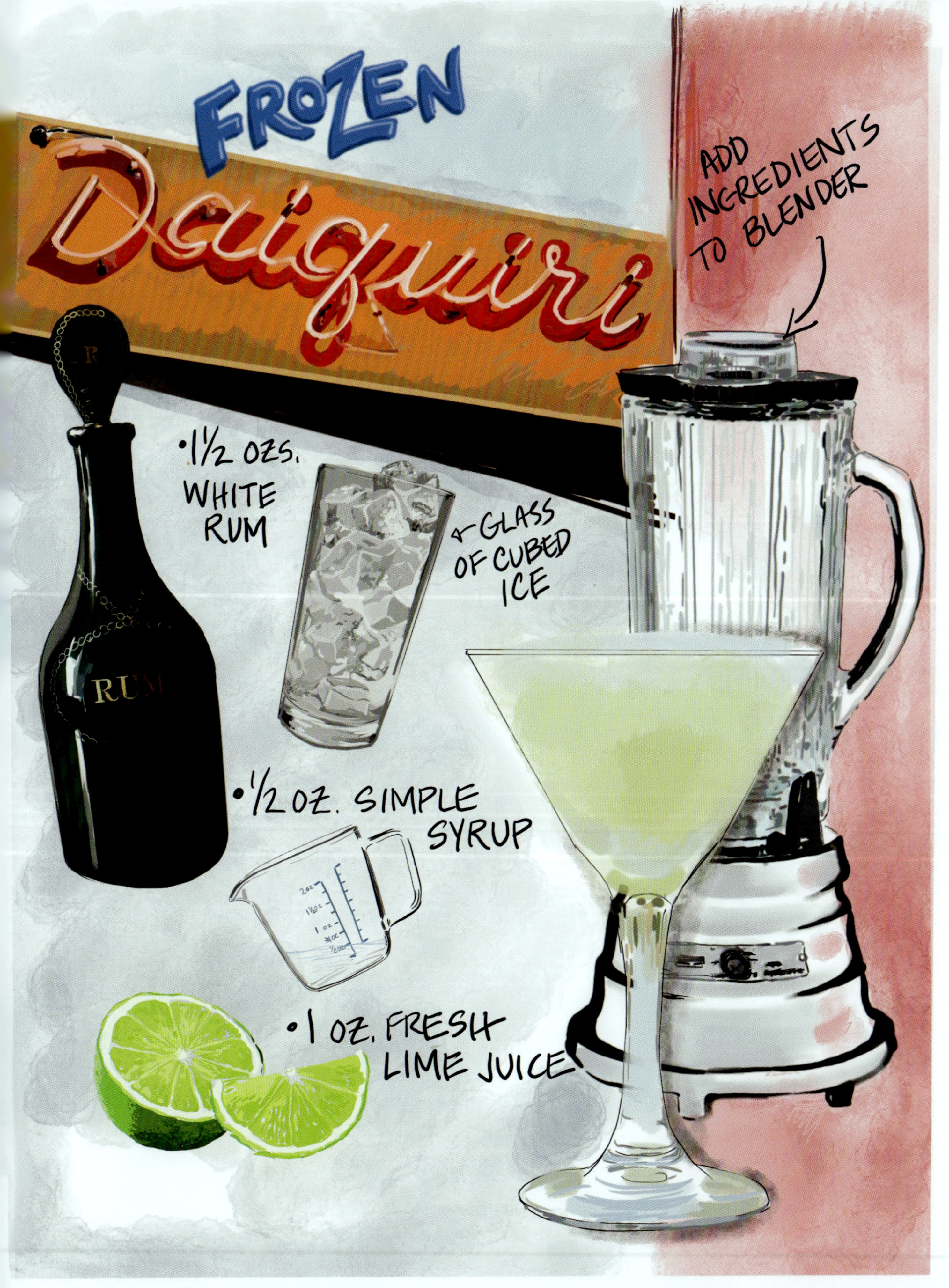
FROZEN
Daiquiri
ADD INGREDIENTS TO BLENDER
•1½ OZS. WHITE RUM
RUM
←GLASS OF CUBED ICE
•½ OZ. SIMPLE SYRUP
•1 OZ. FRESH LIME JUICE

Dark and Stormy

Gaze upon this cocktail and you are transported.

The setting sun is obscured by the clouds rolling in. The sea turns grey, the rain begins to come down, you take cover in a small grass shack on the beach… Ok, maybe I'm getting a little crazy but this rum cocktail is extra tasty. The trick to the Dark and Stormy is the slow pour over the barspoon, which creates a beautiful ombre effect. Alas, it will last only until you stir and enjoy.

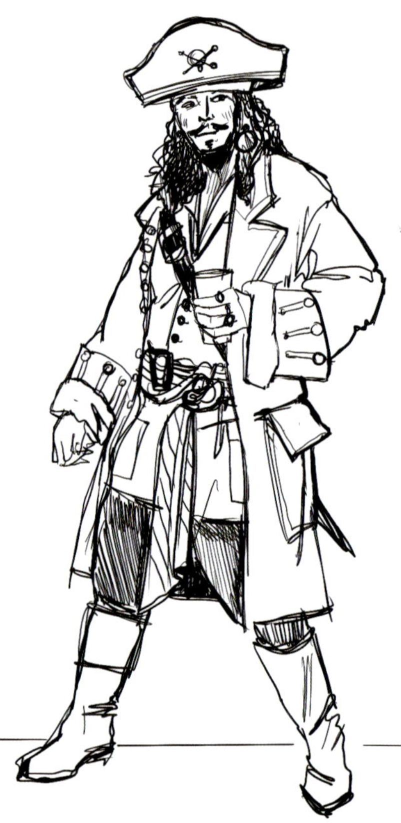

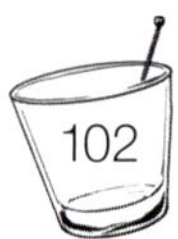

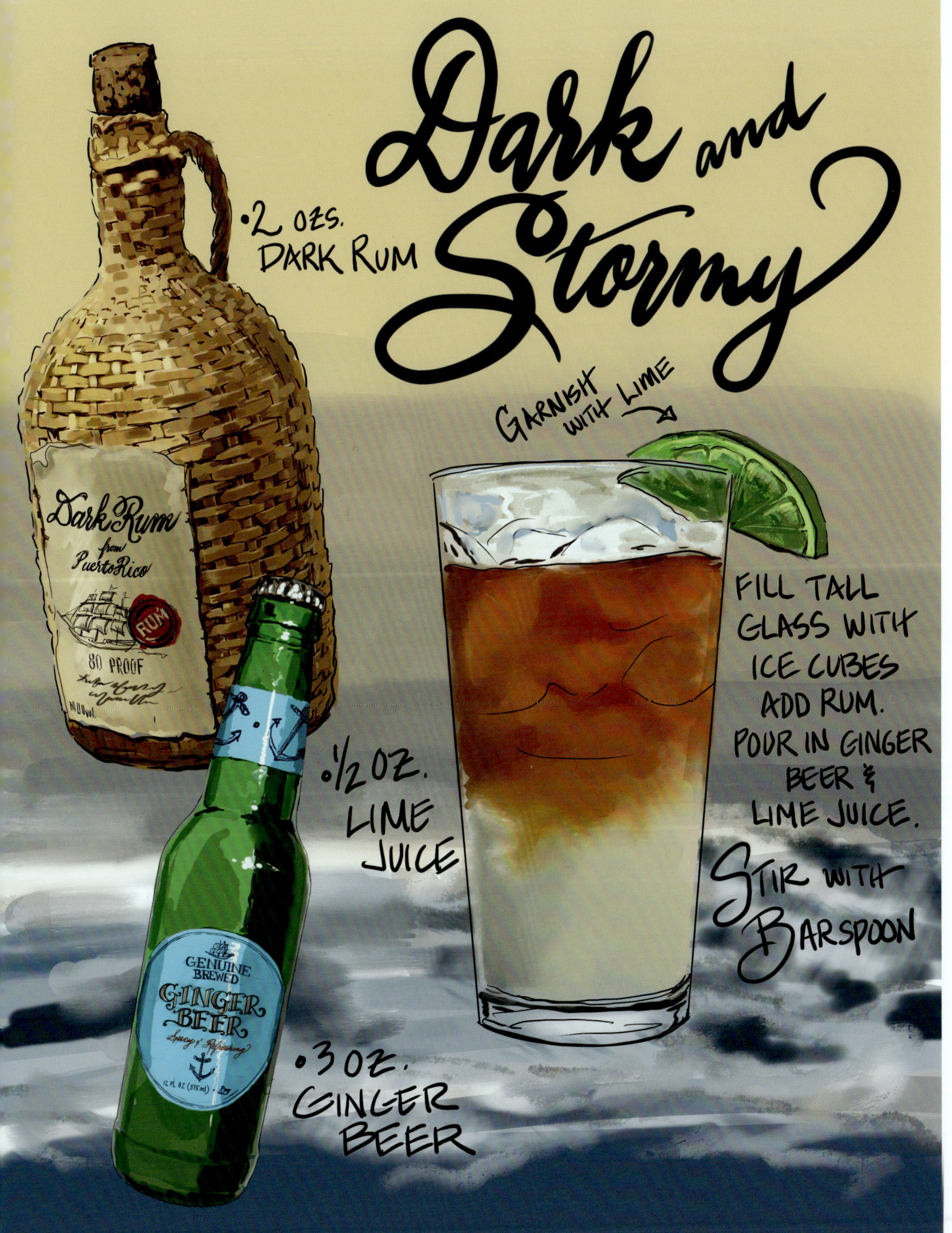
Dark and Stormy
•2 ozs. Dark Rum
Garnish with lime
Dark Rum from Puerto Rico
RUM
80 PROOF
•1/2 oz. Lime Juice
Fill tall glass with ice cubes add rum. Pour in ginger beer & lime juice.
Stir with Barspoon
Genuine Brewed Ginger Beer
•3 oz. Ginger Beer

Mai Tai

There are two reasons I love the Royal Hawaiian Hotel on Waikiki Beach in Honolulu, Hawaii. One is its alliterative nickname, "The Pink Palace of the Pacific". The other is its Mai Tai. The original Mai Tai was created by "Trader Vic" in 1944, and brought to Hawaii in 1953, where it was first served at the Royal Hawaiian Hotel. And while it may be nice to know the drink's history, it's so much better to know the recipe. Then, with the help of an audio of ocean waves crashing into the shore, a lounge chair, beach umbrella and a good furnace or space heater, even the dreariest of winter days can be a day at the beach — once you make this Mai Tai. Oh, and don't forget the sunscreen.

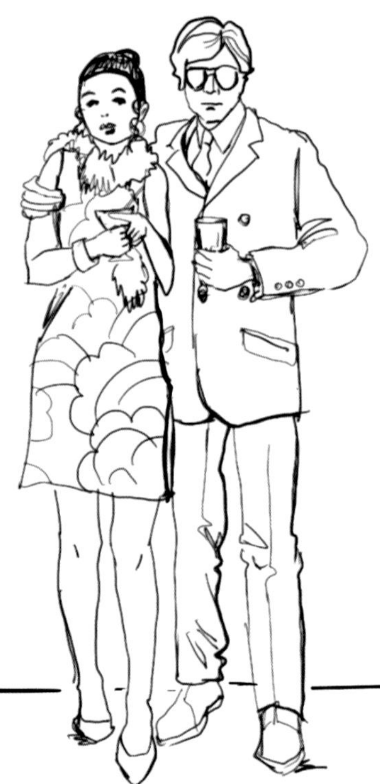

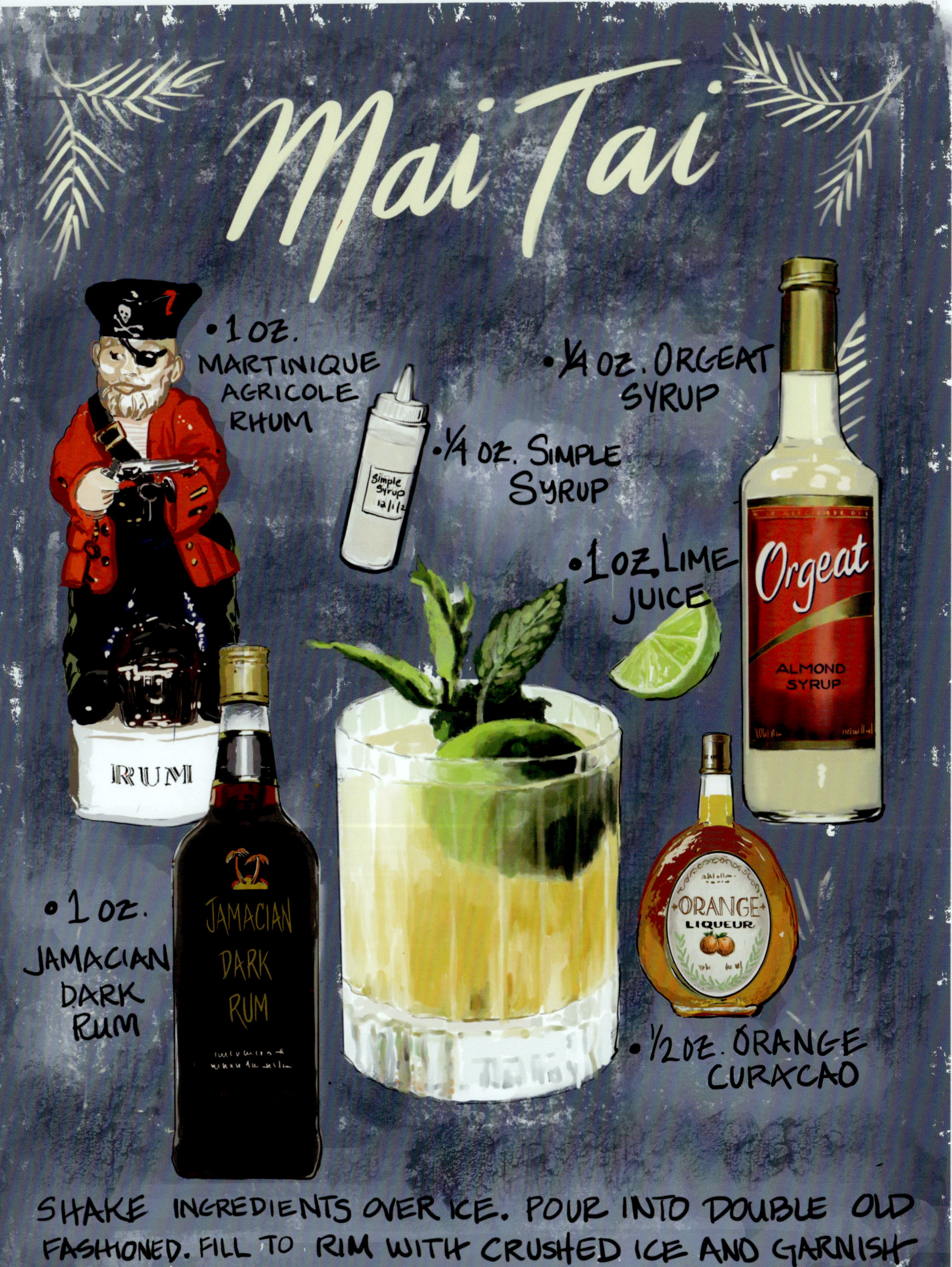
Mai Tai
• 1 oz. MARTINIQUE AGRICOLE RHUM
RUM
• ¼ oz. ORGEAT SYRUP
Orgeat
ALMOND SYRUP
• ¼ oz. SIMPLE SYRUP
Simple Syrup
• 1 oz LIME JUICE
• 1 oz. JAMACIAN DARK RUM
JAMACIAN DARK RUM
ORANGE LIQUEUR
• ½ oz. ORANGE CURACAO
SHAKE INGREDIENTS OVER ICE. POUR INTO DOUBLE OLD FASHIONED. FILL TO RIM WITH CRUSHED ICE AND GARNISH WITH A LIME SHELL AND SPRIG OF MINT.

The Mojito

Like with any drink, the Mojito has as many variations as there are legends attached to it. But the one constant is the mint. You need a lot of mint and it must be fresh. Period. If you don't have fresh mint, then make a Daiquiri, which is basically a Mojito without the mint.

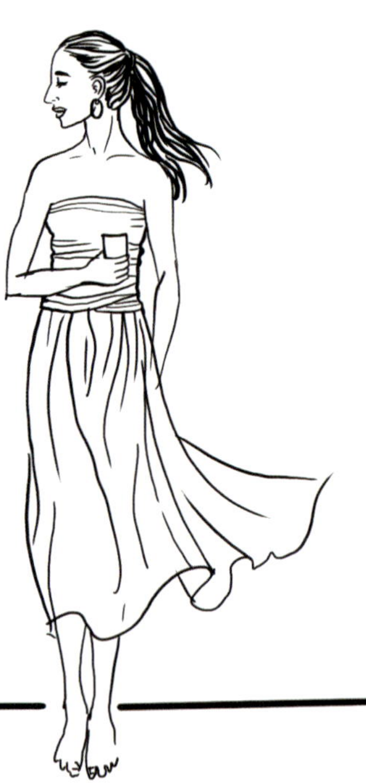

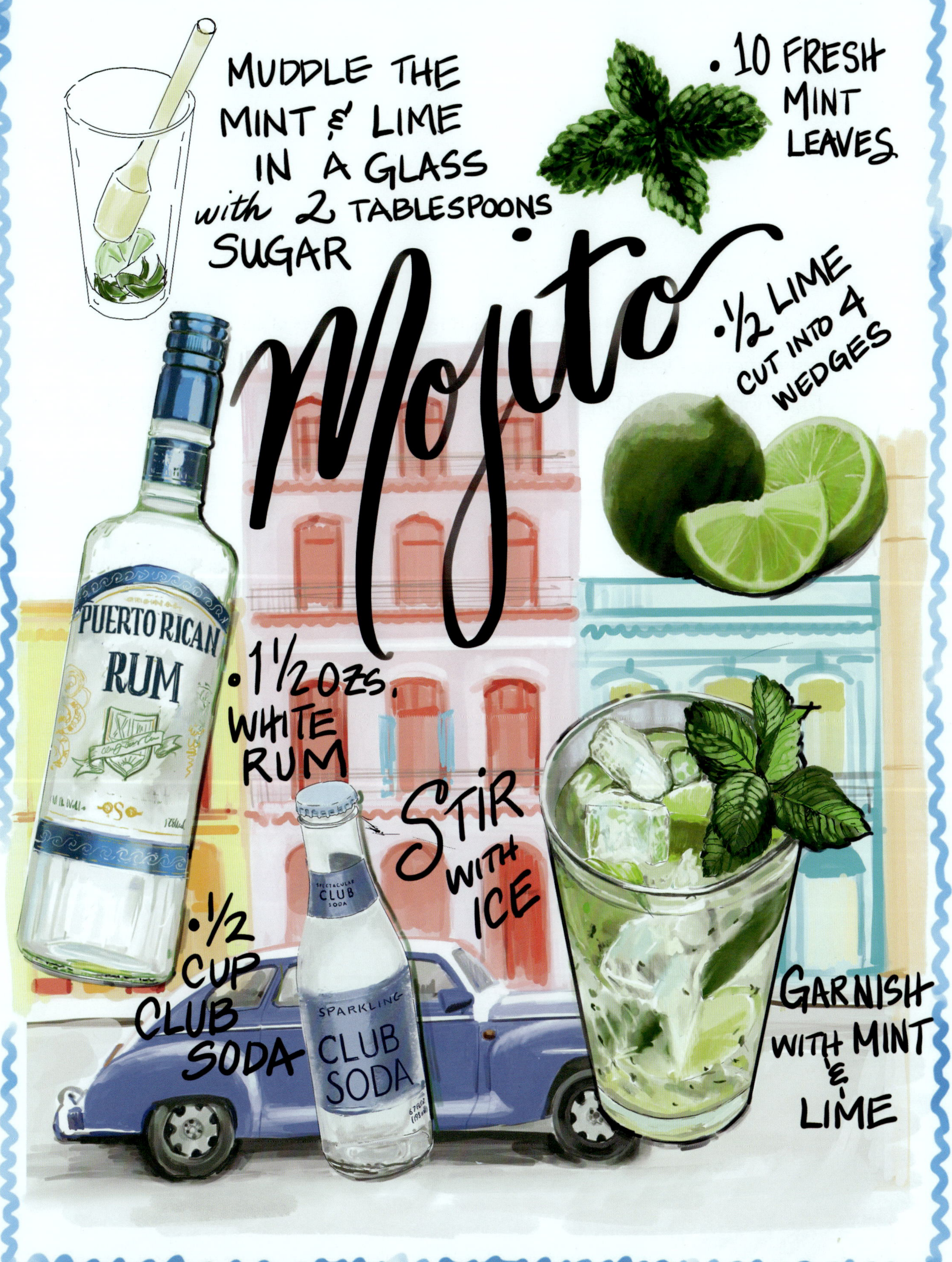

MUDDLE THE MINT & LIME IN A GLASS with 2 TABLESPOONS SUGAR
• 10 FRESH MINT LEAVES.
Mojito
• ½ LIME CUT INTO 4 WEDGES
PUERTO RICAN
RUM
• 1½ OZS. WHITE RUM
STIR WITH ICE
• ½ CUP CLUB SODA
CLUB SODA
SPARKLING
CLUB SODA
GARNISH WITH MINT & LIME

Pina Colada

As I am writing this, it is gloomy and rainy outside my window. I do not remember when I drew this recipe but looking at it today, I am transported to the Caribe Hilton in San Juan, Puerto Rico. The year is 1954, and I want a cocktail that tastes like the beach. I give the bartender discretion to try something new. The result is the Pina Colada. I am happy.

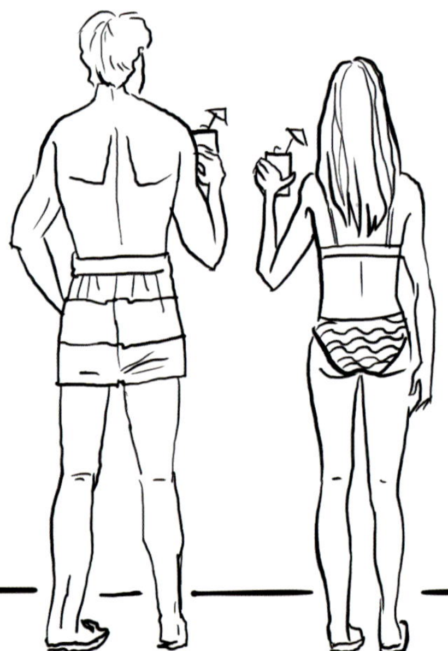

PINA COLADA

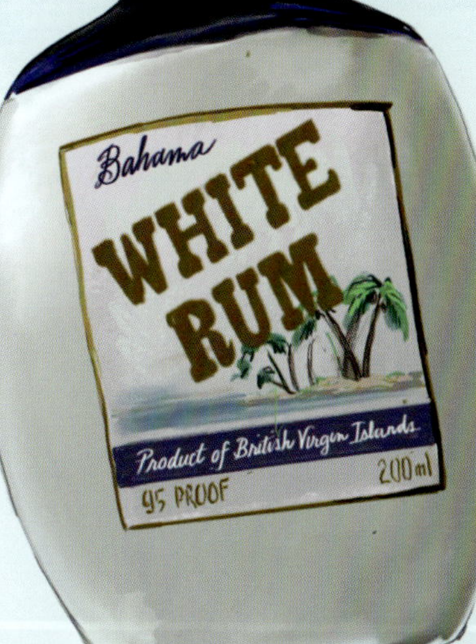

• 2 OZS.
WHITE RUM

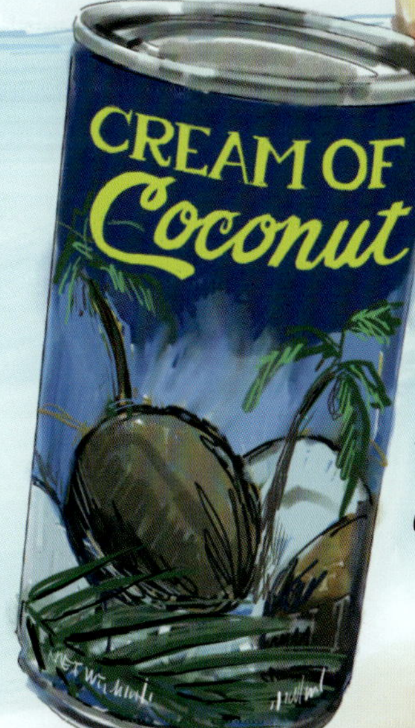

• 1½ OZS.
CREAM OF
COCONUT

COMBINE IN
SHAKER WITH
ICE and
SHAKE 30
SECONDS

GARNISH WITH
FRUIT & AN
UMBRELLA
Toothpick

• 1½ OZS.
PINEAPPLE
JUICE

• ½ OZ.
FRESH
LIME

serve in
Hurricane
GLASS

Zombie

Tiki drinks are awesome! Fruity, sweet, and sour with and lots of rum. The Zombie does not disappoint, but the cinnamon syrup is what puts a special zing in this drink. You will also have to make the effort to get the Falernum Liqueur. It's a combination of rum infused with ginger, lime and almond, so good you will find a way to add it to all your rum based drinks.

Add a bit of 151 rum on top of this cocktail and you can light it on fire! That is pretty awesome.

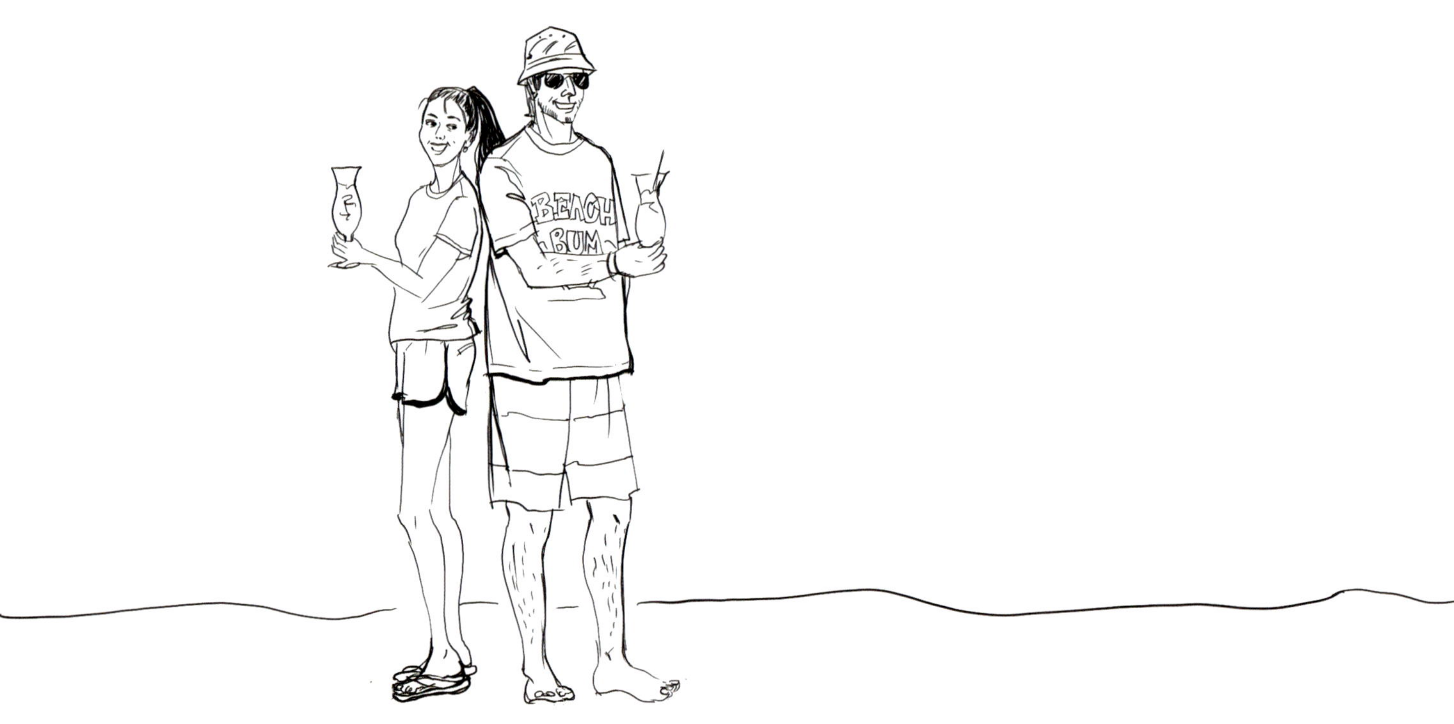

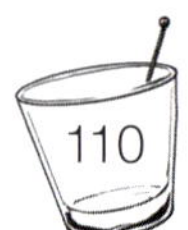

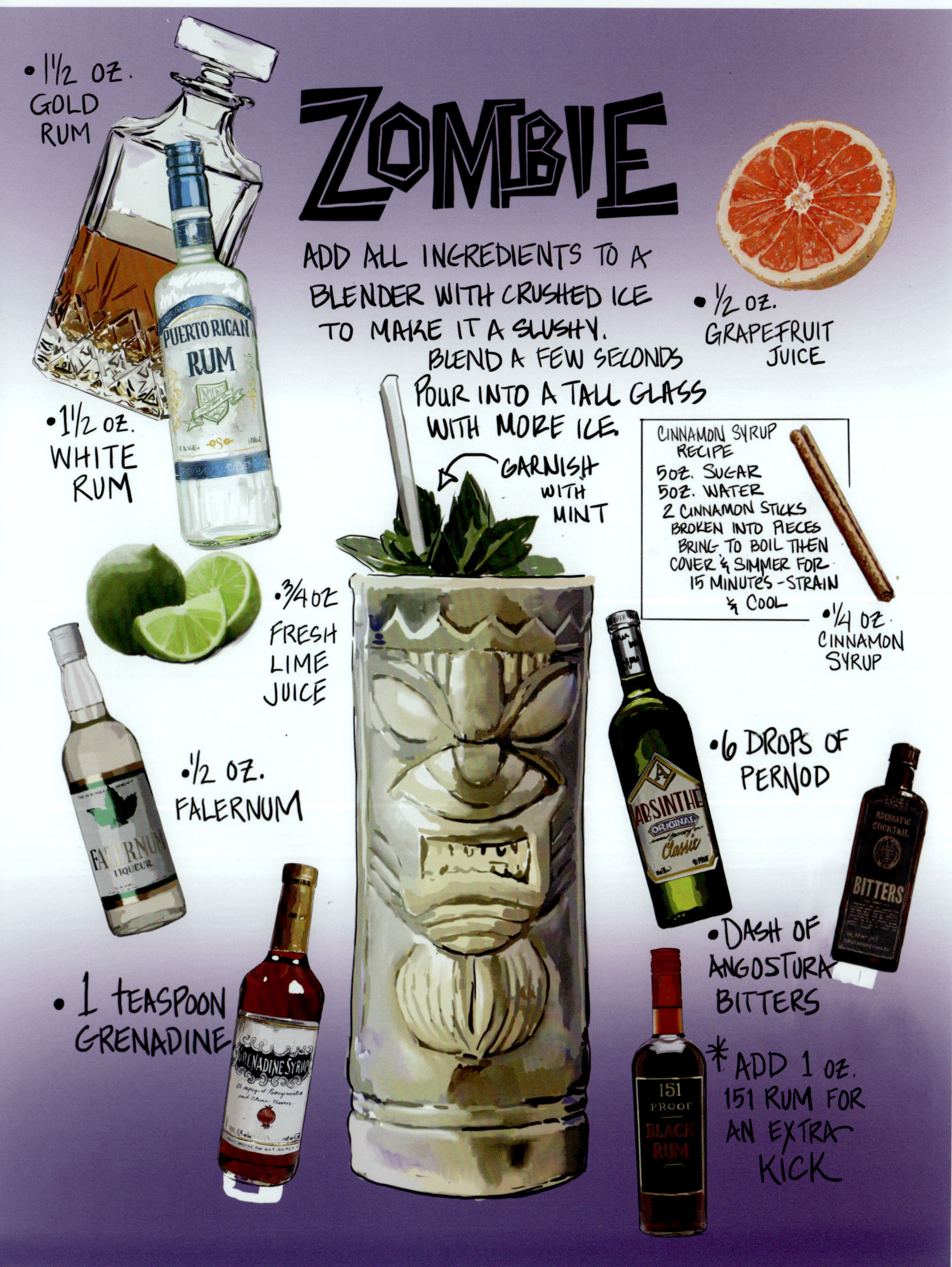

ZOMBIE
• 1½ oz. GOLD RUM
• 1½ oz. WHITE RUM
• ¾ oz FRESH LIME JUICE
• ½ oz. FALERNUM
• 1 TEASPOON GRENADINE
ADD ALL INGREDIENTS TO A BLENDER WITH CRUSHED ICE TO MAKE IT A SLUSHY.
BLEND A FEW SECONDS
POUR INTO A TALL GLASS WITH MORE ICE.
GARNISH WITH MINT
• ½ oz. GRAPEFRUIT JUICE
CINNAMON SYRUP RECIPE
5oz. SUGAR
5oz. WATER
2 CINNAMON STICKS BROKEN INTO PIECES
BRING TO BOIL THEN COVER & SIMMER FOR 15 MINUTES - STRAIN & COOL
• ¼ oz CINNAMON SYRUP
• 6 DROPS OF PERNOD
• DASH OF ANGOSTURA BITTERS
* ADD 1 oz. 151 RUM FOR AN EXTRA KICK
PUERTO RICAN RUM
FALERNUM LIQUEUR
GRENADINE SYRUP
ABSINTHE ORIGINAL Classic
AROMATIC COCKTAIL BITTERS
151 PROOF BLACK RUM

"Nothing says 'I mean business' like using a grocery cart at a liquor store."

—Unknown

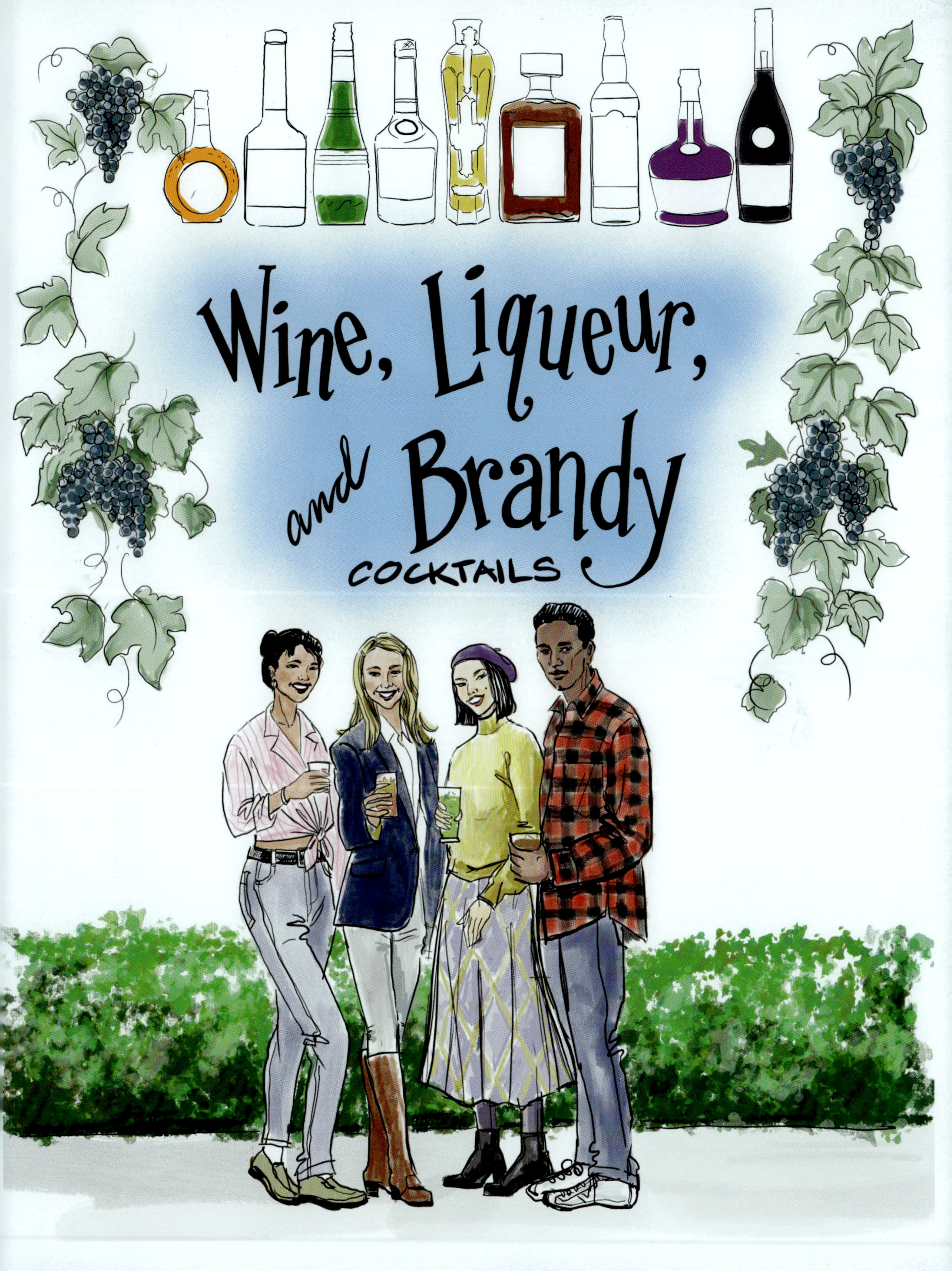
Wine, Liqueur,
and Brandy
COCKTAILS

The Amaretto Sour

I'm going to be honest. This drink is way too sweet for my taste. But the drink gained huge popularity when Amaretto, the Italian almond liqueur, became readily available in the United States during the 1970's. Unlike other Italian liqueurs, like Campari and Aperol, Amaretto is nutty and sweet and Americans went crazy for it. So turn up some disco music and make yourself an Amaretto Sour!

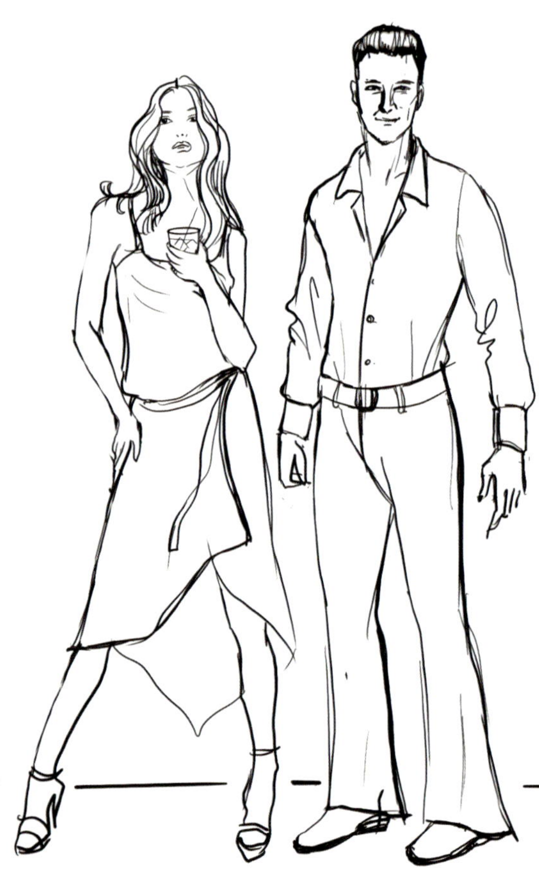

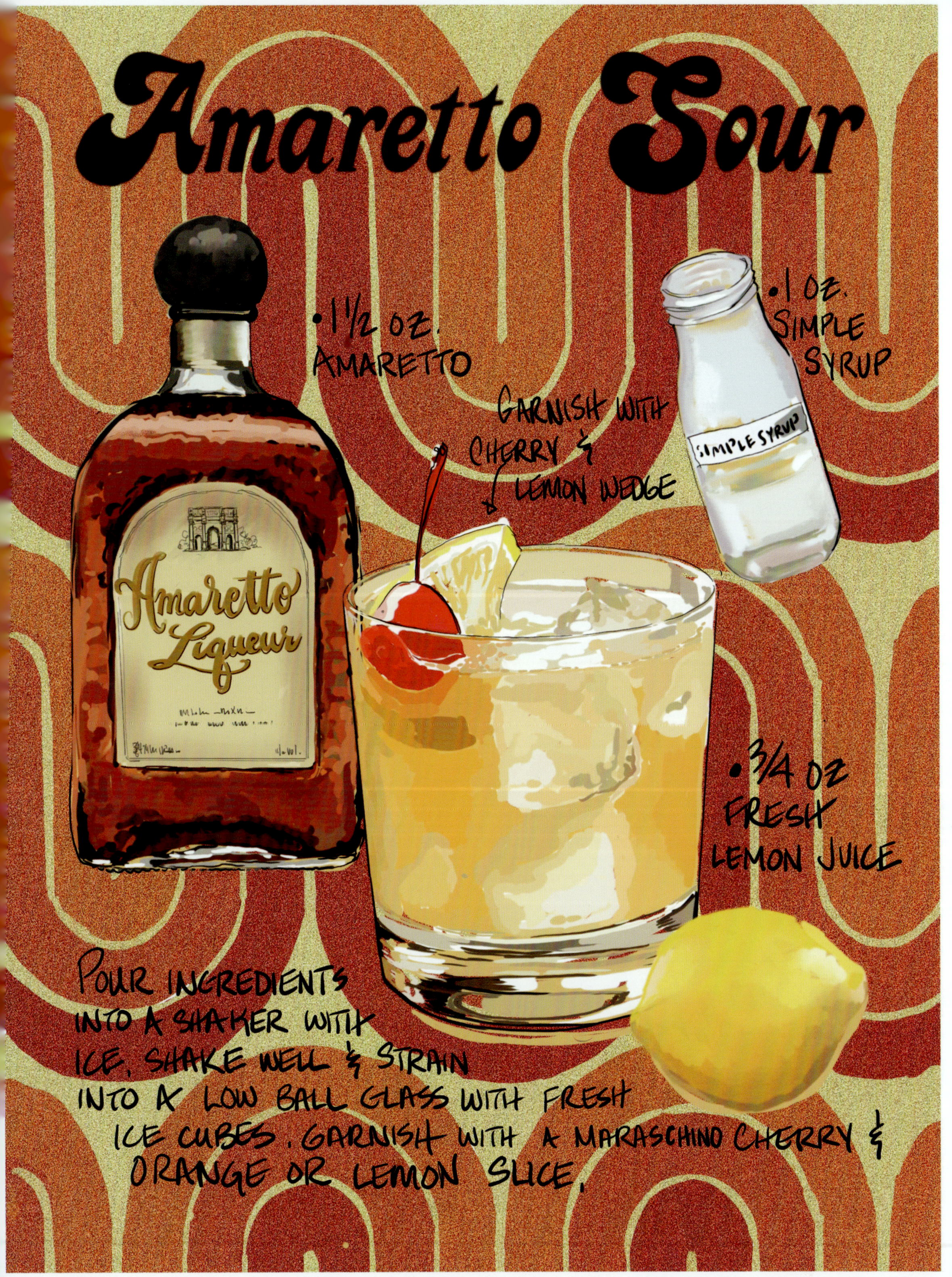
Amaretto Sour
•1½ oz. Amaretto
•1 oz. Simple Syrup
Simple Syrup
Garnish with cherry & lemon wedge
Amaretto Liqueur
•¾ oz Fresh Lemon Juice
Pour ingredients into a shaker with ice. Shake well & strain into a low ball glass with fresh ice cubes. Garnish with a maraschino cherry & orange or lemon slice.

The Americano

The Americano is a great brunch drink or a drink before dinner. It's not sweet and doesn't ruin your appetite. Of course, it is also a James Bond cocktail, making several appearances in the books and the movies. Bond's Americano is as follows, Campari, Cinzano and a large lemon peel. Top it off with Perrier because, "...in his opinion, expensive soda water was the cheapest way to improve a poor drink." (*From a View To a Kill*, Fleming, 1960)

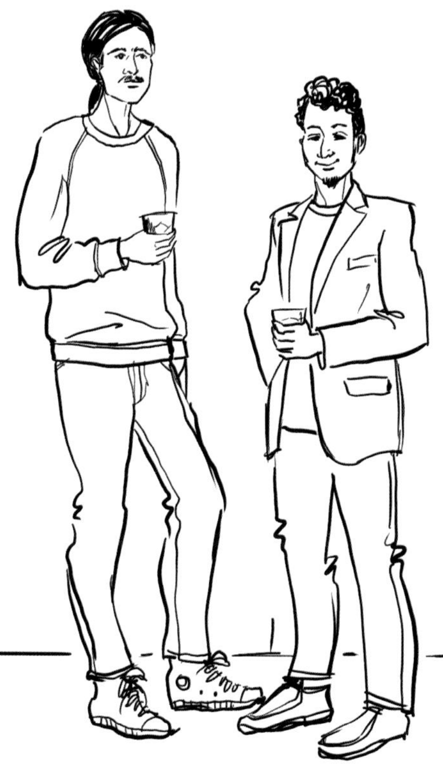

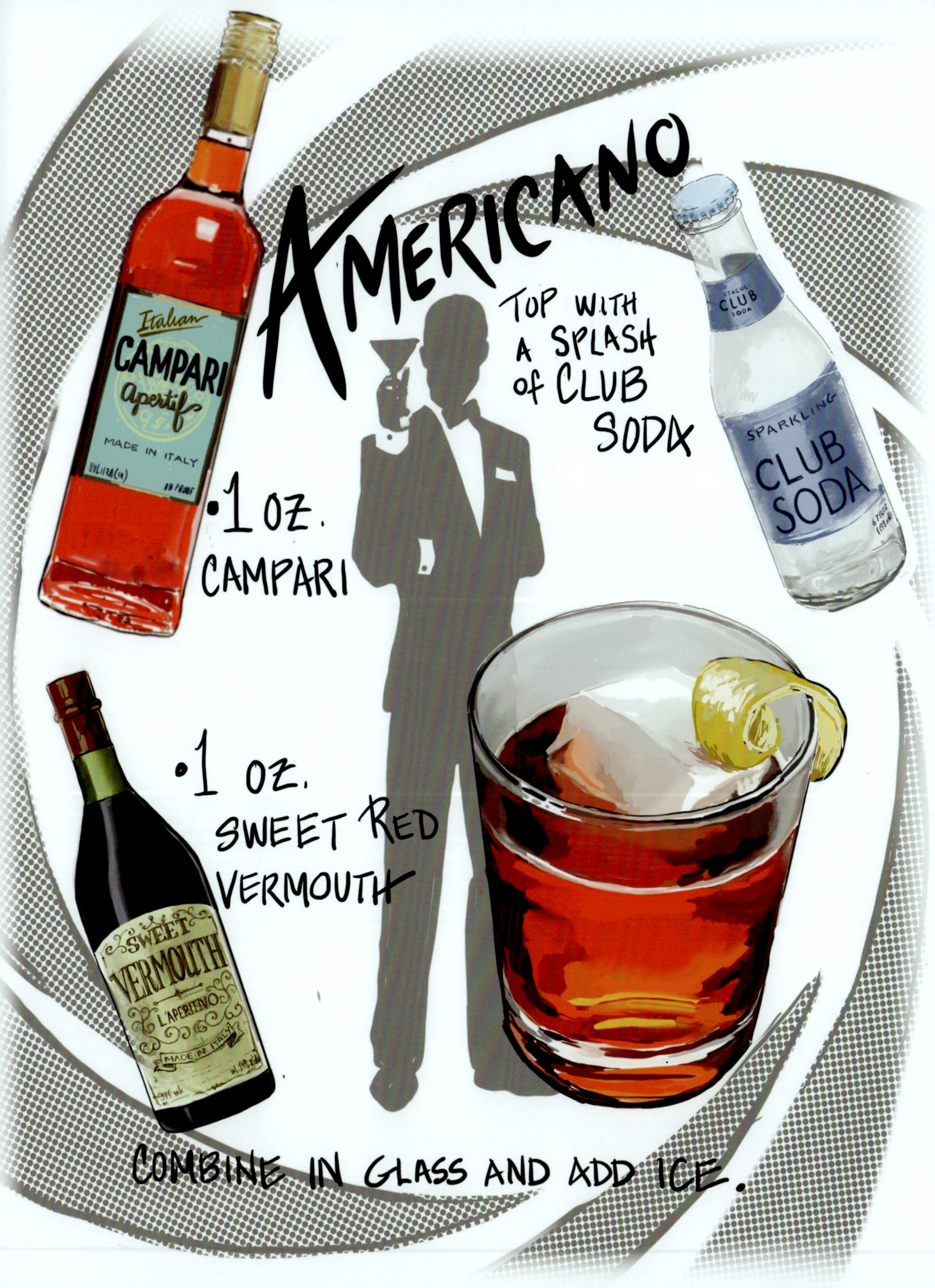
AMERICANO
TOP WITH A SPLASH OF CLUB SODA
•1 OZ. CAMPARI
•1 OZ. SWEET RED VERMOUTH
COMBINE IN GLASS AND ADD ICE.
Italian
CAMPARI
apertif
MADE IN ITALY
CLUB SODA
SPARKLING
CLUB SODA
SWEET
VERMOUTH
L'APERITIVO
MADE IN ITALY

The Aperol Spritz

Dreaming of sitting at a café in the Piazza Navona after a beautiful day of sightseeing and shopping? This drink will take you right to the heart of Rome. It's the perfect aperitif for a summer's day (or any day really.) Don't forgot the orange slice – it's a must!

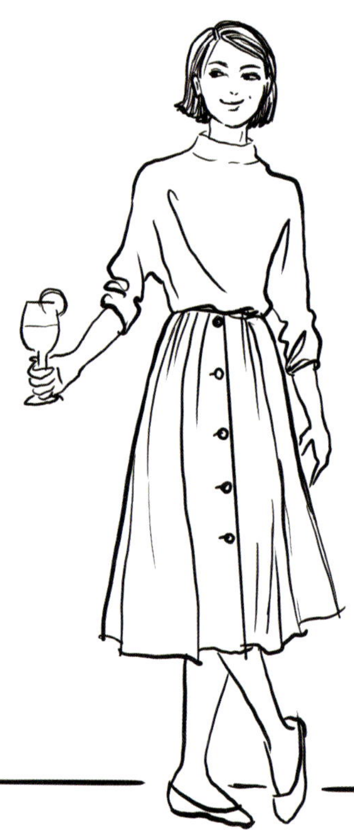

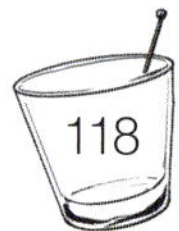

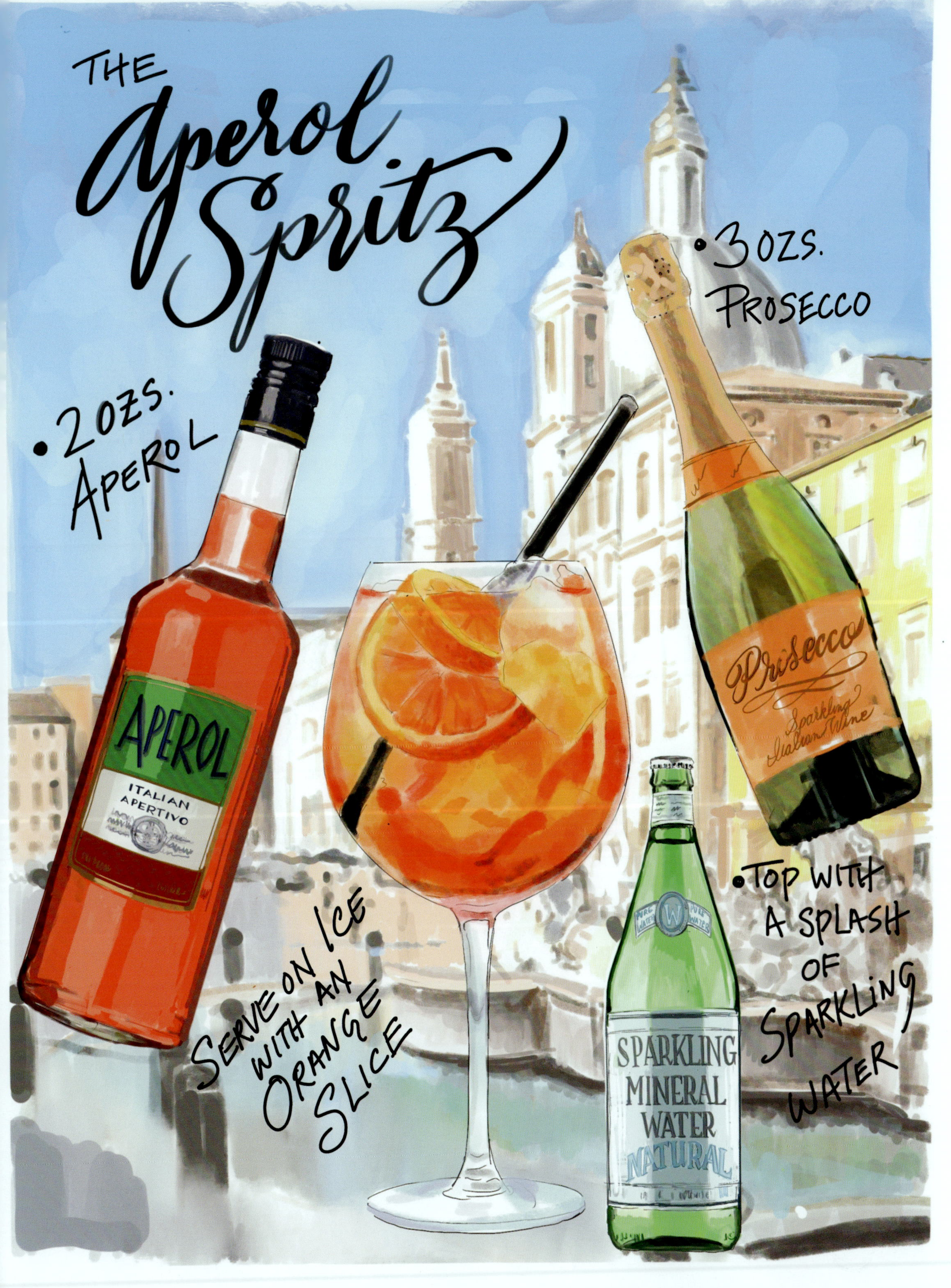
THE
Aperol Spritz
• 2 OZS.
APEROL
• 3 OZS.
PROSECCO
APEROL
ITALIAN
APERTIVO
Prosecco
Sparkling
Italian Wine
SERVE ON ICE
WITH AN
ORANGE
SLICE
• TOP WITH
A SPLASH
OF
SPARKLING
WATER
SPARKLING
MINERAL
WATER
NATURAL

The Brandy Alexander

It is unclear when this cocktail was created or who it was named for. But the nuanced flavors of a Brandy Alexander meld into a delicious whole. This is a truly decadent drink that can double as desert, and in my home often does.

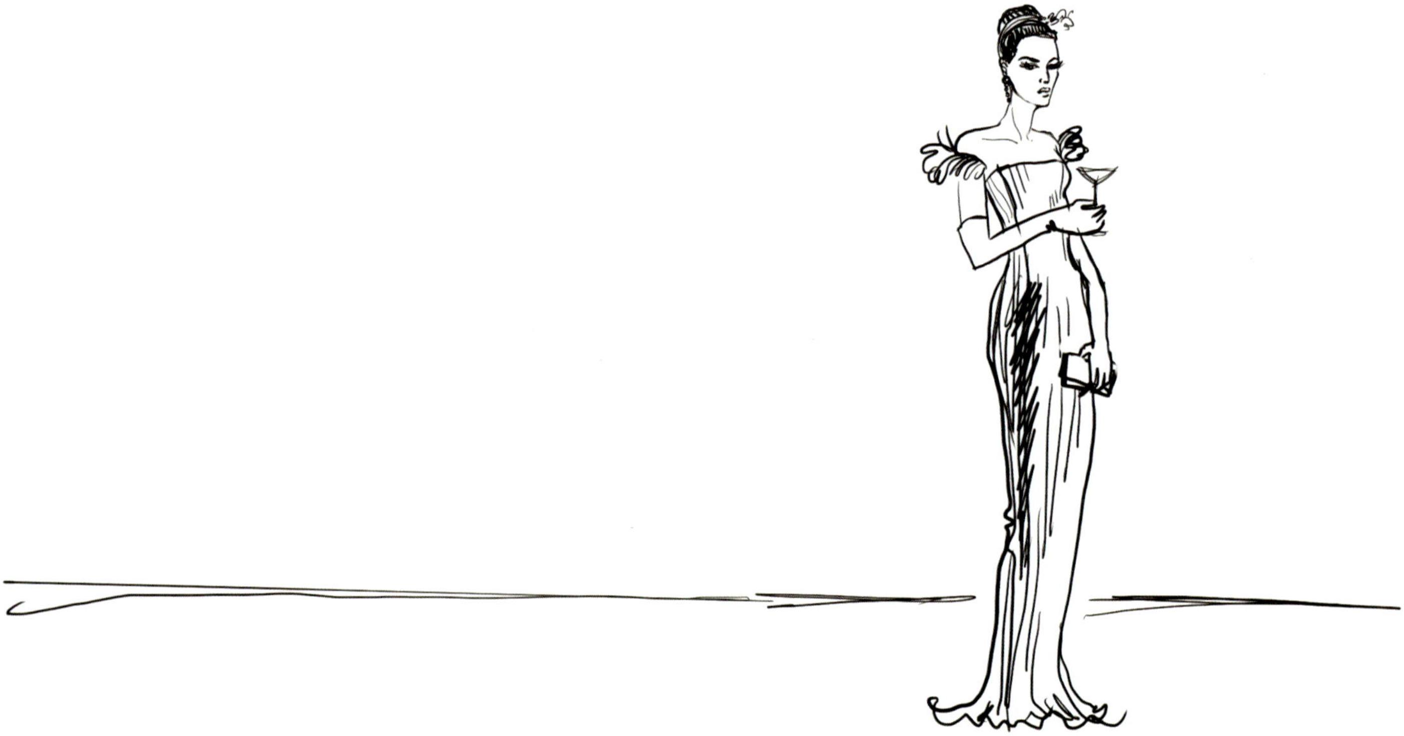

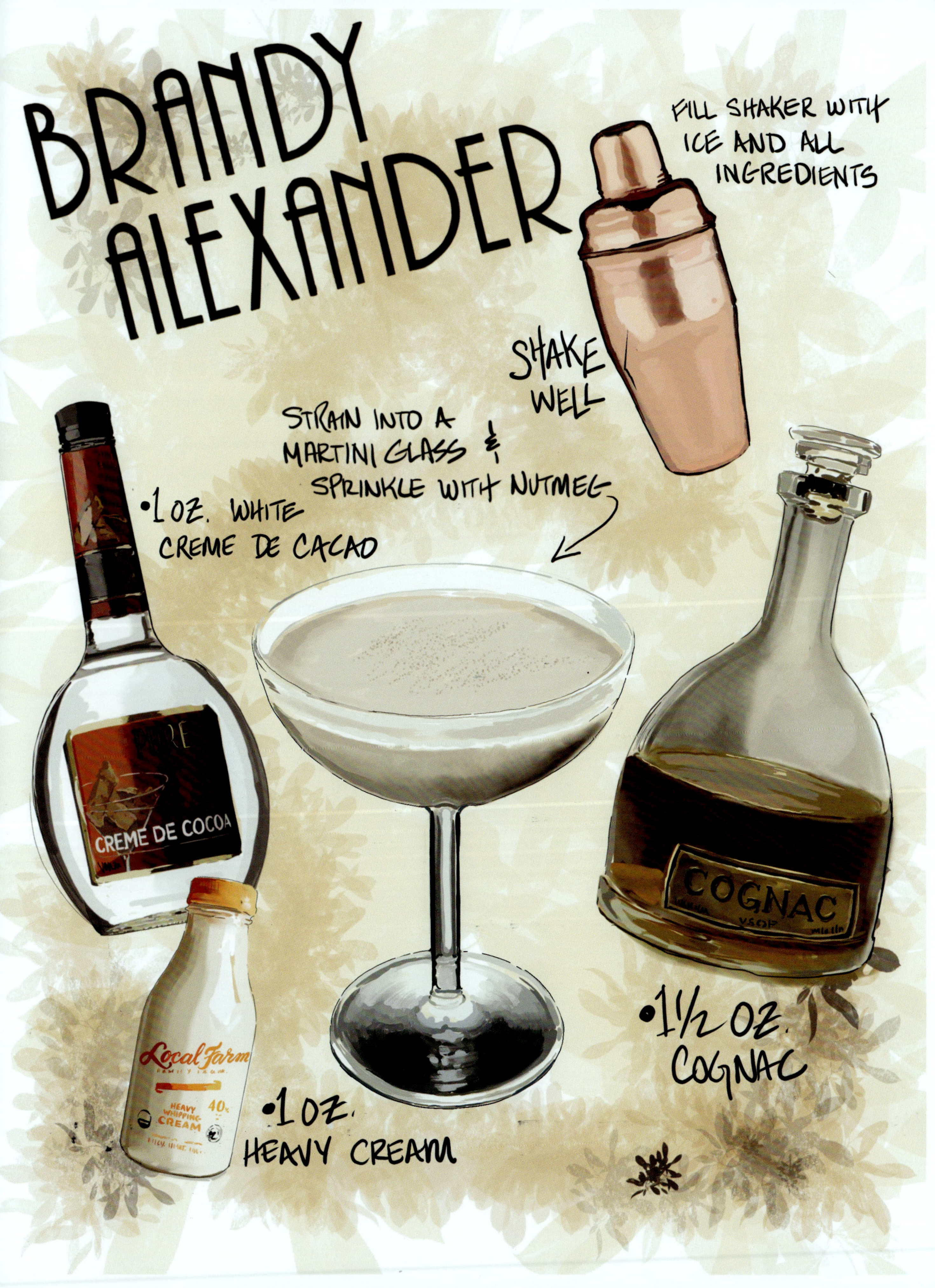
BRANDY ALEXANDER
FILL SHAKER WITH ICE AND ALL INGREDIENTS
SHAKE WELL
STRAIN INTO A MARTINI GLASS & SPRINKLE WITH NUTMEG
•1 OZ. WHITE CREME DE CACAO
CREME DE COCOA
COGNAC
VSOP
•1½ OZ. COGNAC
Local Farm
HEAVY WHIPPING CREAM
40%
•1 OZ. HEAVY CREAM

Egg Nog

When I think of Egg Nog, I am at a holiday party dipping into a punchbowl filled with "Nog". If you like to indulge in this holiday classic and don't have a crowd coming over, this recipe is for one, indulgent, serving. I make mine with 2% milk and it is wonderfully creamy, but you can substitute whole milk or a combination of milk and cream to make it even more rich. And if dairy is a problem, try making this with unsweetened cashew or oat milk. It's equally delicious and decadent. So now, even solo, you can enjoy this holiday standard.

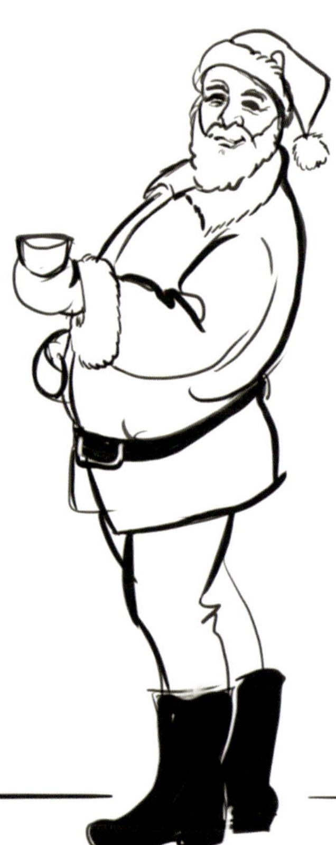

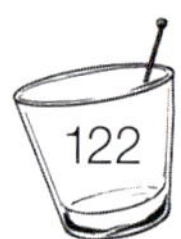

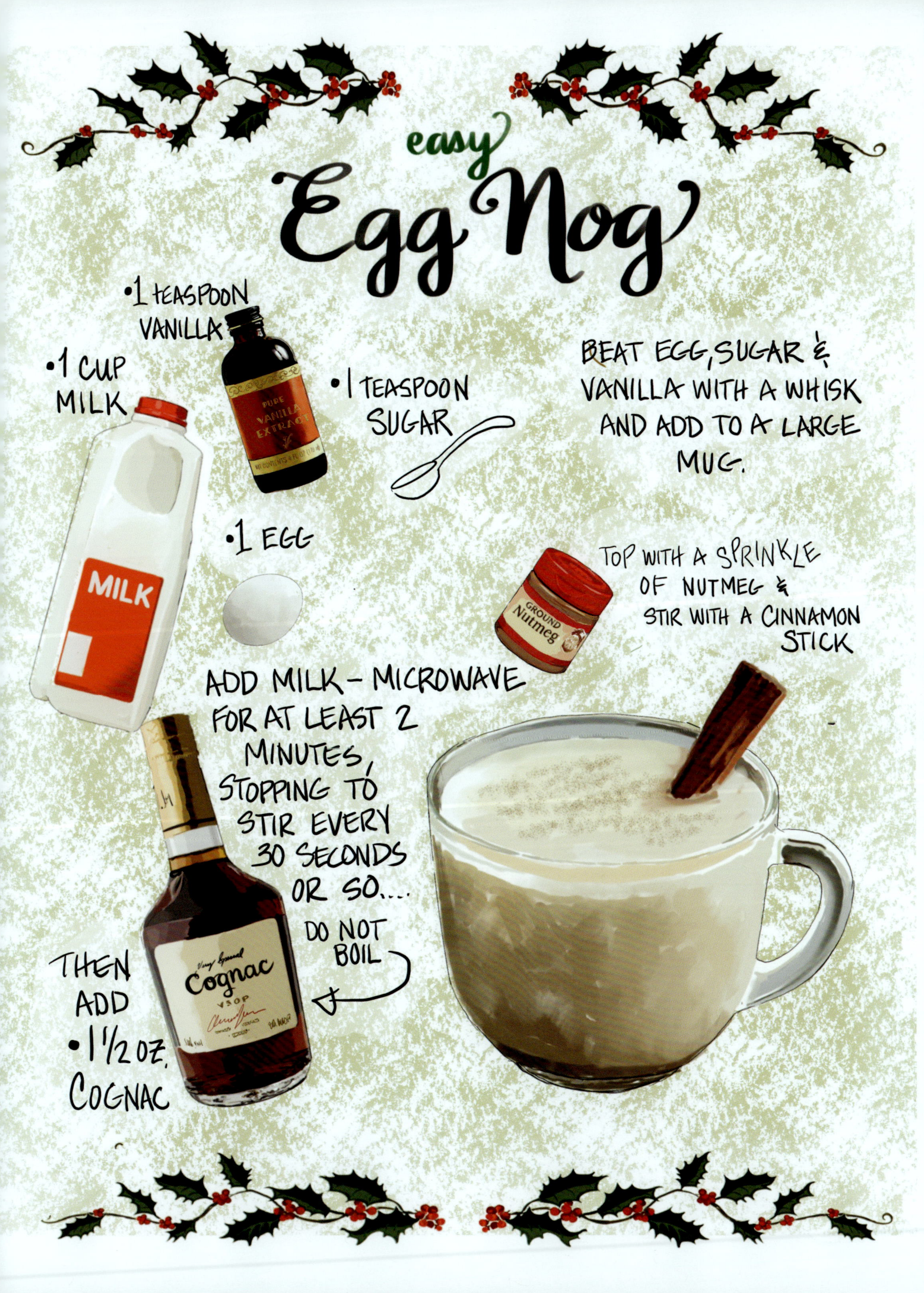
easy
Egg Nog
•1 TEASPOON VANILLA
•1 CUP MILK
PURE VANILLA EXTRACT
•1 TEASPOON SUGAR
BEAT EGG, SUGAR & VANILLA WITH A WHISK AND ADD TO A LARGE MUG.
MILK
•1 EGG
TOP WITH A SPRINKLE OF NUTMEG & STIR WITH A CINNAMON STICK
GROUND Nutmeg
ADD MILK - MICROWAVE FOR AT LEAST 2 MINUTES, STOPPING TO STIR EVERY 30 SECONDS OR SO....
DO NOT BOIL
THEN ADD
•1½ OZ. COGNAC
Cognac
VSOP

The Grasshopper

When I was a kid, it was a treat to go out to lunch with my mom and grandma at the restaurant in the department store. Mom would let me drink the cream that came with her coffee, but I was more intrigued by the pretty green cocktails that the ladies at the next table had ordered. When Grandma told me they were Grasshoppers, I only got more curious. It would be years later until I tasted one. Now I know how much fun those ladies were having that day.

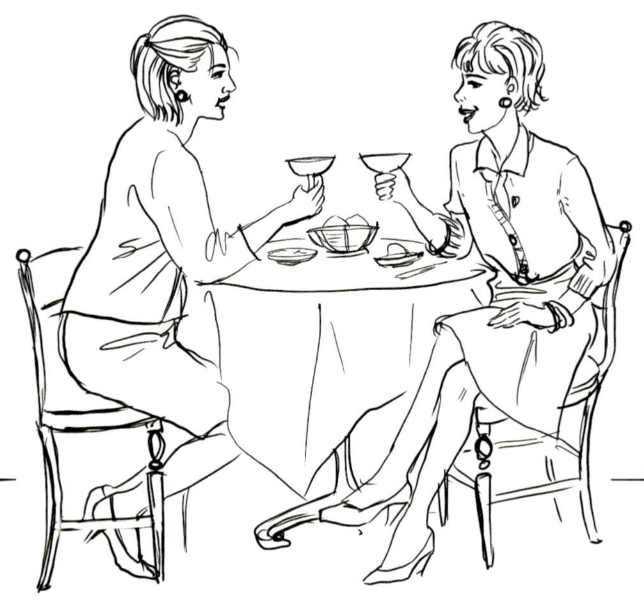

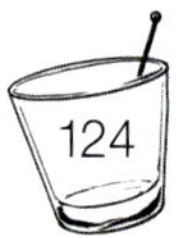

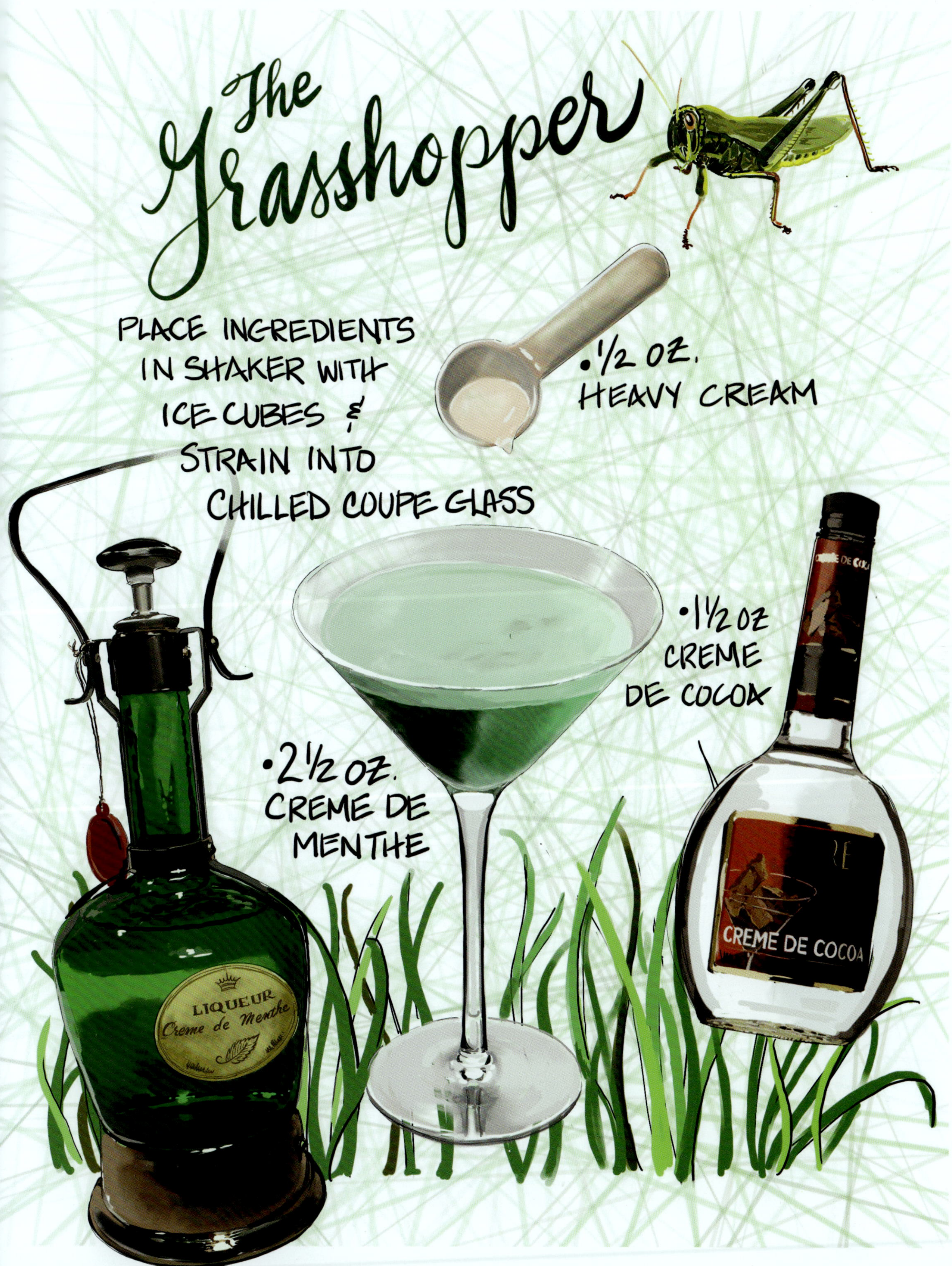
The Grasshopper
PLACE INGREDIENTS IN SHAKER WITH ICE CUBES & STRAIN INTO CHILLED COUPE GLASS
•½ OZ. HEAVY CREAM
•1½ OZ CREME DE COCOA
•2½ OZ. CREME DE MENTHE
LIQUEUR
Creme de Menthe
CREME DE COCOA

Kir Royale

"The night they invented Champagne, as plain as it could be, they thought of you and me." Those are the words to the wonderful Lerner and Lowe song from the musical *Gigi* (1958). And though I wouldn't turn down a glass to celebrate, why not take it up a notch and try this champagne cocktail which adds Crème de Cassis. "Cause since the world began, no woman or a man, will ever be as happy as we are tonight."

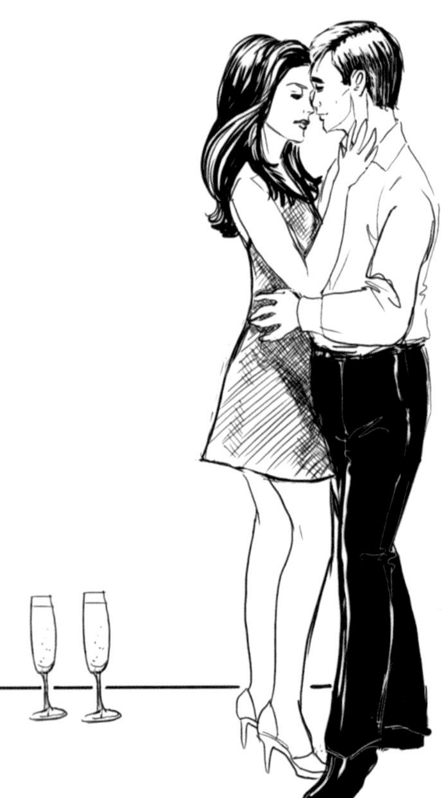

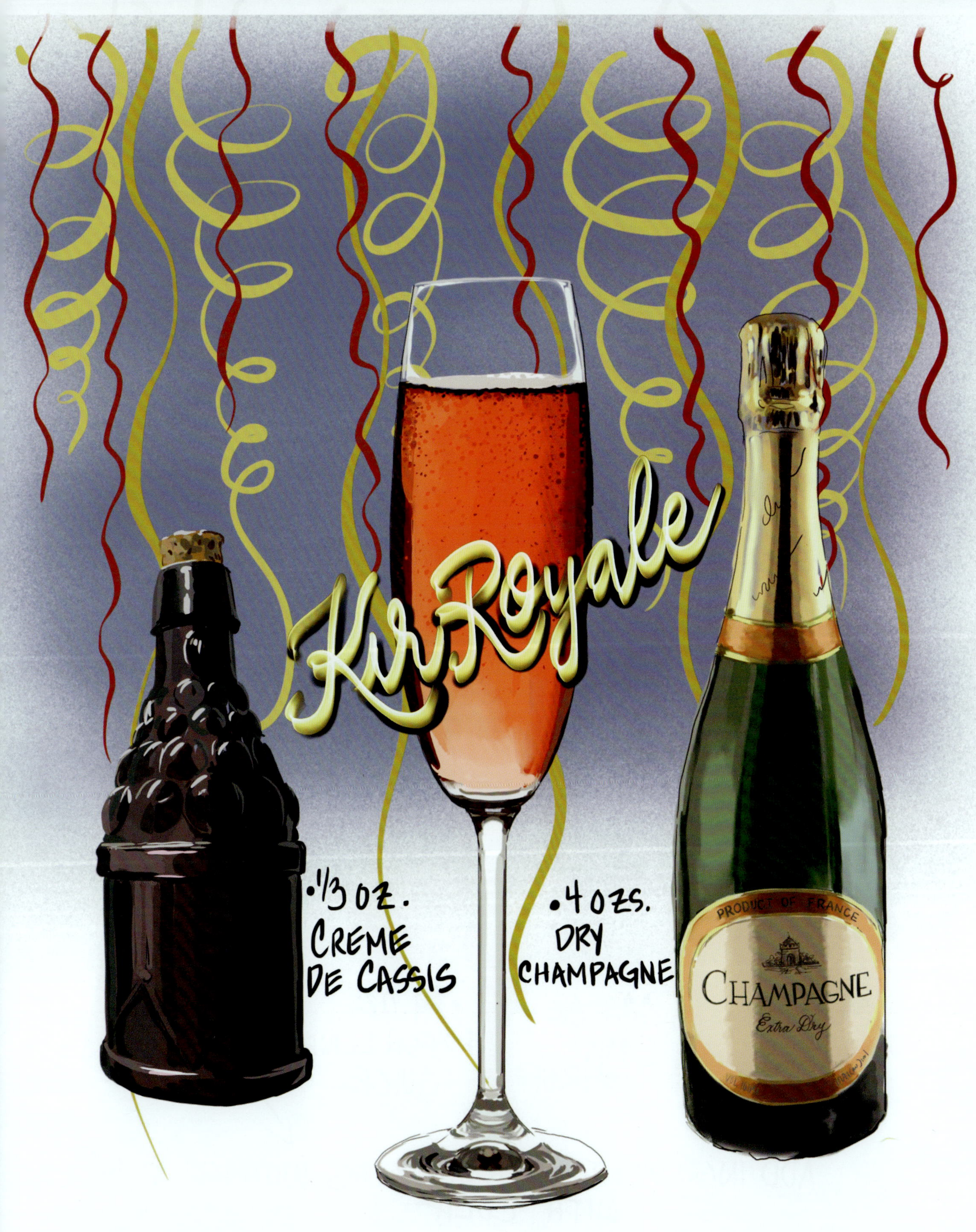

POUR CREME DE CASSIS IN FLUTE. TOP WITH CHAMPAGNE.

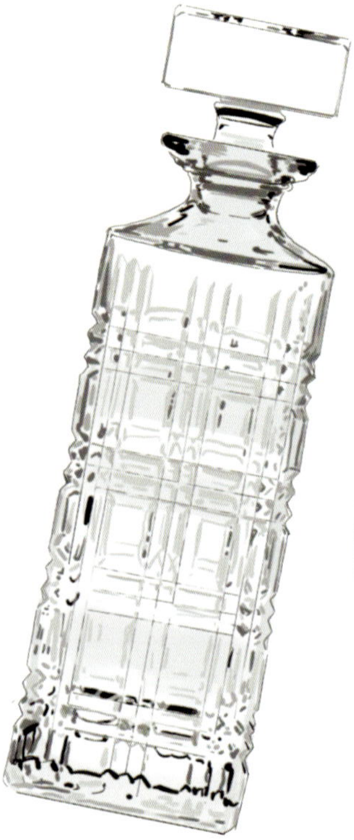

• 3/4 OZ. VODKA

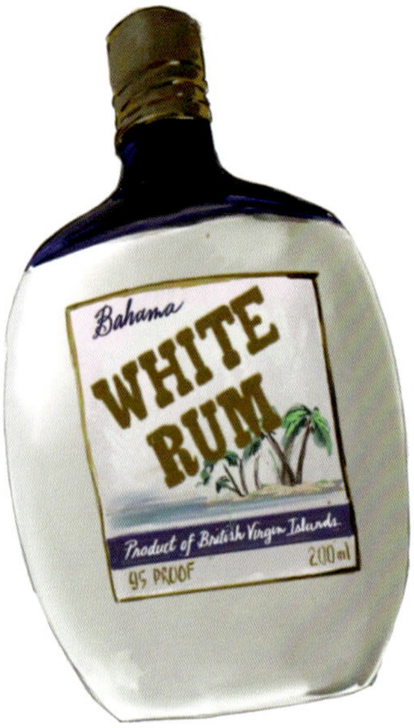

• 3/4 OZ WHITE RUM

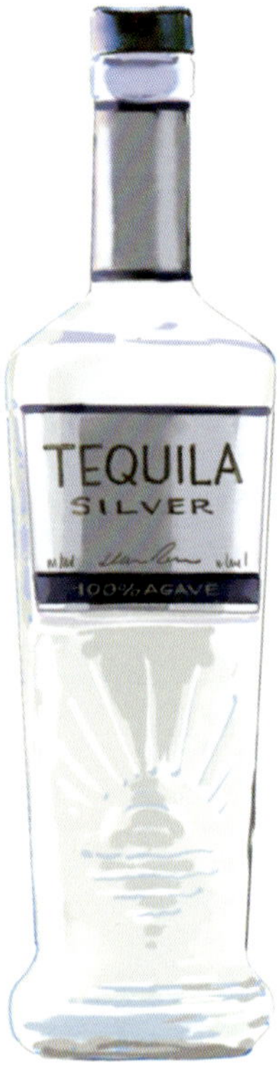

• 3/4 OZ SILVER TEQUILA

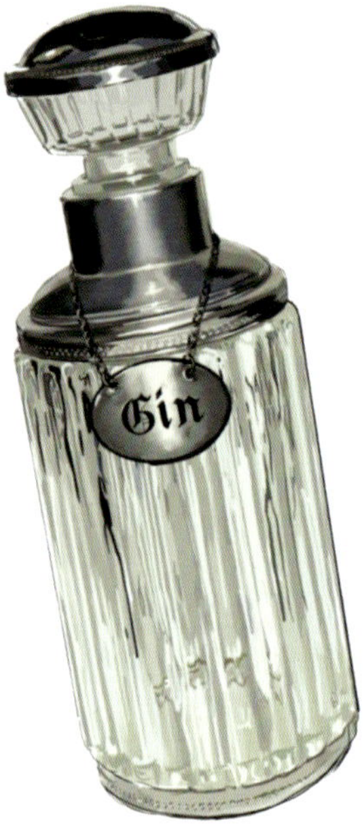

• 3/4 OZ. GIN

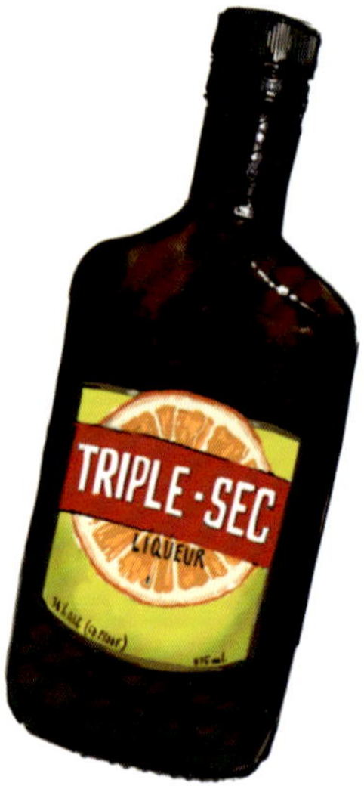

• 3/4 OZ TRIPLE SEC

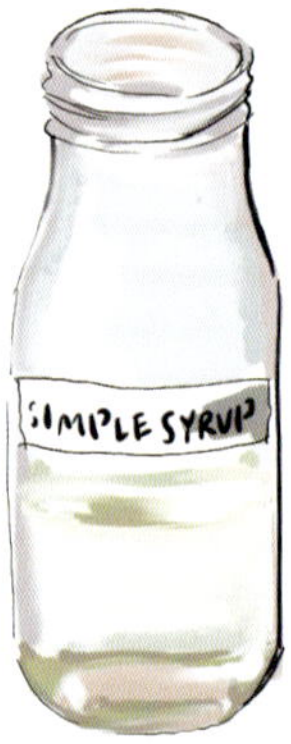

• 3/4 OZ SIMPLE SYRUP

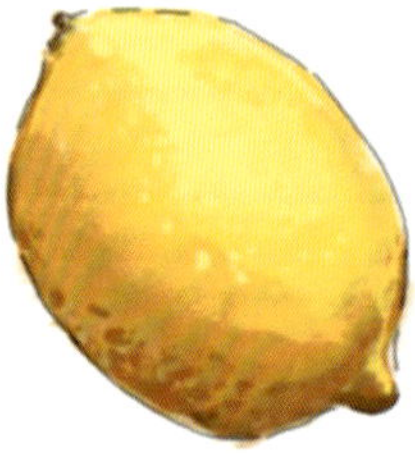

• 3/4 OZ FRESH LEMON JUICE

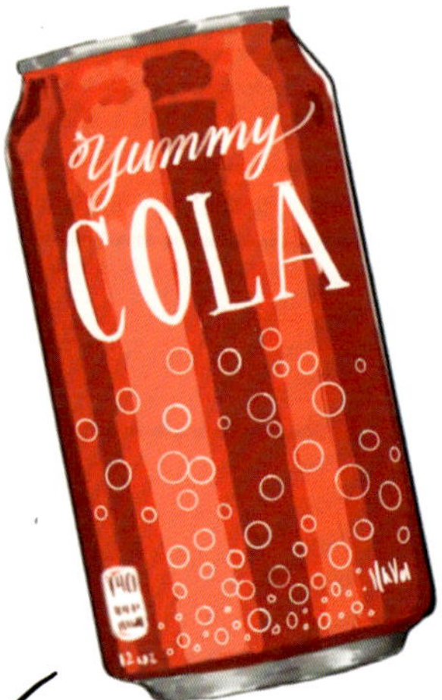

ADD INGREDIENTS TO A TALL GLASS WITH ICE & TOP WITH COLA

Vodka, Rum, Gin, & Tequila

Long Island Iced Tea

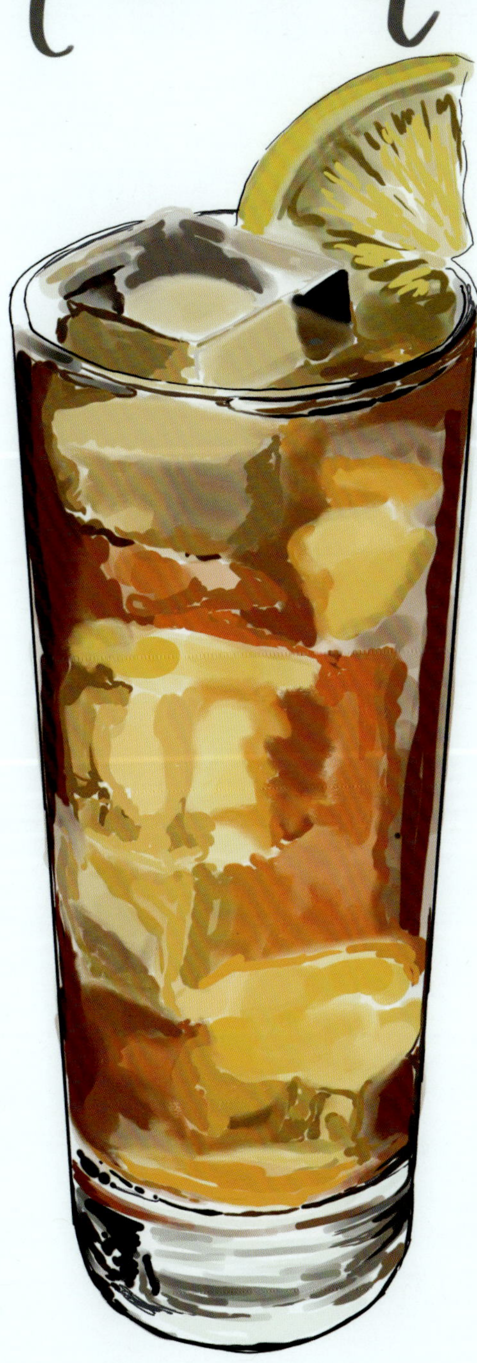

So many ingredients

Pimm's Cup No. 1

Why are Pimm's Cup No.1 popular at Wimbledon and Polo matches? Maybe it's because Pimm's is a gin-based liqueur infused with a secret mix of herbs, spices and caramelized oranges. Maybe it's because it is a light refreshing drink that has less alcohol content than other cocktails so you can indulge and still follow the action on the court or lawn. Maybe because it's made in Great Britain. Maybe it's because it's delicious. Or maybe it's all of the above.

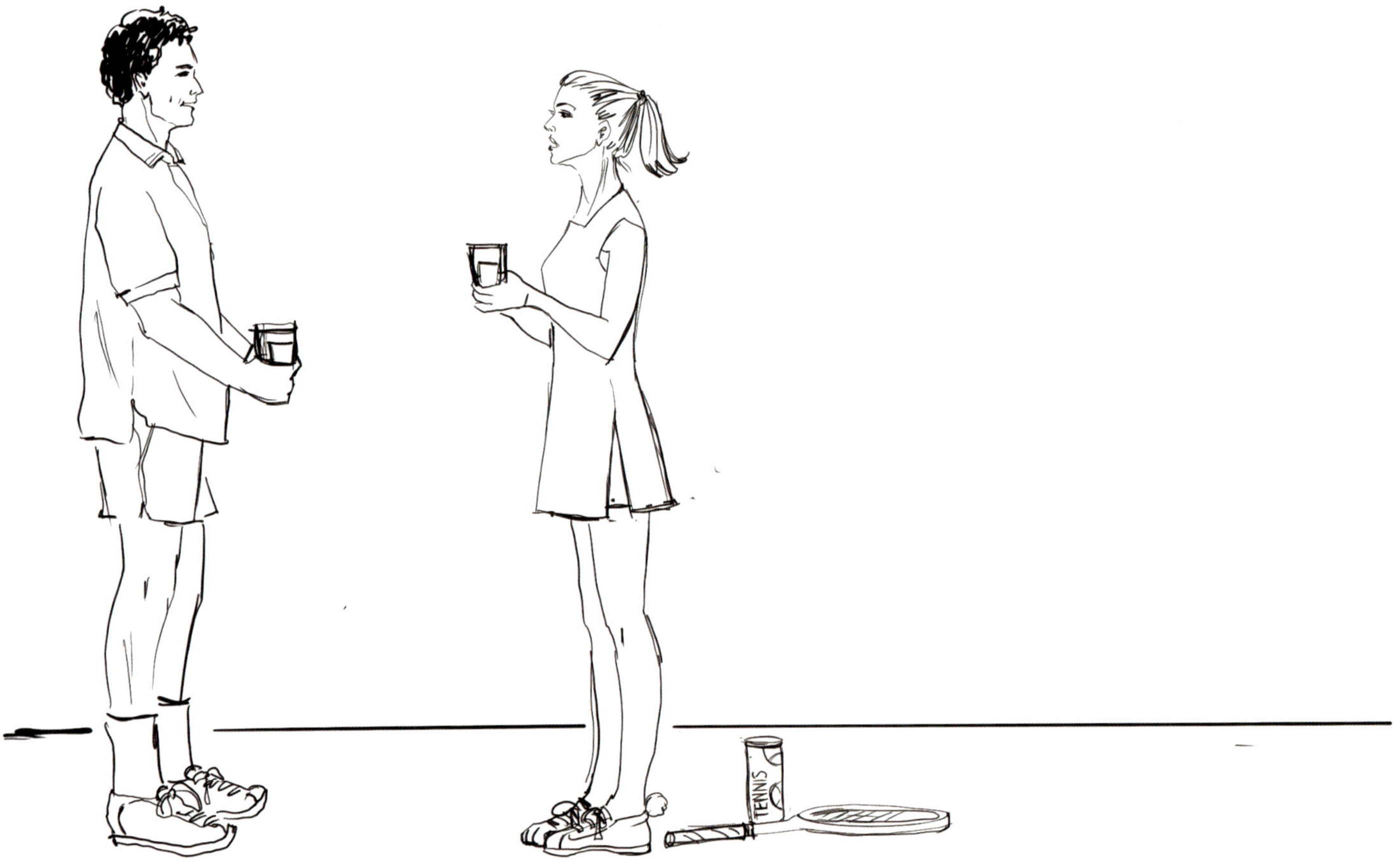

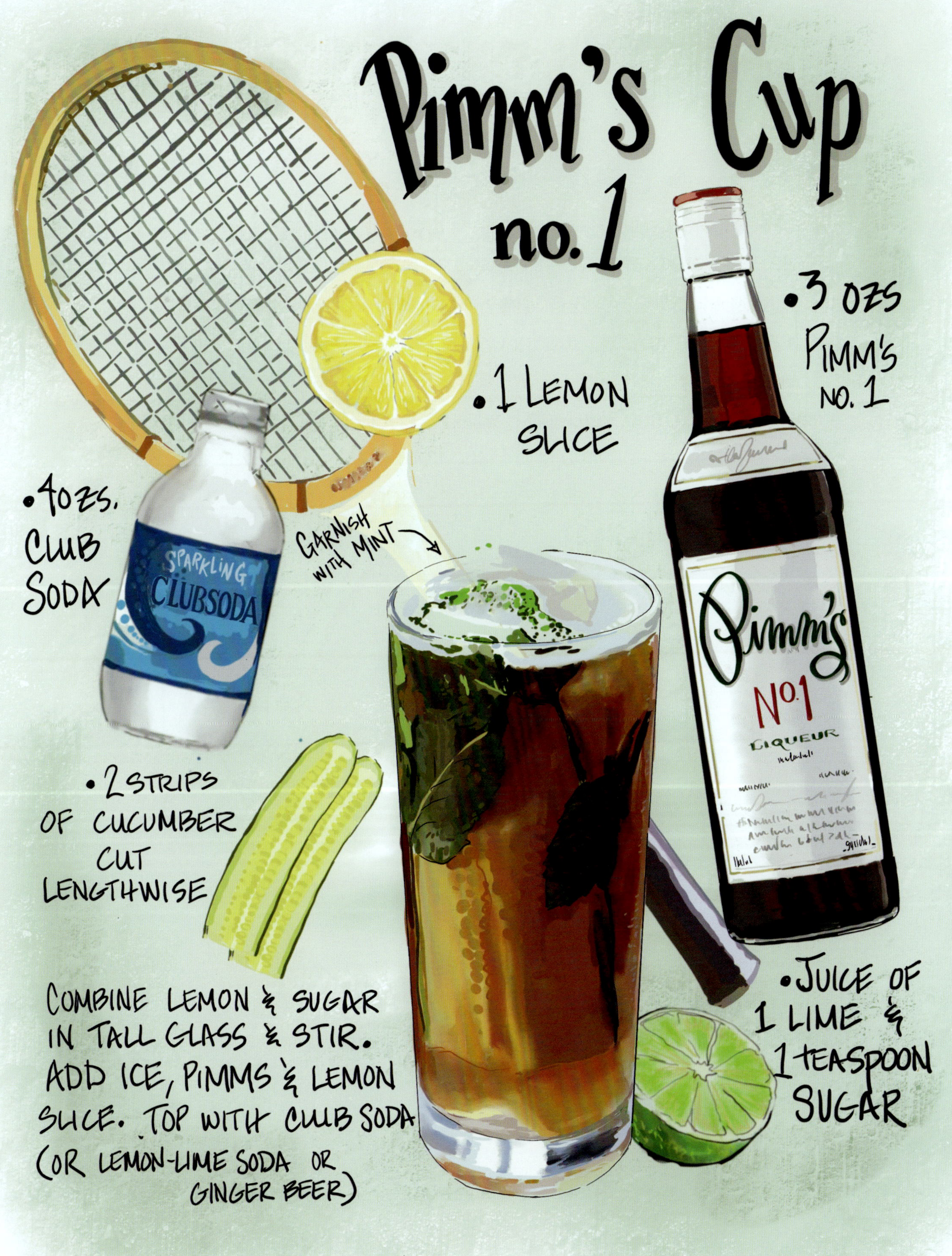
Pimm's Cup
no. 1
•3 ozs
Pimm's
no. 1
•1 Lemon
Slice
•4 ozs.
Club
Soda
Sparkling
Clubsoda
Garnish
with mint
Pimm's
No. 1
Liqueur
•2 strips
of cucumber
cut
lengthwise
Combine lemon & sugar
in tall glass & stir.
Add ice, Pimms & lemon
slice. Top with club soda
(or lemon-lime soda or
ginger beer)
•Juice of
1 lime &
1 teaspoon
sugar

Pisco Sour

Chile and Peru both claim the Pisco Sour as their national cocktails. This long-standing rivalry about who makes the best Pisco Sour is matched only by their rivalry on the football (read soccer) field. This is the Peruvian version, which is made with simple syrup, a dash of bitters, and Peruvian Pisco. The Chilian version substitutes powdered sugar and lime and Pisco from Chile. Either way, add an egg white and shake well to create the froth.

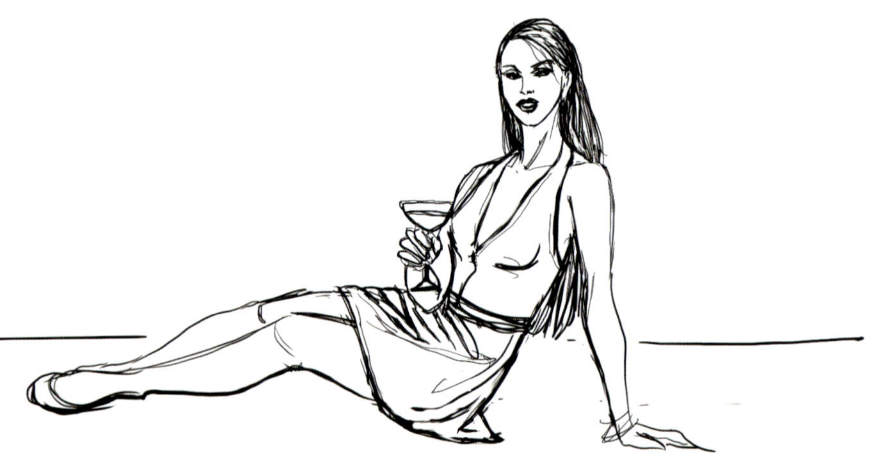

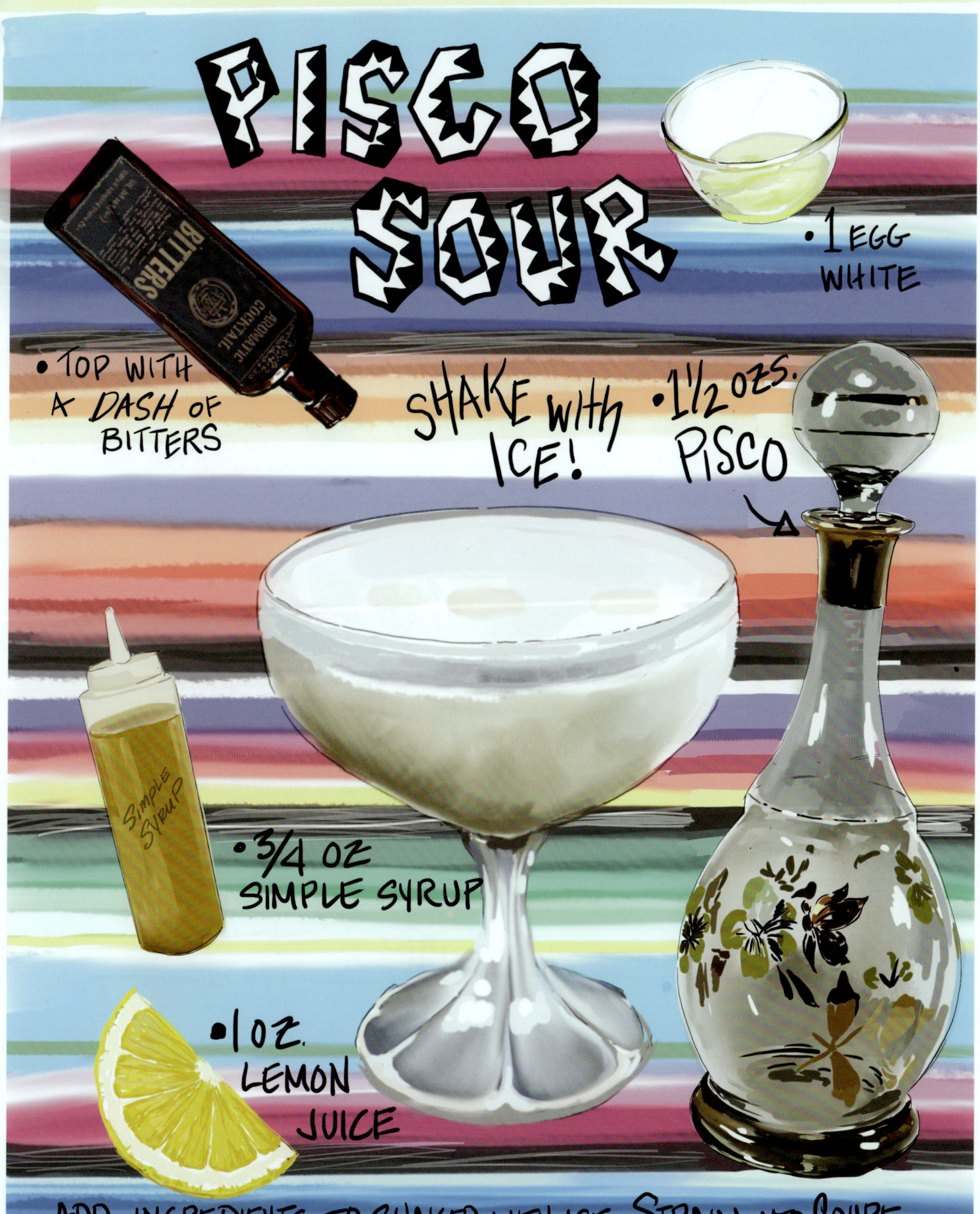
PISCO SOUR
• 1 EGG WHITE
• TOP WITH A DASH OF BITTERS
SHAKE with ICE!
• 1½ OZS. PISCO
Simple Syrup
• 3/4 OZ SIMPLE SYRUP
• 1 OZ. LEMON JUICE
ADD INGREDIENTS TO SHAKER WITH ICE. STRAIN INTO COUPE.

Red Sangria

There is no wrong way to make Sangria. It can be made with red, white or rose wine, any assortment of fruits, and whichever additional flavorings/liquors you like. It can be sparkling or not, sweet or tart, red or white, etc. You can even use frozen fruit if you like – it's a great way to cool the Sangria without diluting it. This is a basic recipe for you to adapt as you like and is based on the Sangria introduced at the New York World's Fair (1964-65).

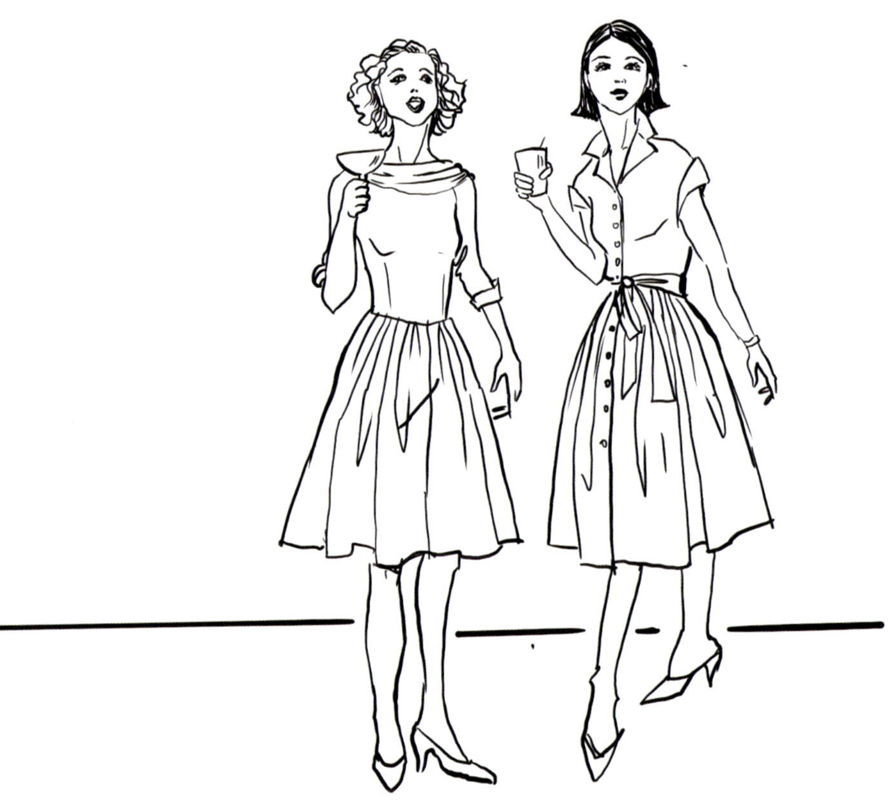

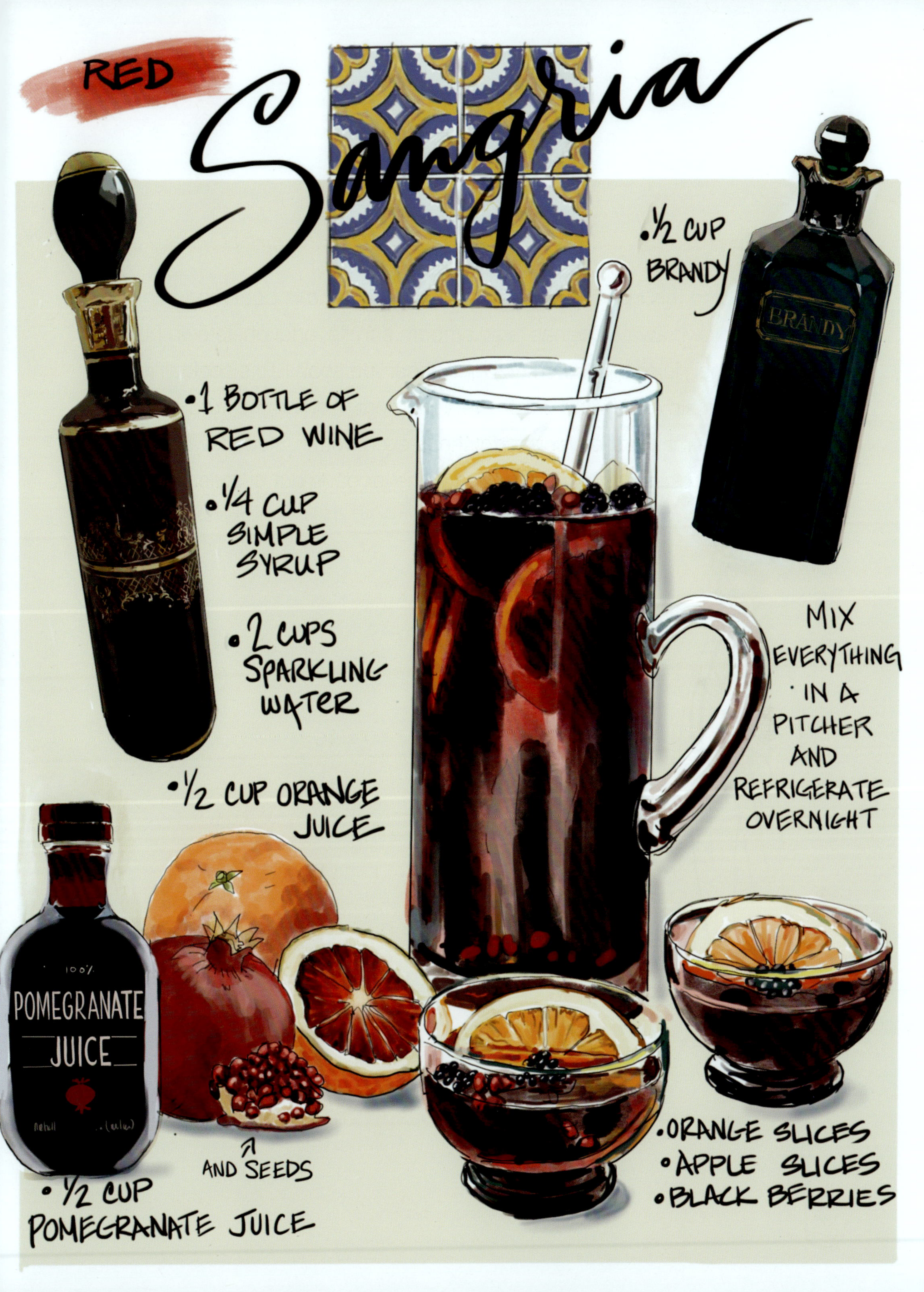
RED
Sangria
•½ CUP
BRANDY
BRANDY
•1 BOTTLE OF
RED WINE
•¼ CUP
SIMPLE
SYRUP
•2 CUPS
SPARKLING
WATER
•½ CUP ORANGE
JUICE
MIX
EVERYTHING
IN A
PITCHER
AND
REFRIGERATE
OVERNIGHT
100%
POMEGRANATE
JUICE
AND SEEDS
•½ CUP
POMEGRANATE JUICE
•ORANGE SLICES
•APPLE SLICES
•BLACK BERRIES

Sidecar

I prepared this classic cocktail while researching this book and frankly I was blown away. Cognac is so smooth and flavorful on its own but add lemon juice and some orange liqueur and wow. This cocktail is meant to sip slowly and savor every moment. Adding the Turbinado sugar rim makes the whole experience even better. Slow down and enjoy this classic cocktail. Good taste never goes out of style.

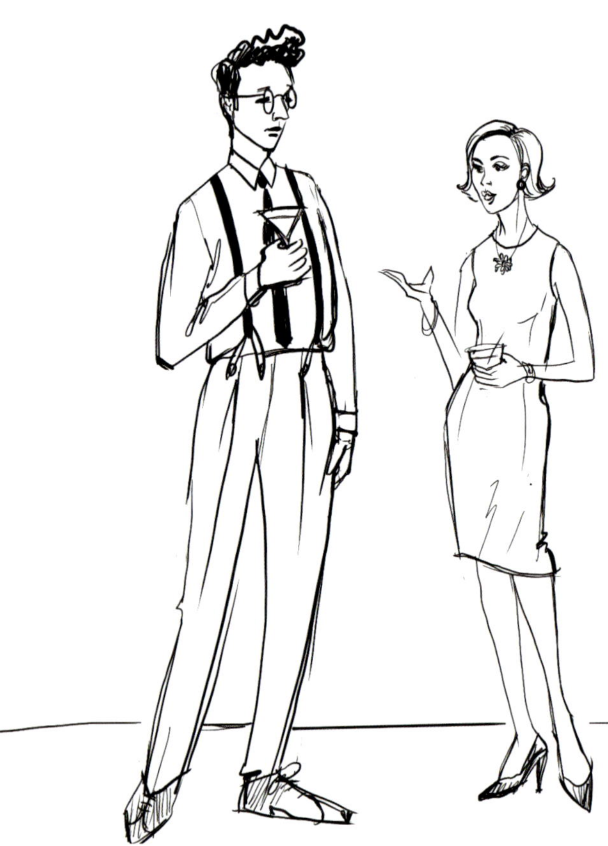

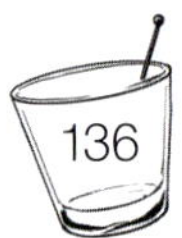

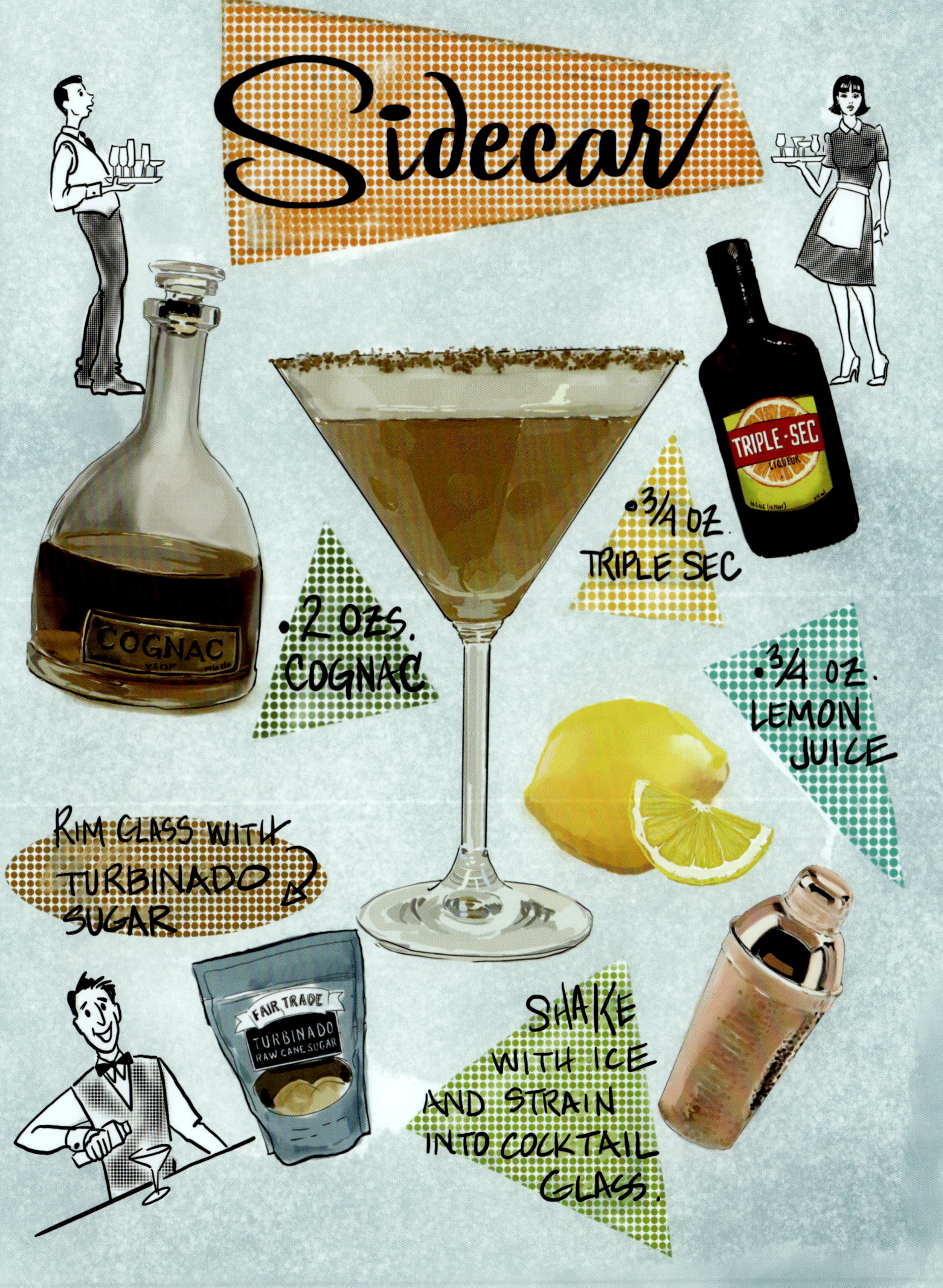

Sidecar
TRIPLE·SEC
LIQUEUR
COGNAC
VSOP
•2 OZS.
COGNAC
•3/4 OZ.
TRIPLE SEC
•3/4 OZ.
LEMON
JUICE
RIM GLASS WITH
TURBINADO
SUGAR
FAIR TRADE
TURBINADO
RAW CANE SUGAR
SHAKE
WITH ICE
AND STRAIN
INTO COCKTAIL
GLASS.

*"I doubt alcohol is the answer,
but it's worth a shot.."*

—Unknown

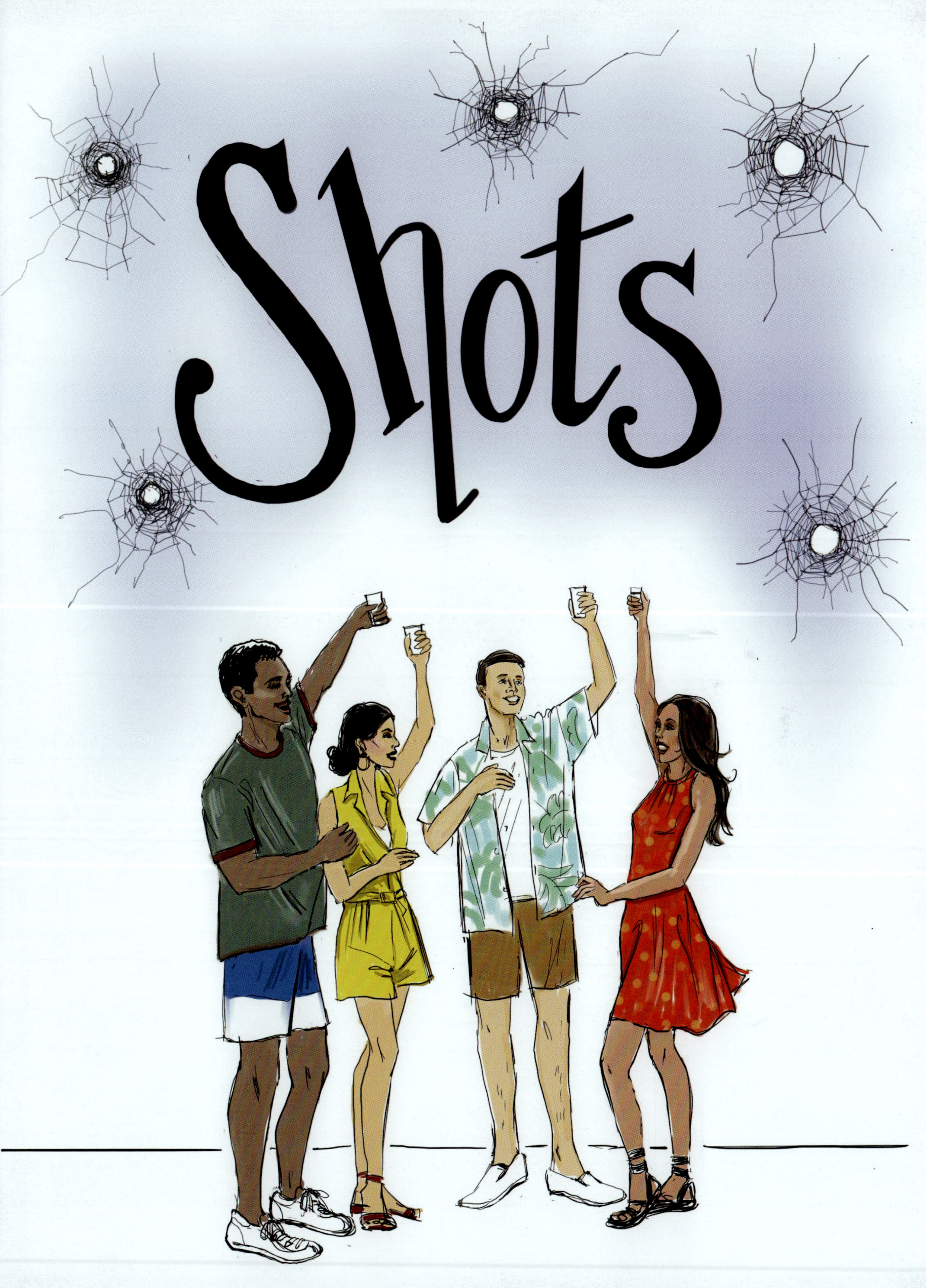
Shots

B-52

Just what is a B52? A: An American long-range, subsonic, jet-powered strategic bomber; B: An opening chess move; C: A hair style; or D: A legendary rock band? The answer is… E: All the above. A B-52 is also the name of a very cool looking cocktail shot that is extremely sweet and goes down easy. So put on some dance music and get the party started.

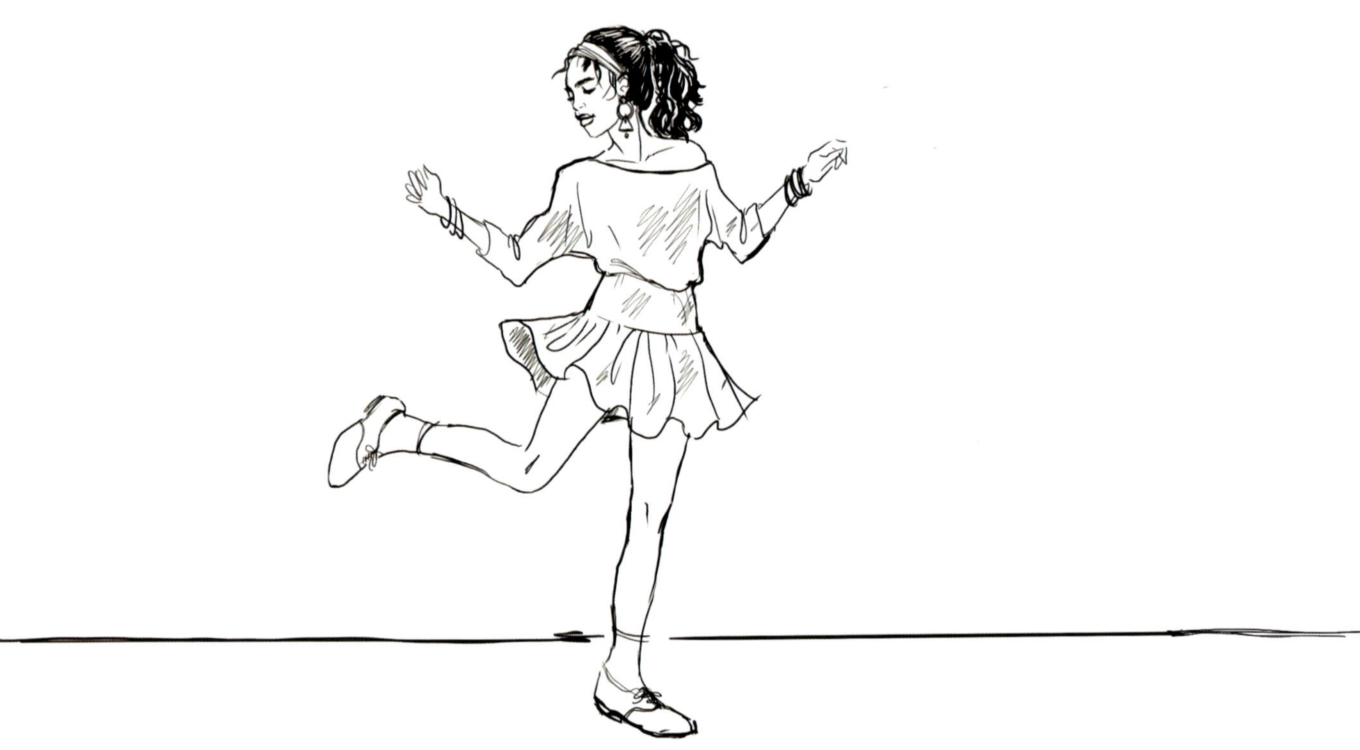

B-52

- 1 PART KAHLUA
- 1 PART IRISH CREME
- 1 PART ORANGE LIQUEUR

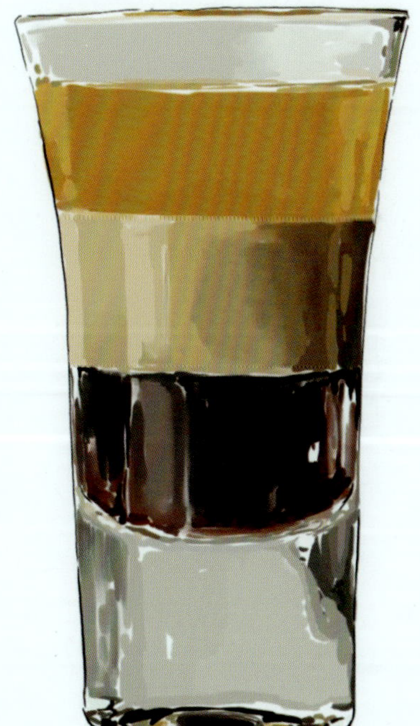

ADD KAHLUA TO SHOT GLASS. FOLLOW WITH IRISH CREME, POURED SLOWLY, OVER A BARSPOON. FINALLY, TOP WTH ORANGE LIQUEUR.

Gelatin Shots

The best thing about gelatin (AKA "Jello") shots is not how they taste, after all, they are commonly slurped, so you don't really taste much. And while maybe no one ever said, "I love Jello so much, I wish they made a drink with it," someone did have a brilliant idea. A platter of different flavored gelatin shots, their deep, translucent hues sparkling under the lights, really gets the party going. And isn't that the point sometimes?

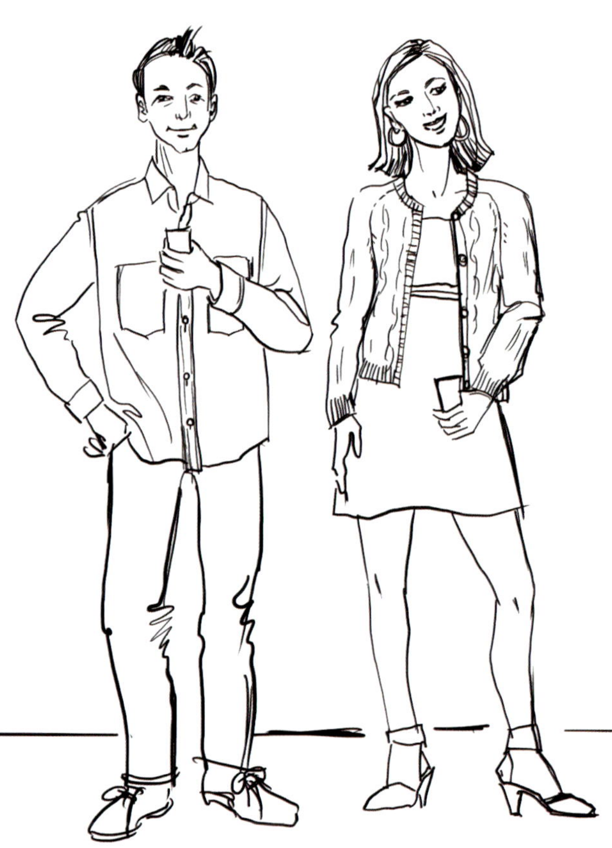

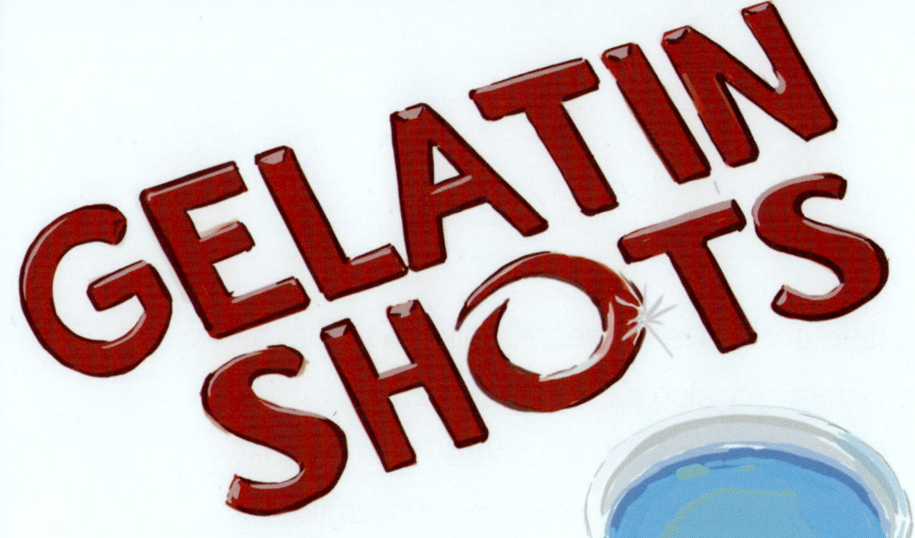

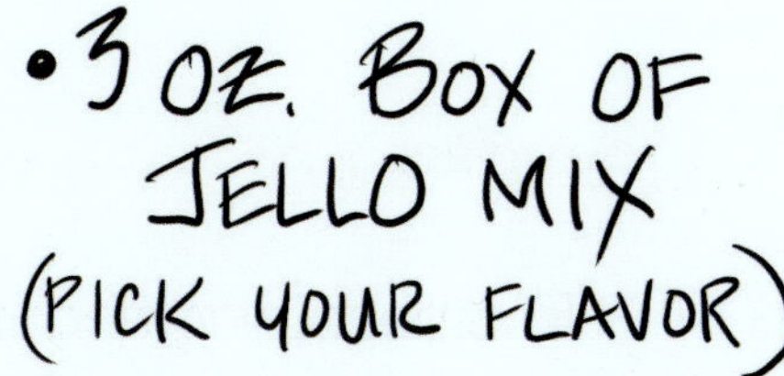

- 3 OZ. BOX OF JELLO MIX (PICK YOUR FLAVOR)
- ½ CUP VODKA
- WATER

HEAT 1 CUP WATER TO BOIL. POUR INTO BOWL, ADD JELLO POWDER & WHISK TILL DISSOLVED. ADD ½ CUP COLD WATER & ½ CUP VODKA.

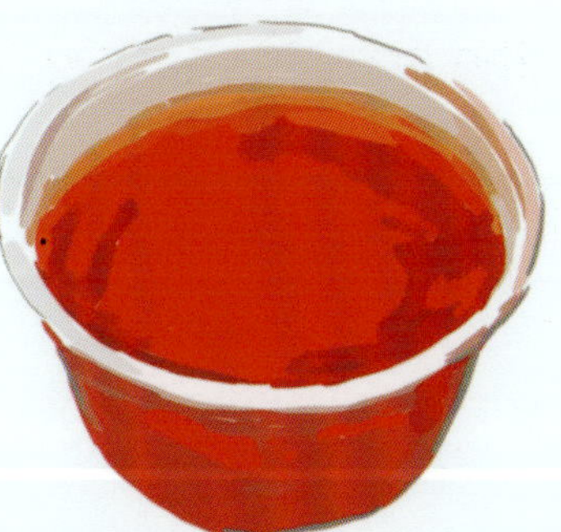

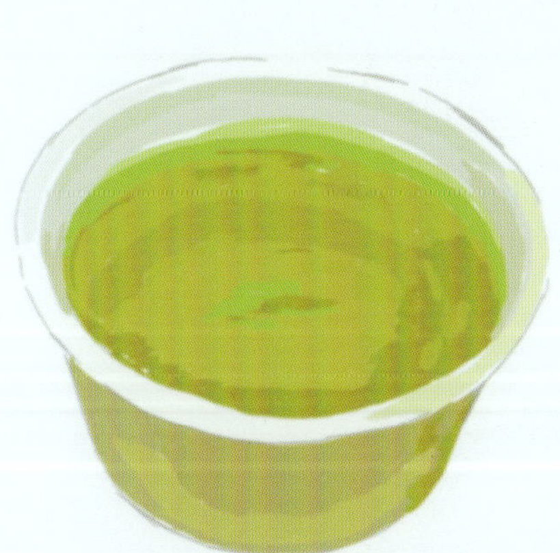

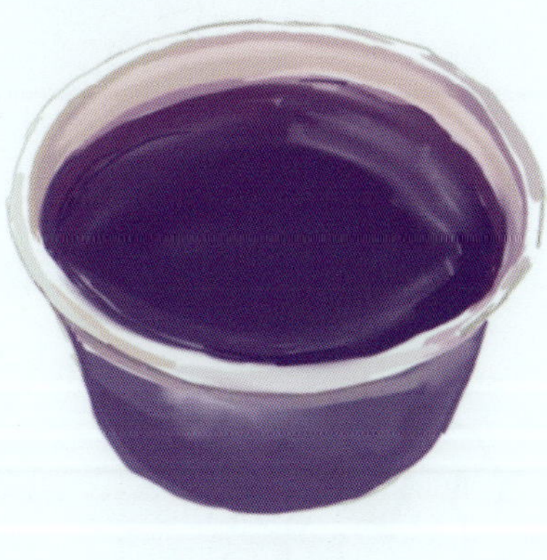

POUR INTO PLASTIC SHOT CUPS - OR USE A TURKEY BASTER TO EASILY DIVIDE INTO CUPS.

REFRIGERATE FOR 1½-2½ HOURS UNTIL FIRM.

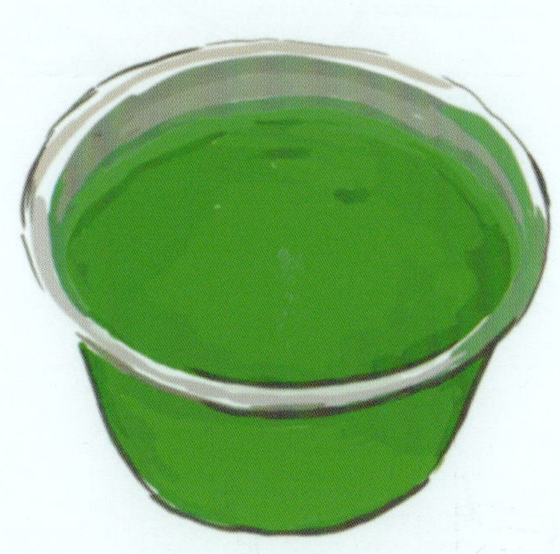

Kamikaze

In college, my friends Steve and Dave hosted Kamikaze nights at their apartment. They filled an old juice jar with crushed ice and poked a small hole in the lid for pouring. This created a makeshift cocktail shaker. They filled the juice jar with batches of Kamikazes and poured them out for their guests. Kamikazes still remind me of great friends and good times.

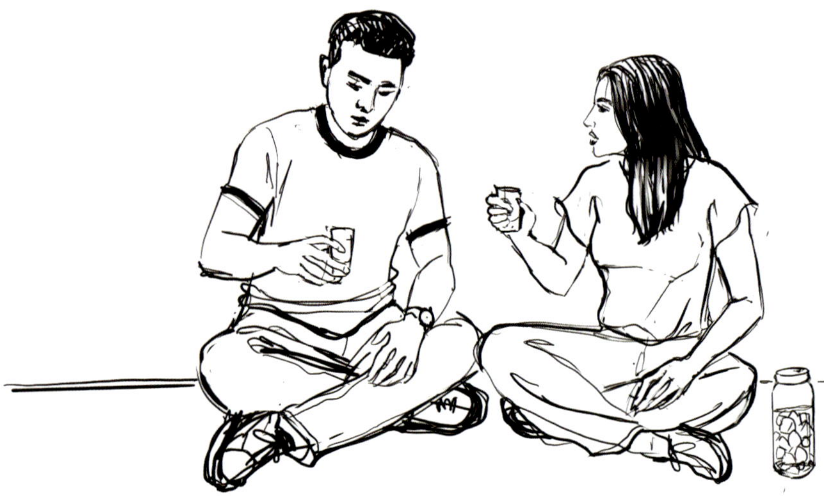

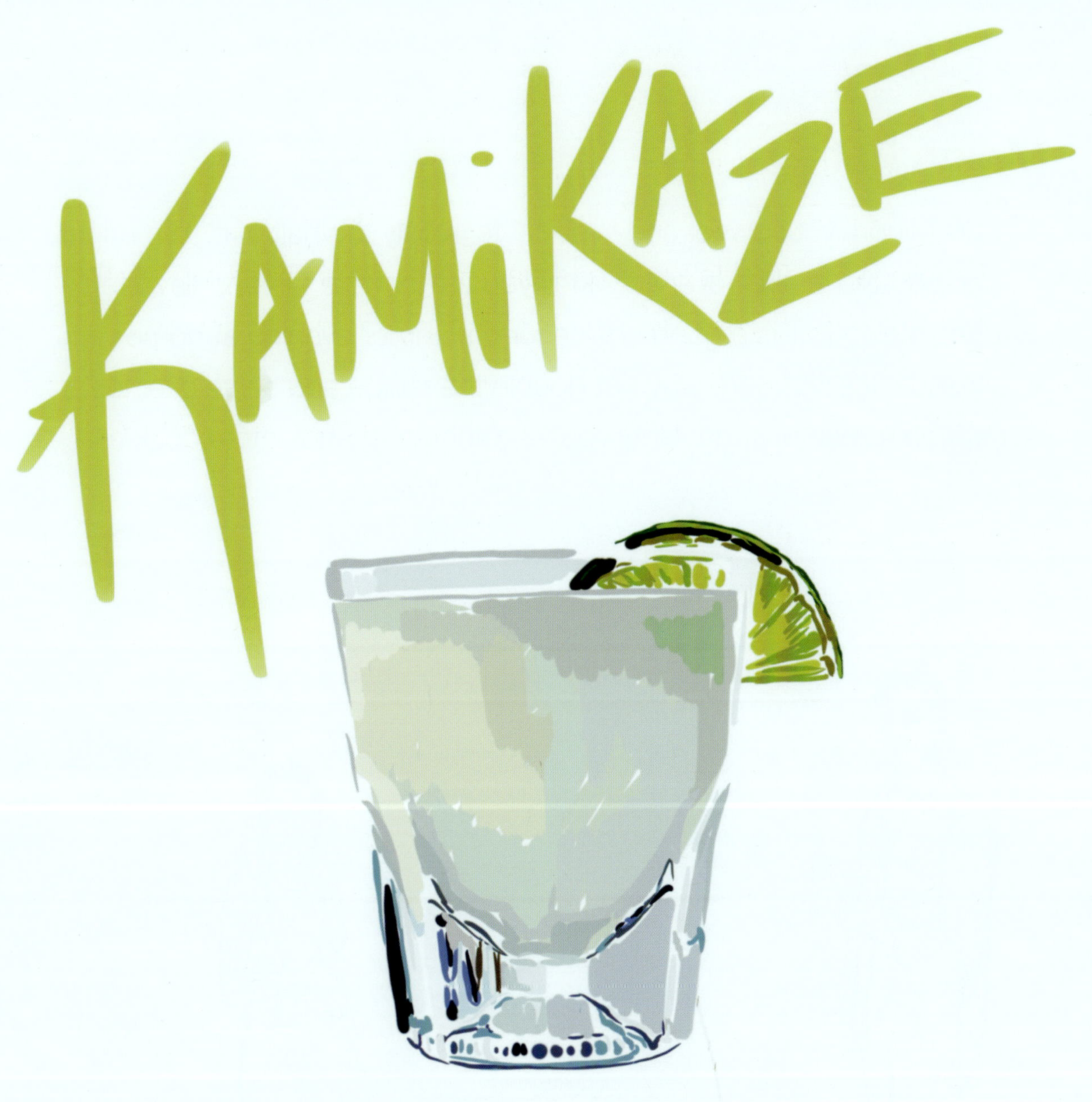

- 1 PART VODKA
- 1 PART LIME JUICE
- 1 PART TRIPLE SEC

ADD TO SHAKER WITH ICE. SHAKE WELL AND STRAIN INTO A SHOT GLASS.

Melon Ball

Oh Midori, your sweet and fresh taste is only the half of it. The bright green color makes every cocktail you are in more fun and flavorful. The Melon Ball is a good choice for a summer evening at home with friends. It's so good, why not double the recipe and serve over ice with a splash of soda. Now you've turned that shot into a cocktail.

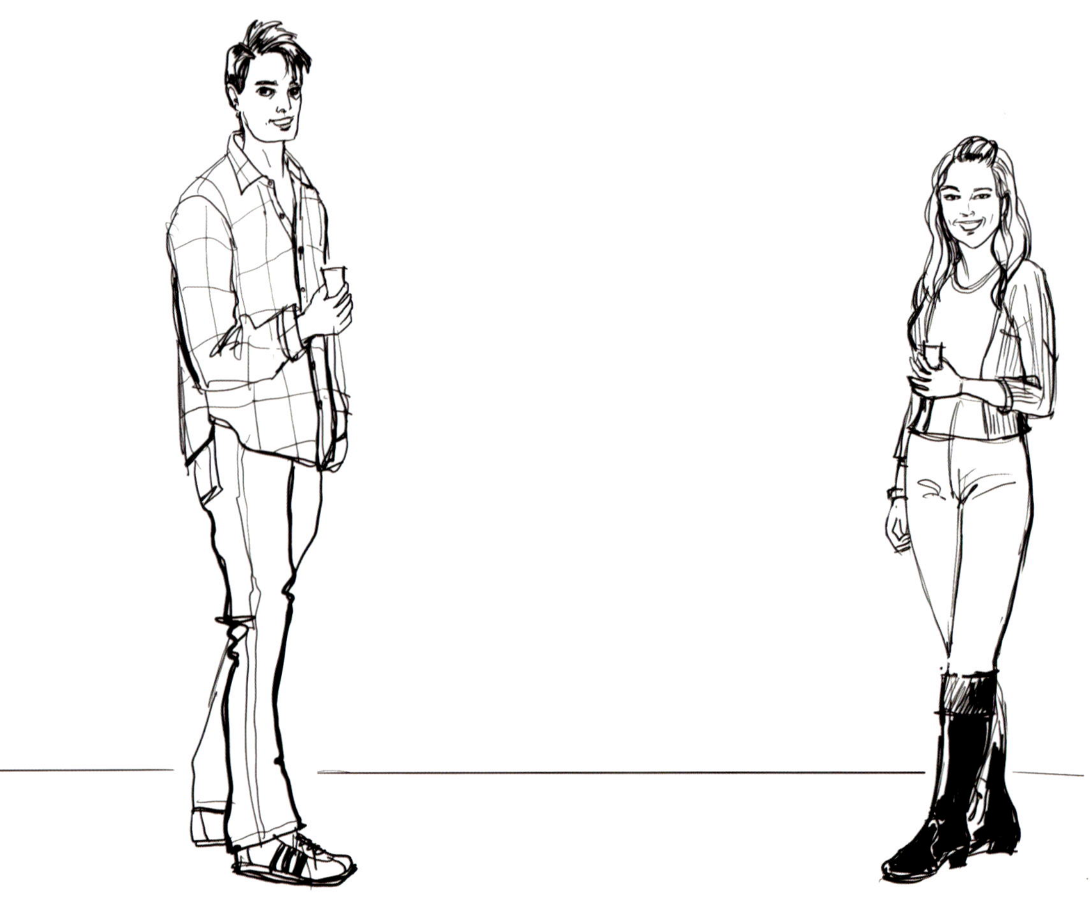

Melon Ball

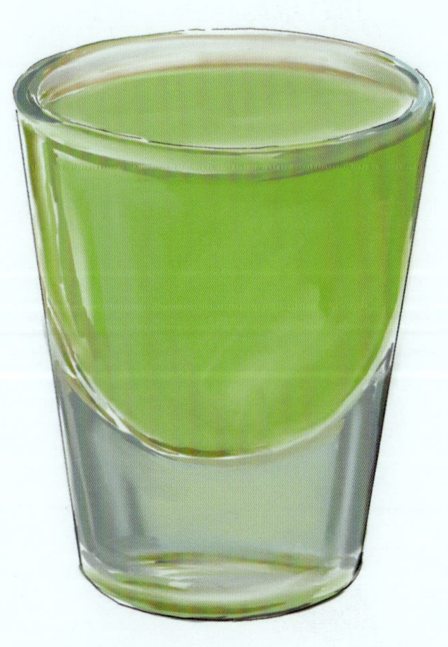

- 1/4 oz. Midori
- 1/4 oz. Pineapple Juice
- 1/2 oz. Vodka

Add ingredients to shaker with ice. Shake well and strain into shot glass.

Sex On The Beach

Was this invented to sell Peach Schnapps? Was it named for spring breakers in Florida? Or is it just a way to separate the "in" crowd from those who are too embarrassed to order this drink in a bar? I don't know the answer, but this sweet shot is as easy to drink as it is to make. Just be careful not to have too many or you might regret it in the morning.

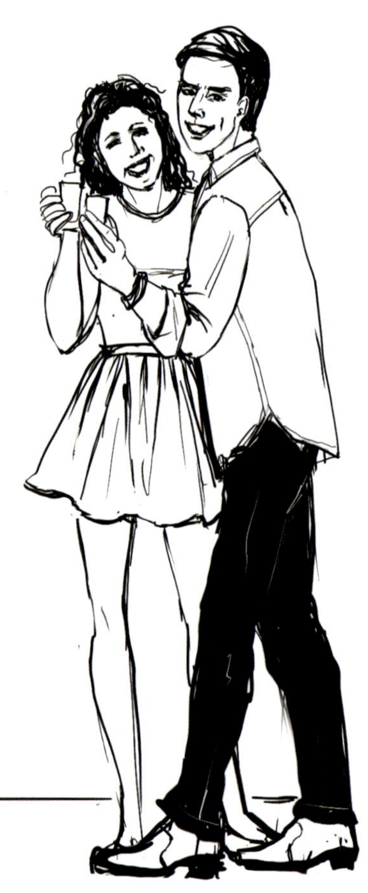

Sex on the Beach

- 1 PART VODKA
- 1 PART PEACH SCHNAPS
- 1 PART CRANBERRY JUICE
- 1 PART PINEAPPLE JUICE

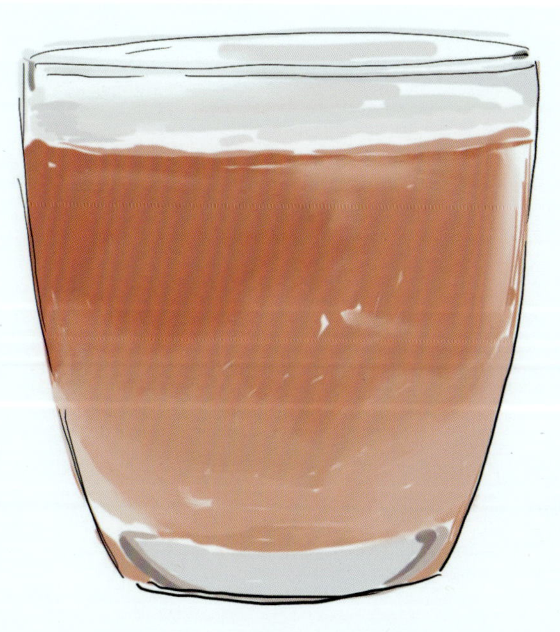

ADD TO SHAKER WITH ICE. SHAKE & STRAIN INTO SHOT GLASS.

Slippery Nipple

Etiquette states that there is only one proper time to try the Slippery Nipple, that would be, the bachelorette party. Ok, there is no etiquette for bachelor parties, which is why they are so fun, but this shot is a magical blend of flavors that when poured correctly is very provocative looking. Of course, the name is almost as good as the taste.

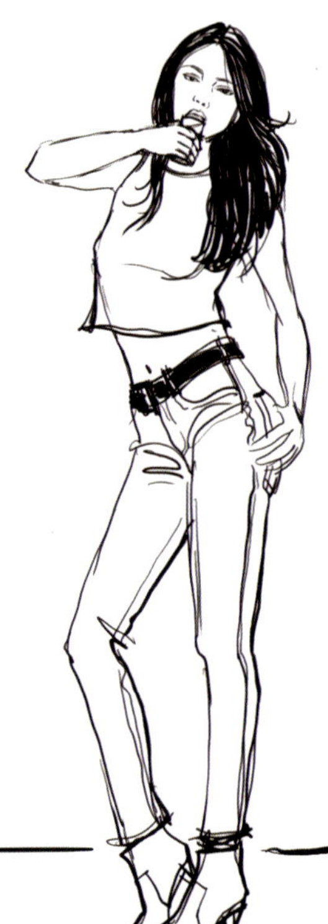

- ½ oz. Sambucca Liqueur
- ½ oz. Irish Creme
- 1 drop of Grenadine

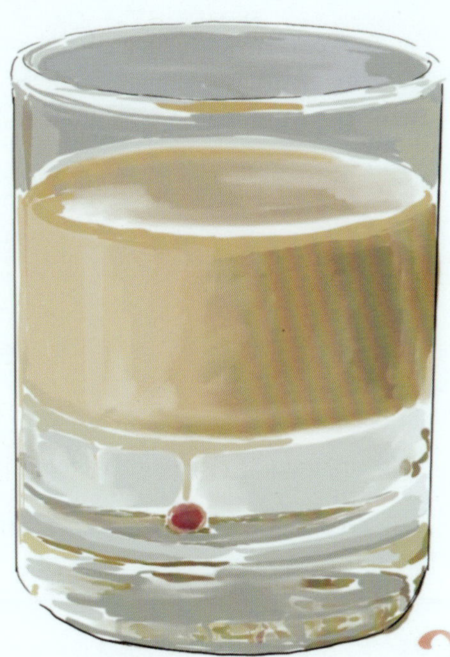

Slippery Nipple

ADD SAMBUCCA TO A SHOT GLASS. SLOWLY POUR IN IRISHCREME OVER A BAR SPOON. FINISH WITH A DROP OF GRENADINE.

"A bartender is just a pharmacist with a limited inventory."

—Albert Einstein

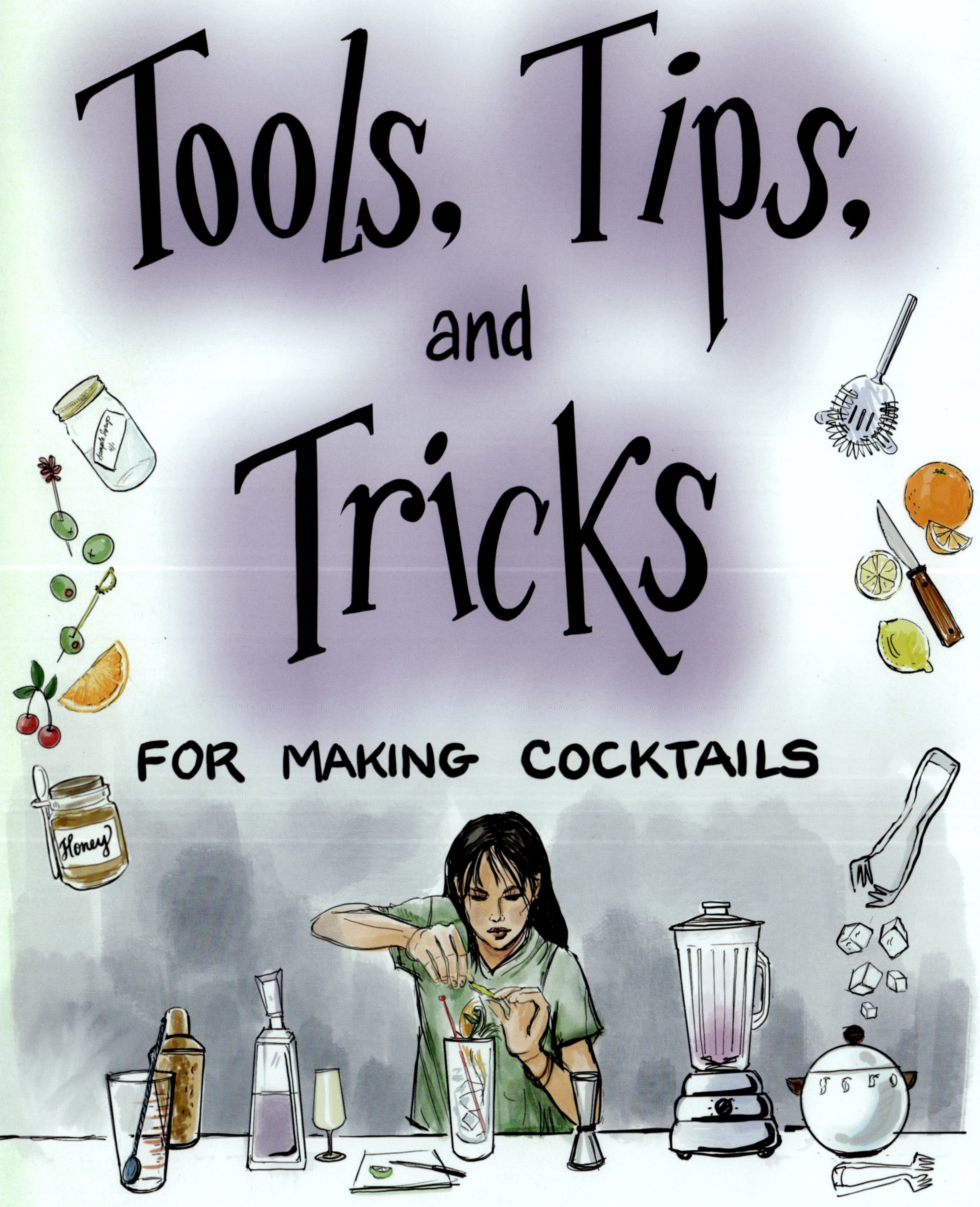
Tools, Tips, and Tricks
FOR MAKING COCKTAILS
Honey

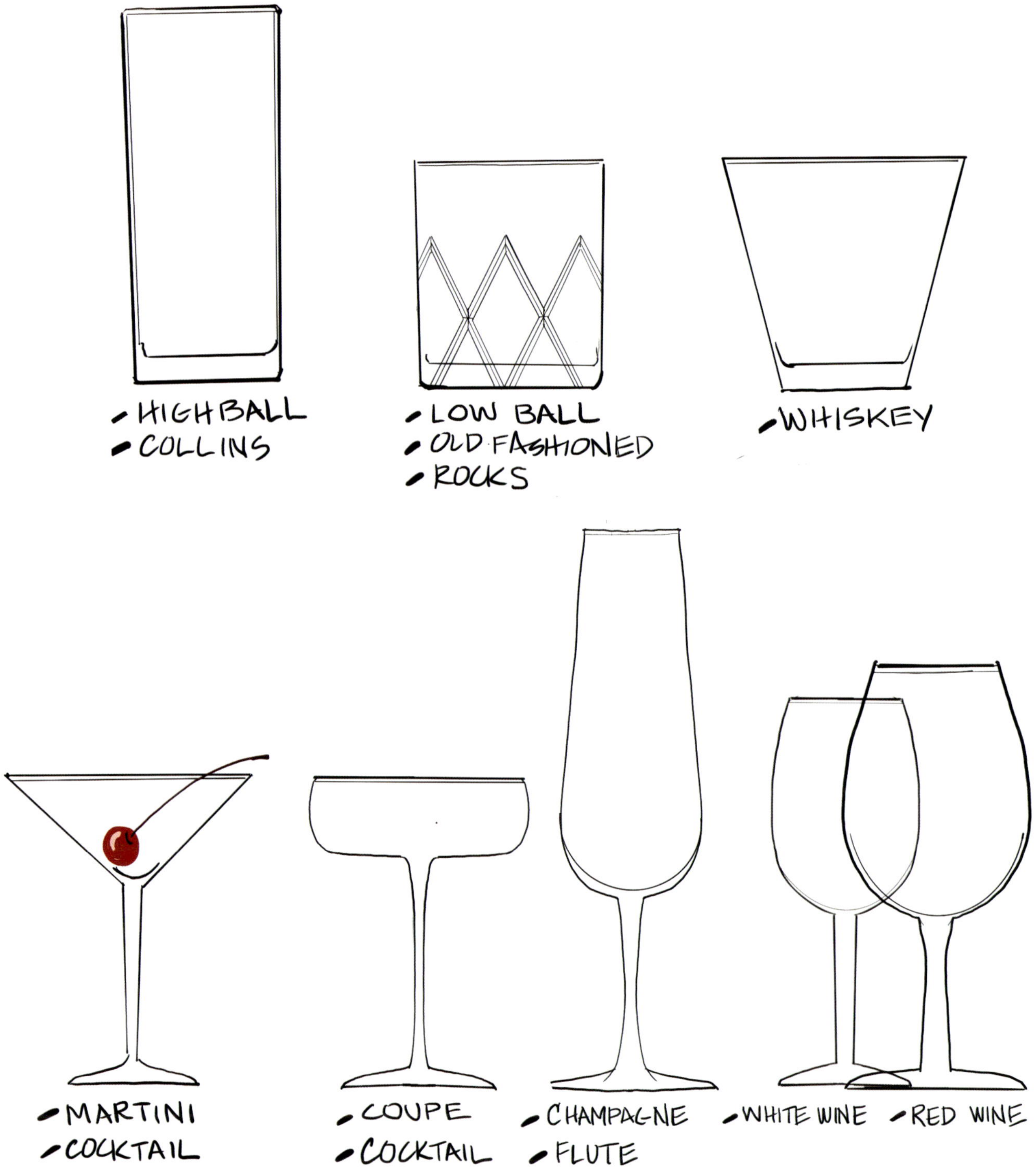

- HIGHBALL
- COLLINS

- LOW BALL
- OLD FASHIONED
- ROCKS

- WHISKEY

- MARTINI
- COCKTAIL

- COUPE
- COCKTAIL

- CHAMPAGNE
- FLUTE

- WHITE WINE

- RED WINE

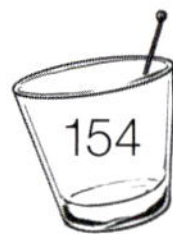

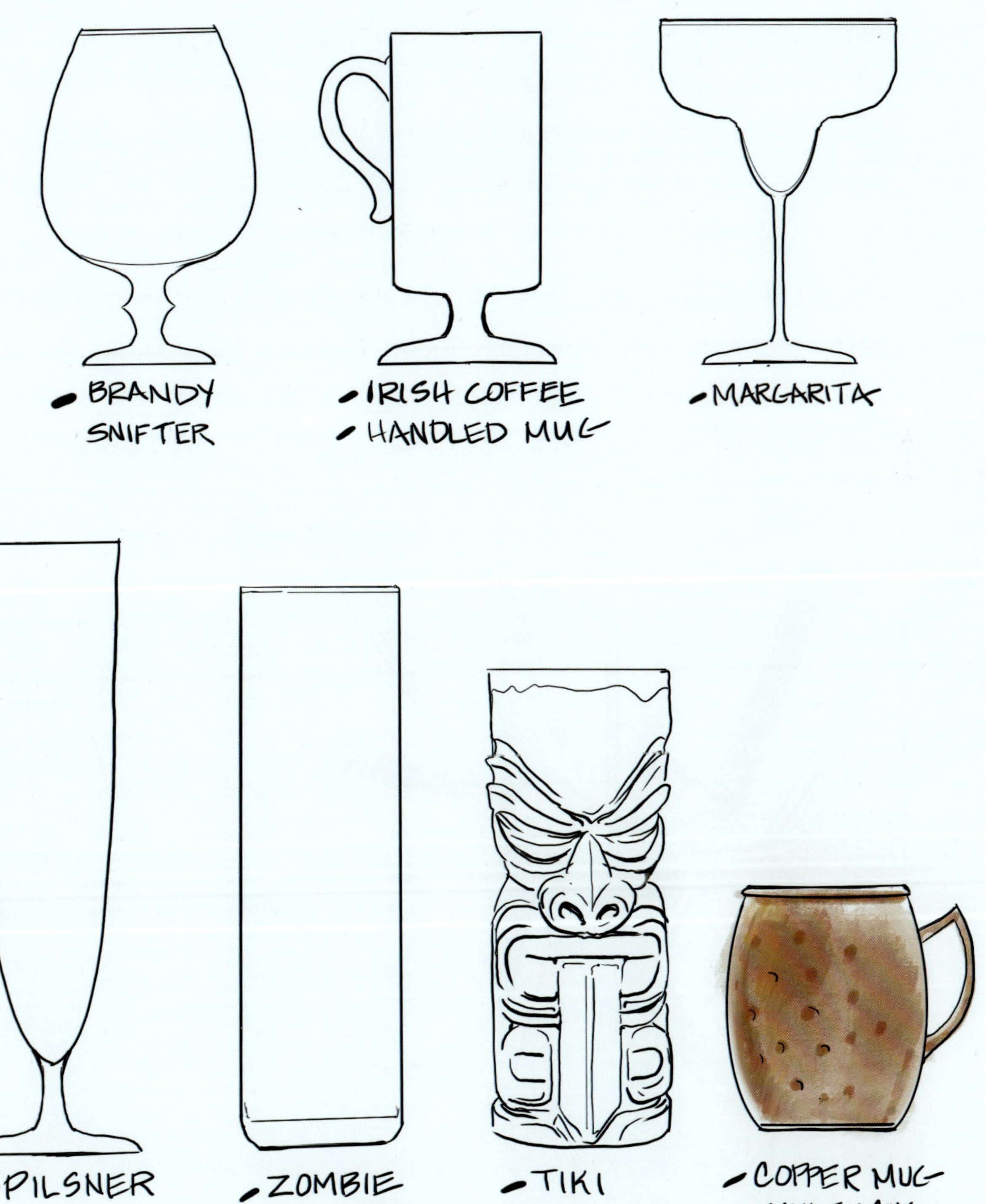
BRANDY SNIFTER
IRISH COFFEE
HANDLED MUG
MARGARITA
PILSNER
ZOMBIE
ICE TEA
TIKI
COPPER MUG
MULE MUG

A basic home bar should be equipped with a few tools, many of which you may already own. You will need a cutting board, a sharp paring knife, a bottle opener, a corkscrew and a long-handled spoon or swizzle stick for stirring your drink. It's nice to use ice tongs instead of your fingers for handling ice. A bar strainer is a nifty tool to have as it fits nicely over most glasses. Of course, in addition you will need something to measure with and make drinks in.

You can find bar accessories online, in local stores, even grocery stores. I like to search for them at antique and thrift shops. Not only can you get some really great buys, but you can find unique designs. Midcentury was a popular era for the home cocktail bar, so there are many great tools still available.

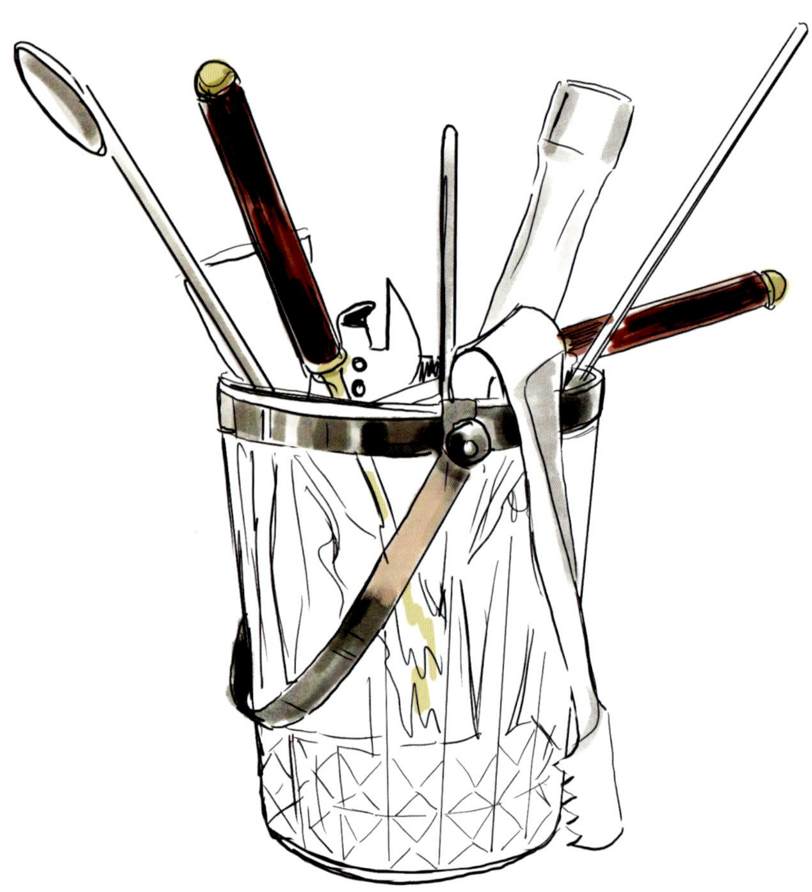

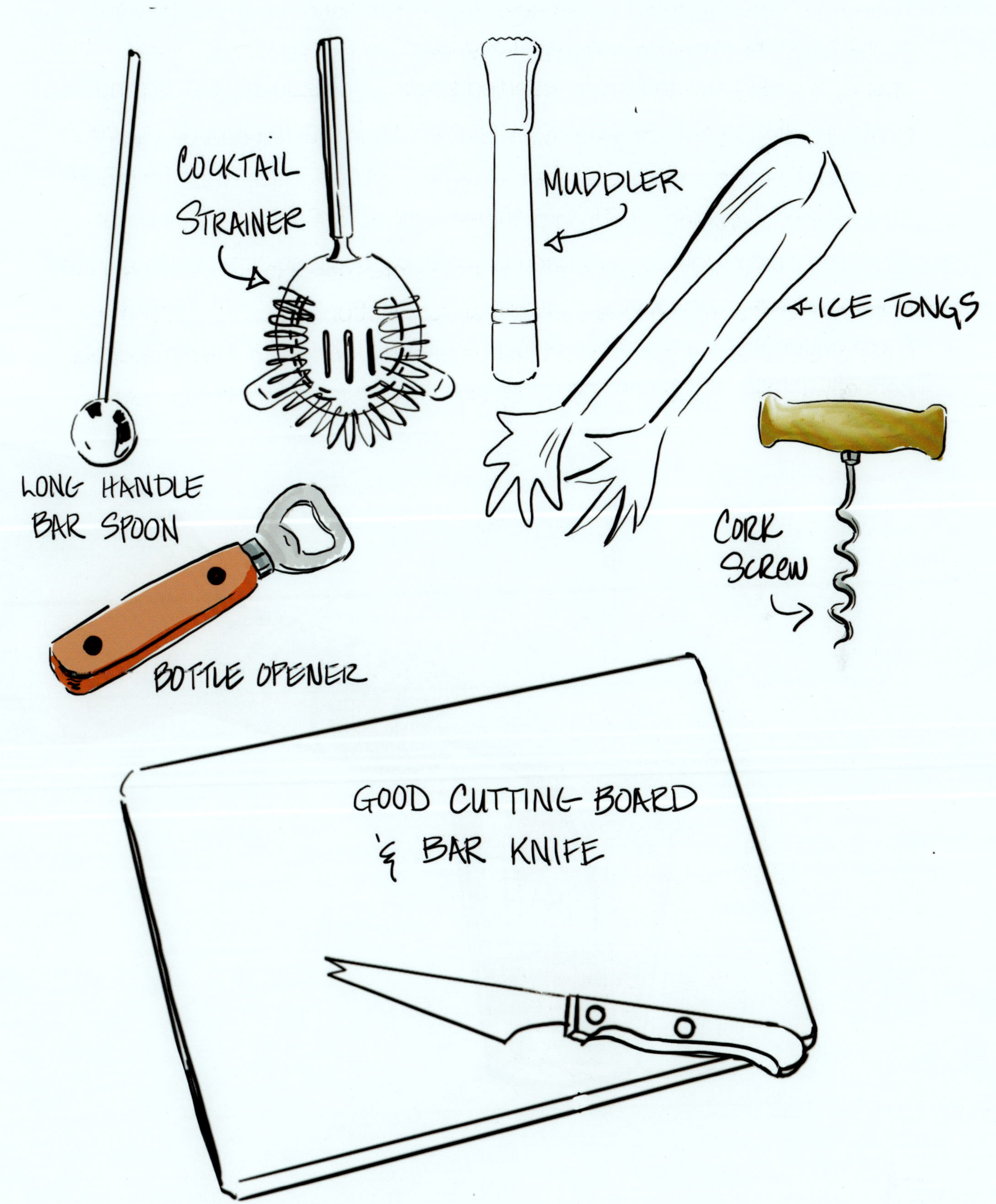
COCKTAIL STRAINER
MUDDLER
ICE TONGS
LONG HANDLE BAR SPOON
CORK SCREW
BOTTLE OPENER
GOOD CUTTING BOARD & BAR KNIFE

I've never been able to figure out how Bartenders pour out an ounce without measuring it. But they do and that is why they are professionals. I need help, so I enlist some of my many shot glasses and tools to figure it out. Unfortunately, not all shot glasses are created equal. A shot and/or a jigger is supposed to be an ounce and a half. Which is fine if that's what the recipe calls for, but eyeballing a fraction of that in a glass with sloped sides is not easy. The classic double jigger can be confusing because although the smaller side measures 1 ounce, the larger side can be 1 ½ oz. or 2 ozs. I suggest you find a device that has various measurements on it to you can make each drink perfectly. It helps if you can find one with a spout for easy pouring.

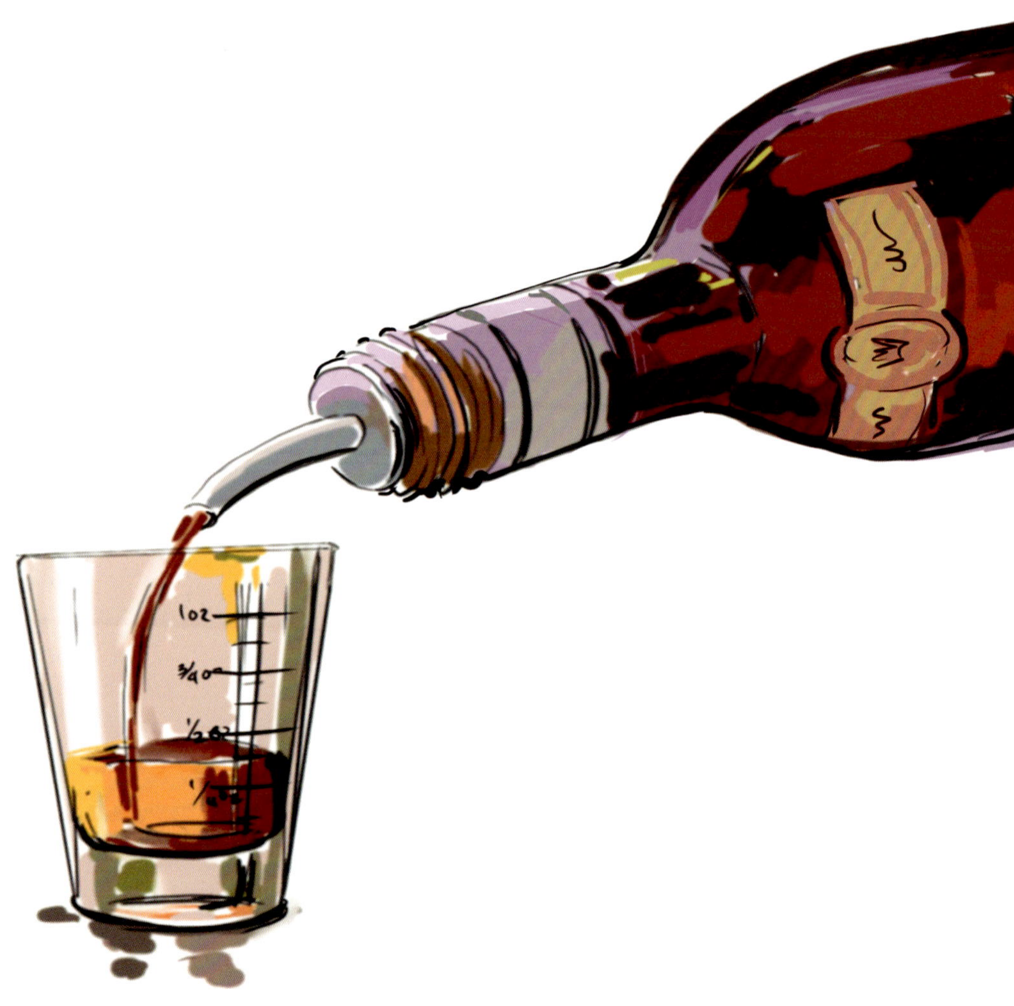

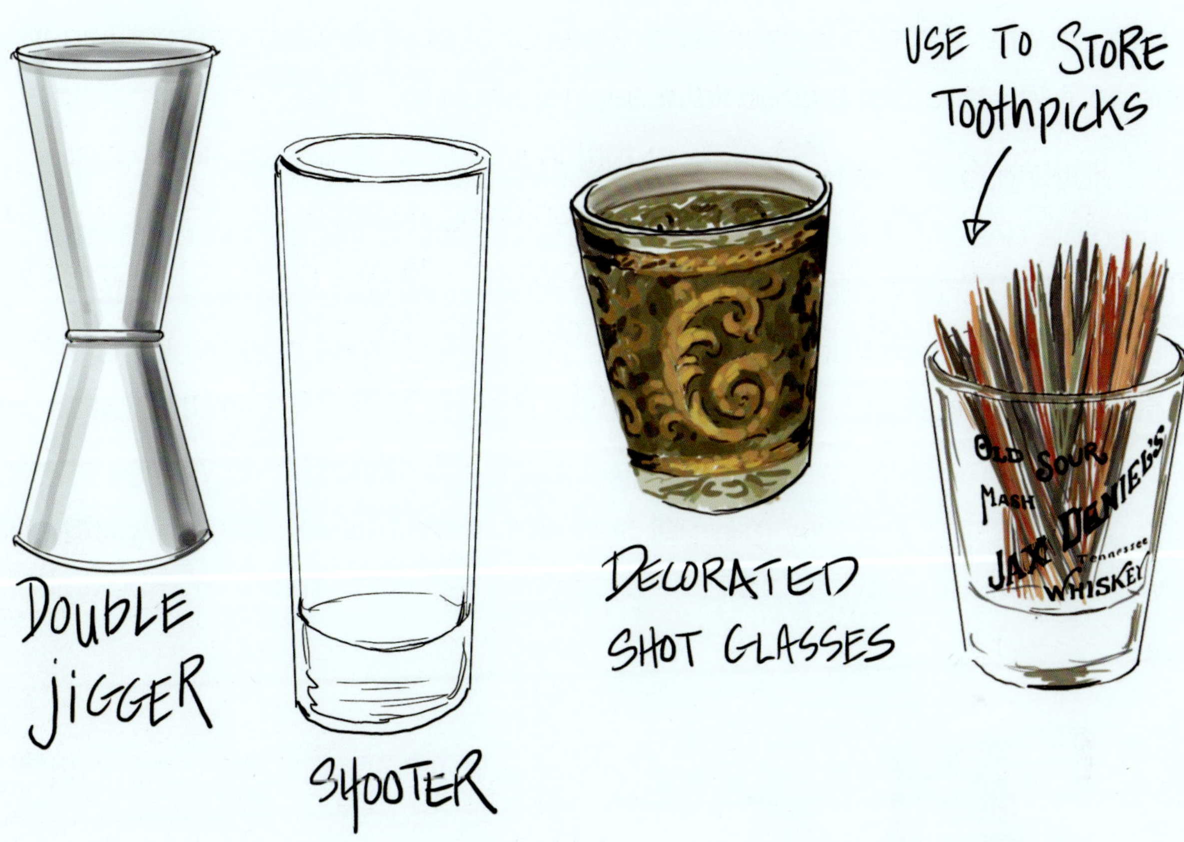
USE TO STORE Toothpicks
DOUBLE JIGGER
SHOOTER
DECORATED SHOT GLASSES
OLD SOUR MASH
JACK DANIEL'S
Tennessee WHISKEY

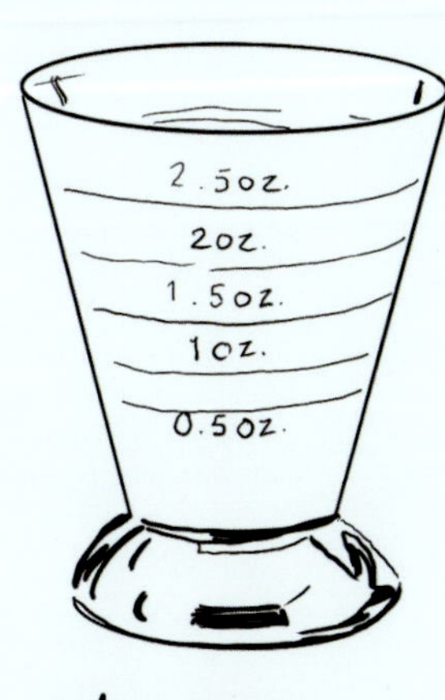
2.5oz.
2oz.
1.5oz.
1oz.
0.5oz.

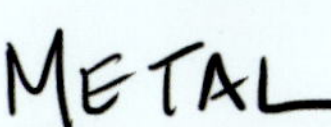
METAL

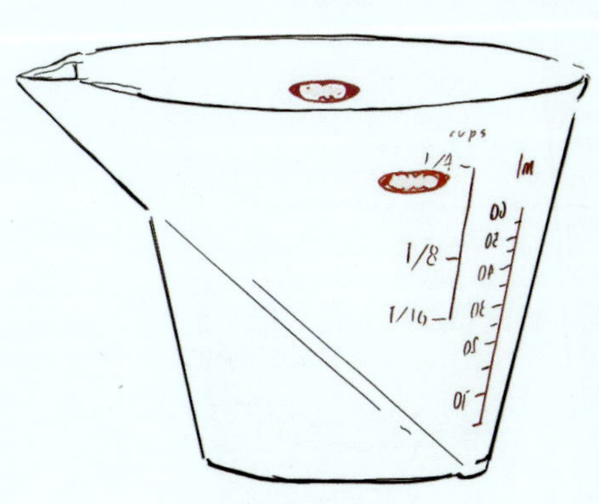
cups
1/4
1/8
1/16
PLASTIC

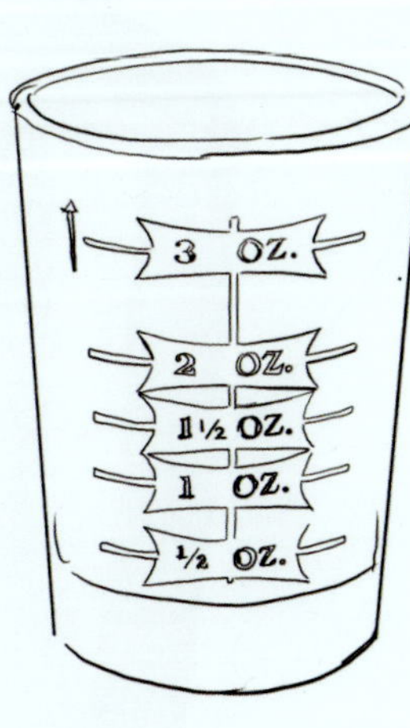
3 OZ.
2 OZ.
1½ OZ.
1 OZ.
½ OZ.
GLASS

Most cocktails require mixing, and that can happen in a container with a spoon or in a shaker. Shaking the ingredients makes the drinks super cold and better tasting. This shaking device does not have to be fancy or even store bought. You can fashion a cocktail out of anything that can contain all the contents and has a good lid or seal for shaking.

Still, nothing looks better in a home bar than a cool shaker. You can find incredible designs in both new products and antique items. If you are going to do some serious cocktail preparation make sure you choose a shaker that is easy to open but also has a good seal. Each type of shaker has its advantages and disadvantages. For instance, the Cobbler, with its built-in strainer is convenient, while the Boston is easy to clean. Many vintage shakers are great looking, but they may not seal well or are missing parts. I actually own many vintage styles, but I use a modern version to make my cocktails.

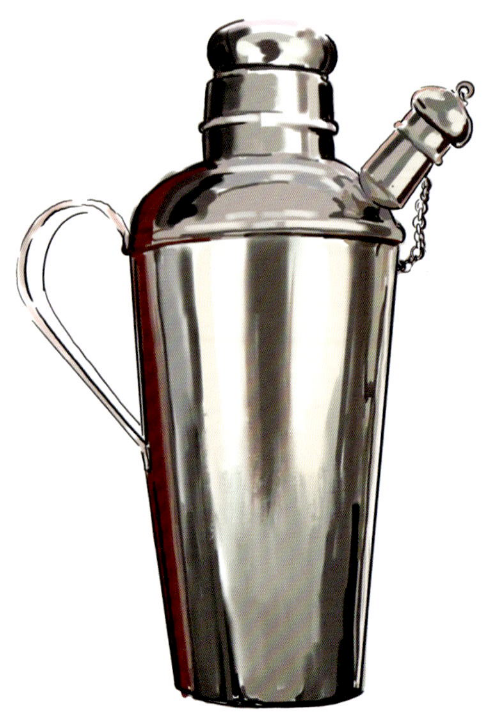

Do I Really Need A Cocktail Shaker?

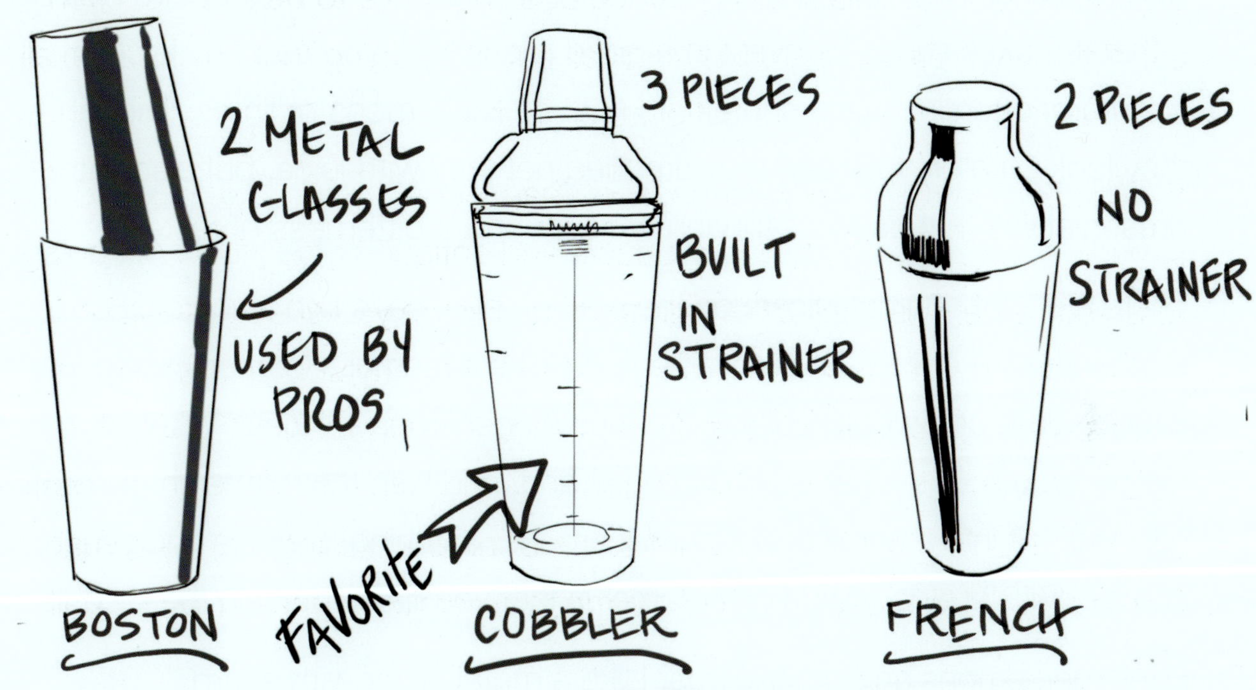

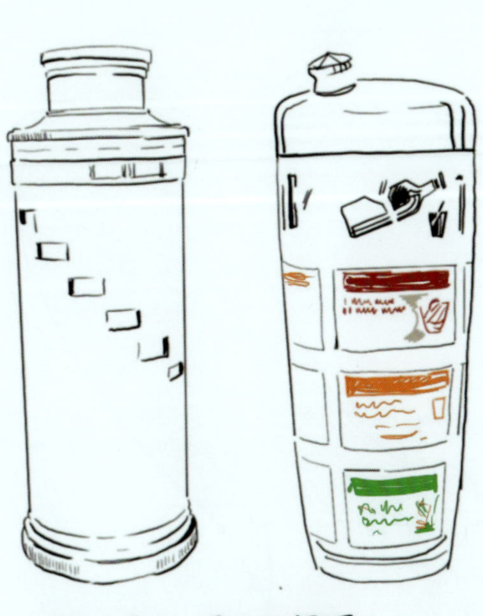

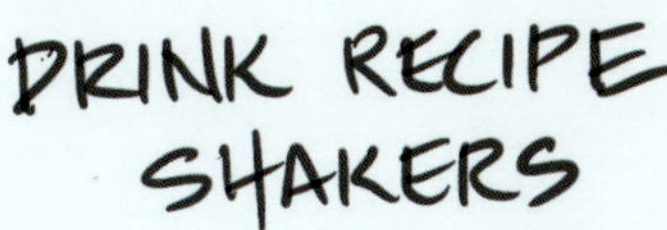

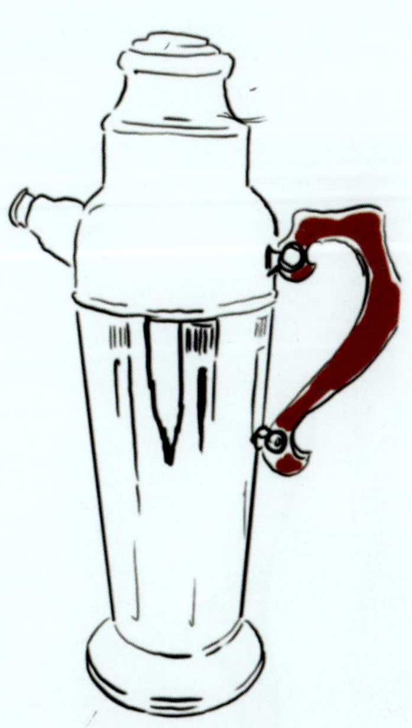

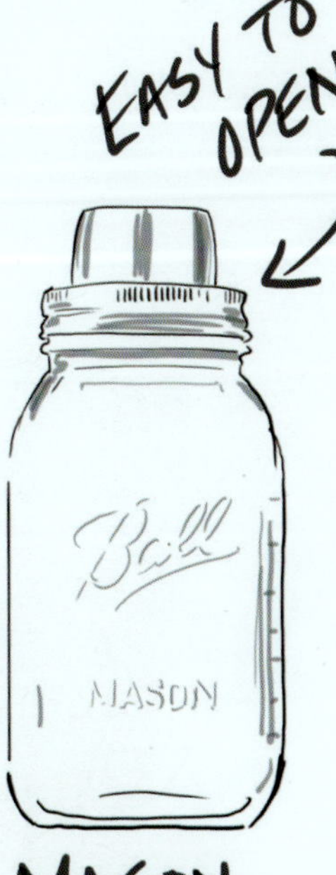

Put Down the Plastic Lemon!

There are so many cocktails that use citrus as an ingredient – a wedge of lime, a splash of lemon juice or even a glassful of orange or grapefruit juice – that it makes sense to invest in a good juicer. Yes, you can buy juice in the store, often in plastic containers shaped like lemons or limes. Though they look cute on your bar, they are filled not only with juice, but also with preservatives that cause a dilution of flavor and a bitterness of taste.

There are a lot of great juicers on the market, but I have two favorites. For smaller fruits like limes and Meyer lemons I like a reamer. Reamers come plastic, glass and wood, but for me, the wooden ones are best. With a reamer, you hold the halved fruit in one hand, and with the reamer in the other hand stick it into the fruit and smush it around, catching the juice and seeds into a bowl. The downside of a reamer is that you have to strain the juice.

For larger lemons and other citrus, I like a metal juicer with sharp, pronounced ridges that really tear into the fruit. These also come in plastic or even wood, but metal is best. Often, this kind of juicer has a strainer and spout built in, which is a nice plus.

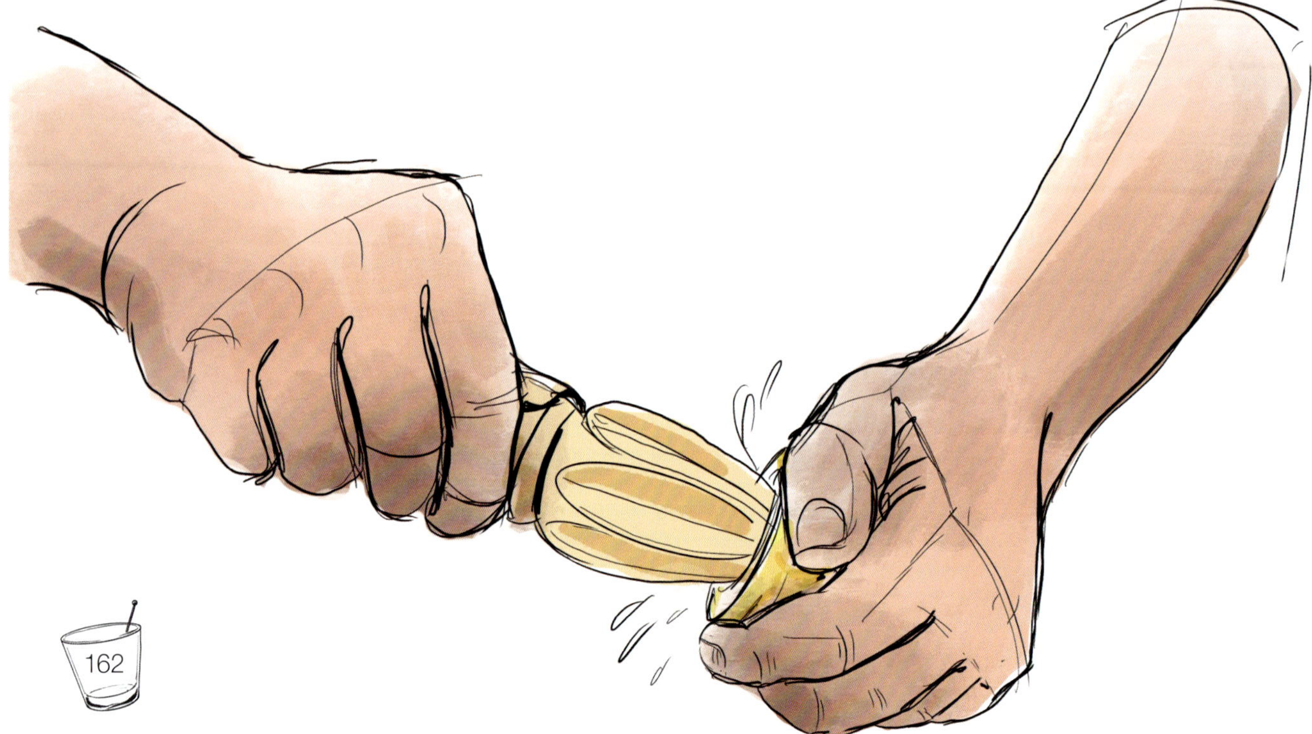

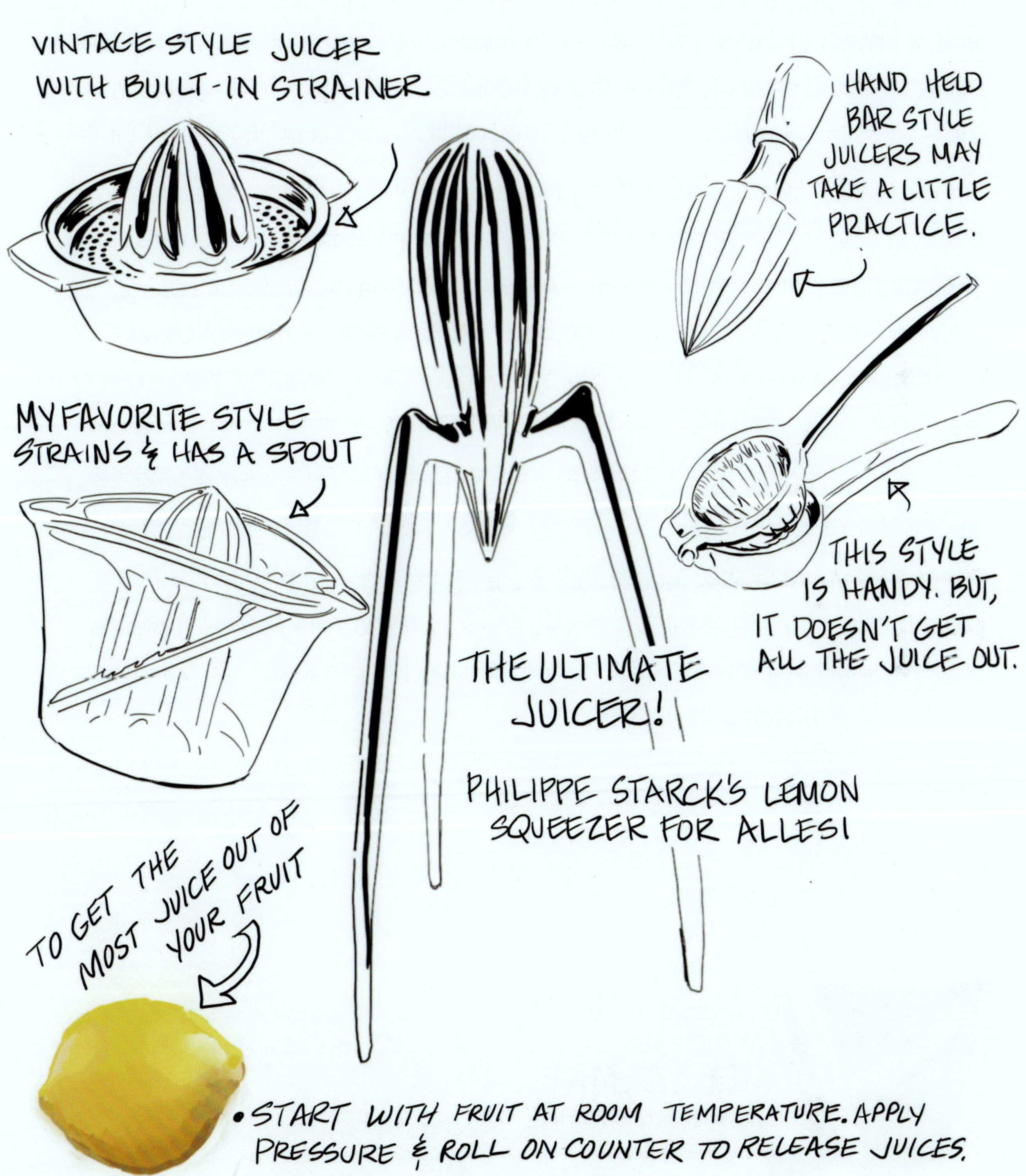

• START WITH FRUIT AT ROOM TEMPERATURE. APPLY PRESSURE & ROLL ON COUNTER TO RELEASE JUICES.

Fancy bars serve their drinks over "clear" ice. As in ice that is perfectly clear – no cloudiness, no imperfections. Crystal clear. Clear ice looks better and allows the look of the cocktail to shine. It also melts more slowly, which keeps the drinks from getting watered down. Clear ice is also made by expensive ice machines in fancy bars. Clear ice can also be made at home, but it is a long and laborious process.

Yet the lack of clear ice should not be a deterrent for the home bartender. You can actually be more creative with your cocktails because you are not in a commercial venue. Ice doesn't have to be made from water. For your Cosmopolitan, make ice out of cranberry juice. A Bloody Mary? Freeze some tomato juice with a little Worcestershire Sauce, celery salt and Tabasco and as your drink chills it will continue to infuse with flavor.

You can even buy specialty ice cube trays in different sizes and shapes. You can also use common household items for making ice. It is thought that larger ice cubes melt more slowly, so use the two ounce "tuppers" for XL size cubes. Clear plastic egg cartons are great for making funky semi-ovals; while long and narrow plastic prescription bottles can be used for ice "logs." Be creative… there is no wrong way to make ice.

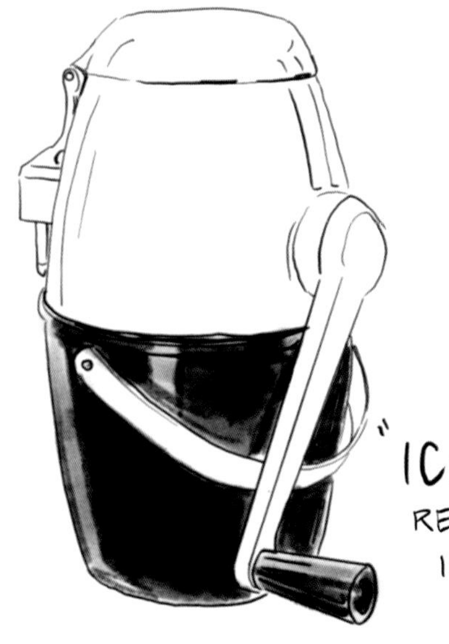

"ICE-O-MAT"
RETRO CRUSHED
ICE MAKER

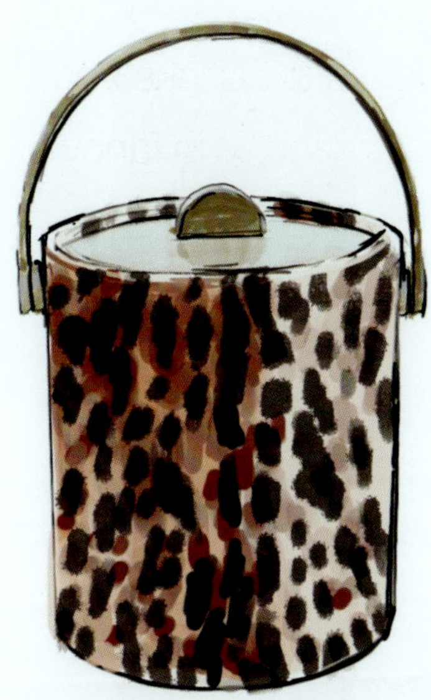
PATTERNED
LUCITE

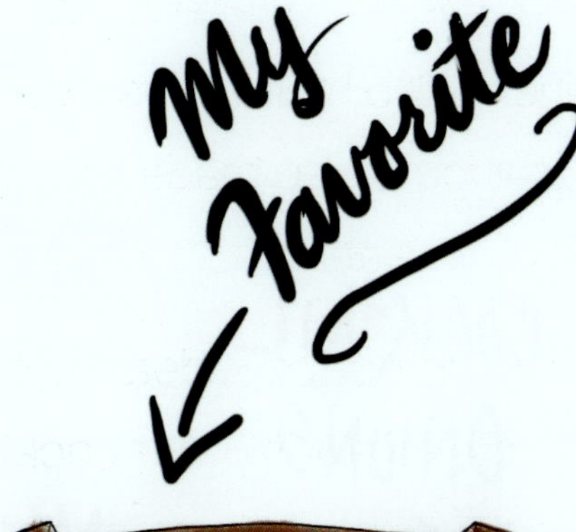
My Favorite

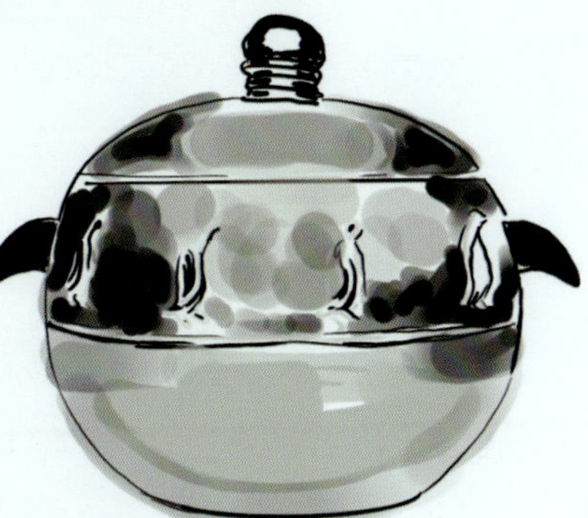
PENGIUN

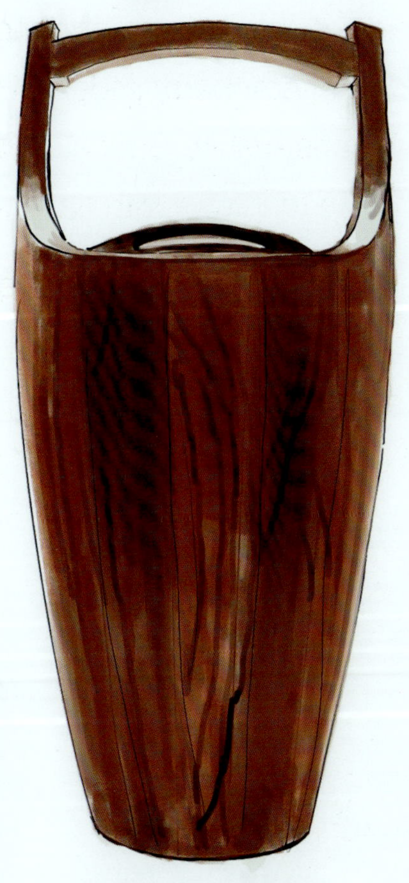
DANSK
CONGO

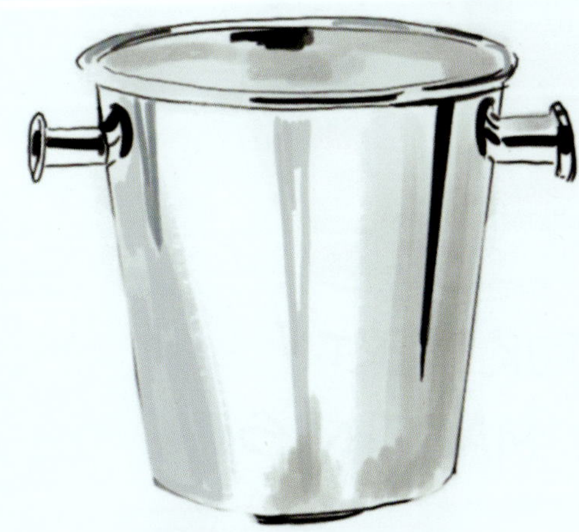
ALESSI

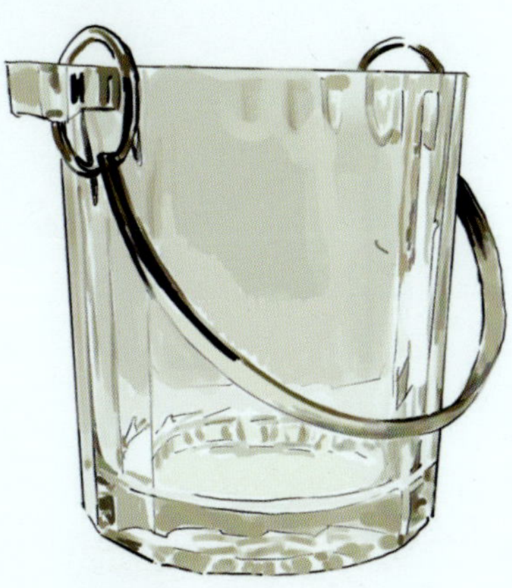
CRYSTAL

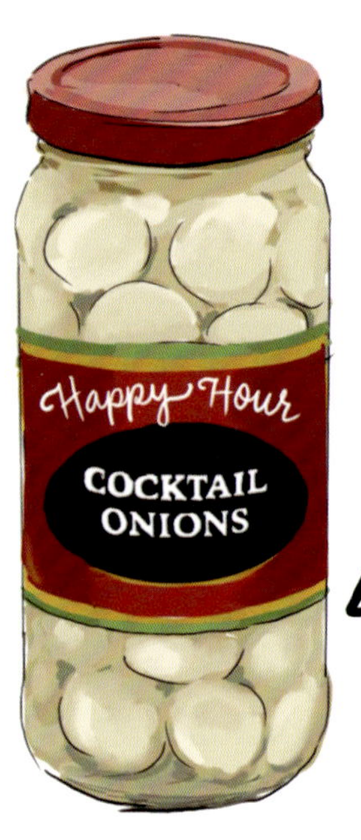

COCKTAIL ONIONS

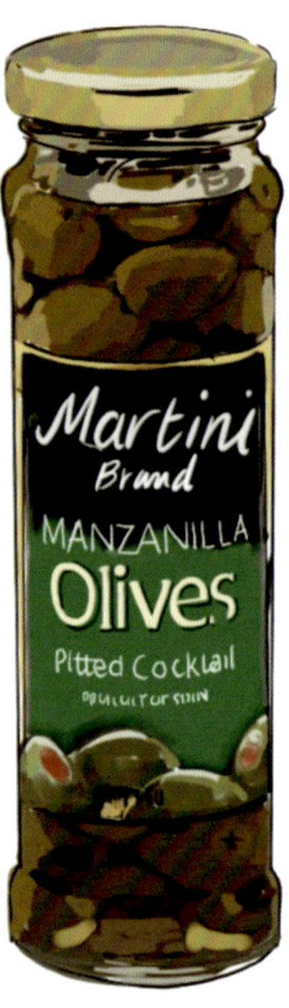

MARTINI OLIVES

BLUE CHEESE STUFFED OLIVES

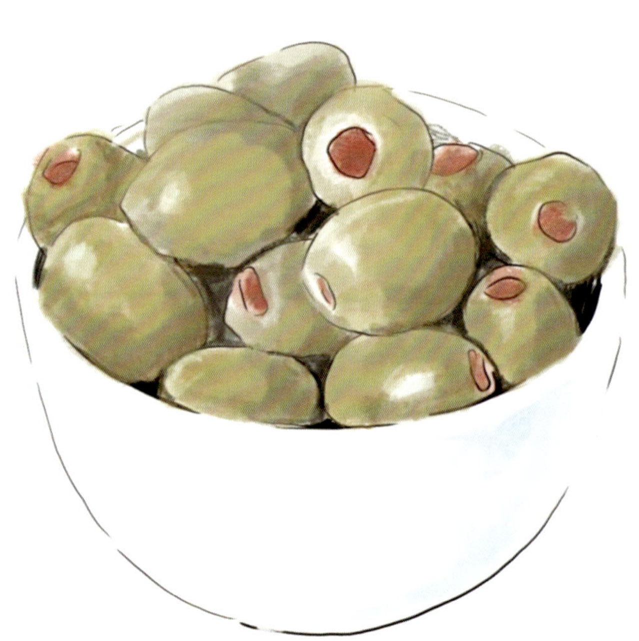

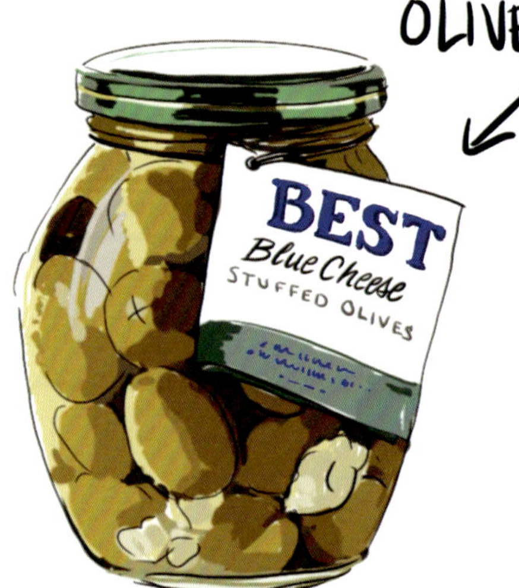

FOR DIRTY MARTINIS

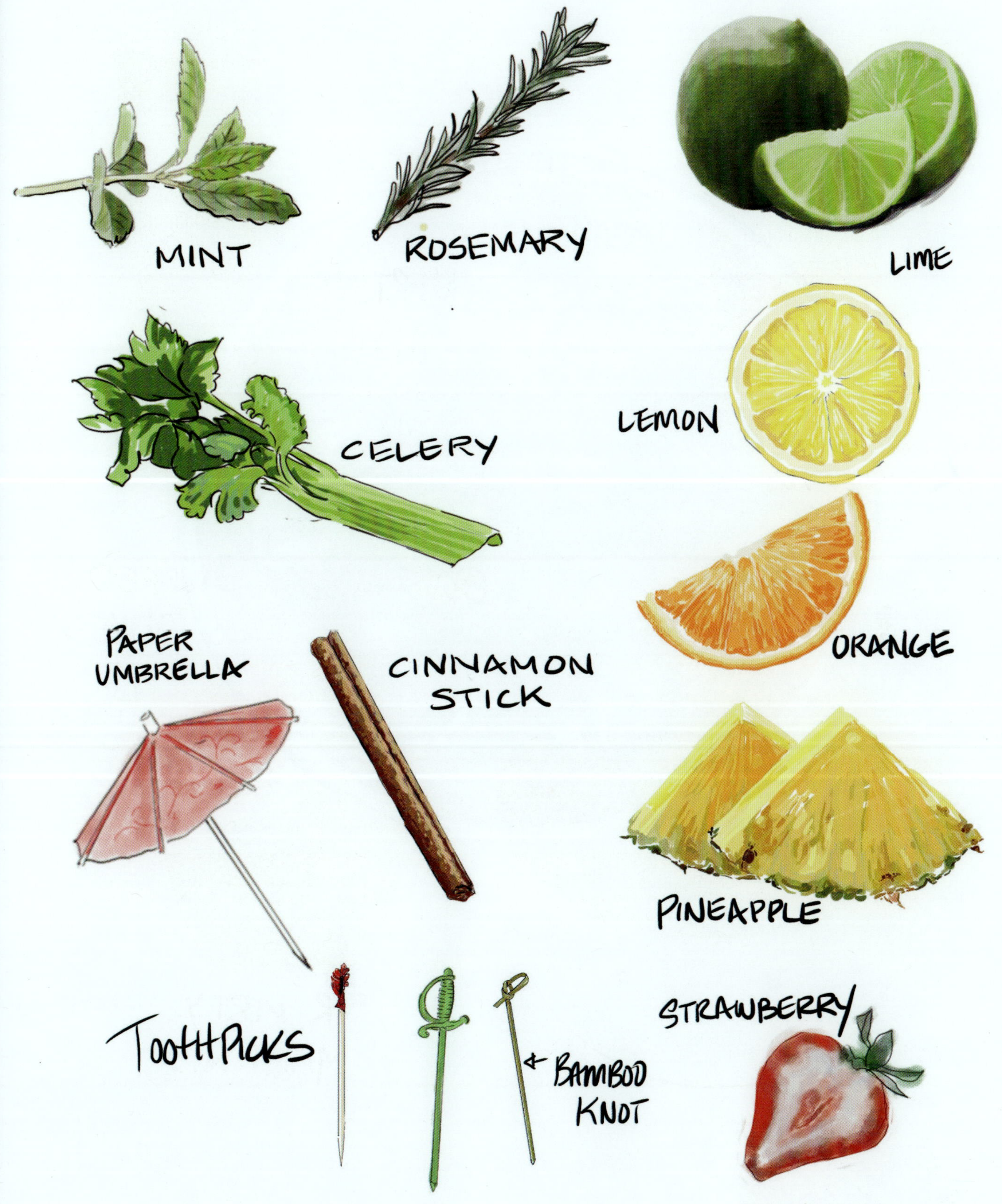
MINT
ROSEMARY
LIME
LEMON
CELERY
ORANGE
PAPER UMBRELLA
CINNAMON STICK
PINEAPPLE
TOOTHPICKS
STRAWBERRY
BAMBOO KNOT

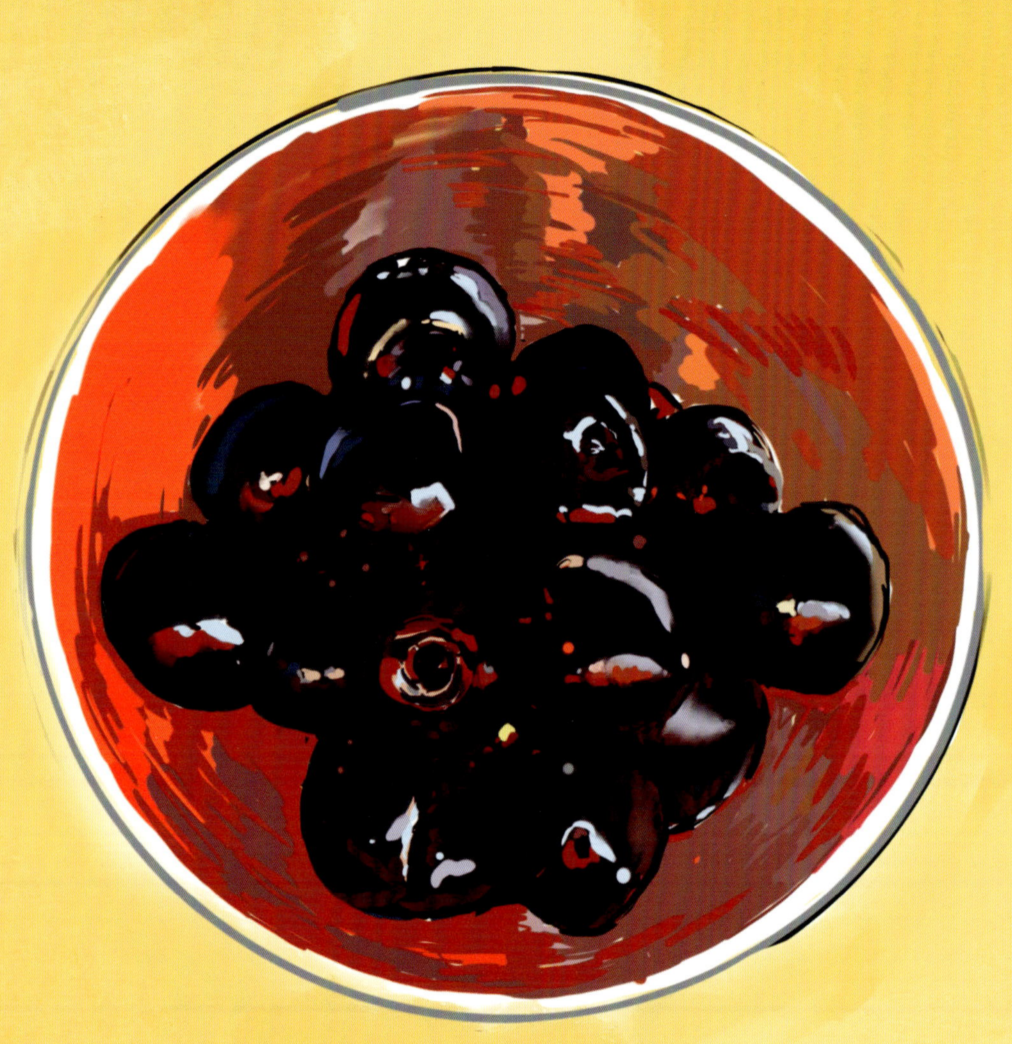

THE LUXARDO CHERRY

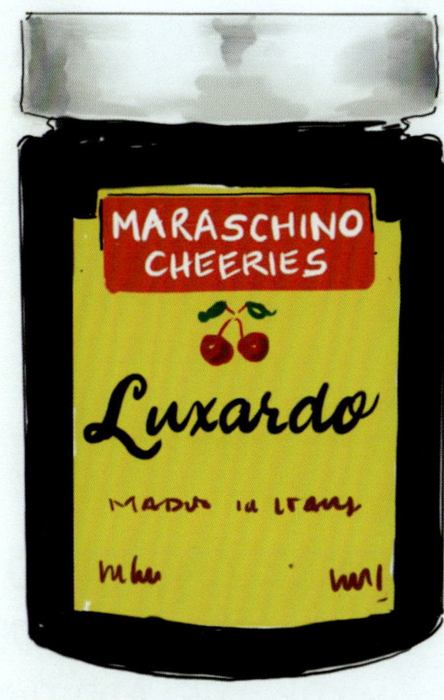

LUXARDO MARASCHINO CHERRIES ARE THE GOLD STANDARD - AND EXPENSIVE! BUT, FOR THE PRICE OF ONE JAR, YOU CAN MAKE YOUR OWN VERSION....

The hardest part of making these is pitting the cherries!

Get a CHERRY PITTER!

HOMEMADE LUXARDO CHERRIES

1 POUND CHERRIES - PITTED & STEMMED
½ CUP WATER
½ CUP SUGAR
1 CINNAMON STICK
JUICE OF 1 LEMON
5 PEPPERCORNS
PINCH OF NUTMEG
PINCH OF KOSHER SALT
1 CUP LUXARDO LIQUEUR

IN A MEDIUM SAUCEPAN, COMBINE WATER, SUGAR, CINNAMON, LEMON, NUTMEG & SALT. HEAT + STIR TO DISOLVE SUGAR. HEAT TO JUST UNDER A BOIL - SIMMER FOR 5 MINUTES. STIR IN THE CHERRIES AND LET COOK FOR ABOUT 3 MINUTES. REMOVE FROM HEAT & STIR IN THE LUXARDO LIQUEUR. LET COOL.

YOU CAN STORE CHERRIES IN REFRIGERATOR FOR UP TO 1 MONTH...... BUT I BET THEY WILL BE EATEN SOONER!

Explaining Bubbly Water

Seltzer • Sparkling Mineral Water • Club Soda

Seltzer is

PLAIN TAP WATER WHICH IS CARBONATED WITH CARBON DIOXDE.

Sparkling Mineral Water is

NATURAL SPRING OR WELL WATER (WITH SALT & SULFUR IN IT) WHICH HAS NATURAL CARBONATION OR CARBONATION ADDED WITH CARBON DIOXDE.

Club Soda is

WATER CARONATED WITH CARBON DIOXDE, WITH THE ADDITION OF POTASSIUM BICARBONATE & POTASSIUM SULFATE. THESE MINERALS GIVE IT A SLIGHTLY SALTY TASTE, PREFERED IN MANY DRINKS.

TONIC WATER IS TOTALLY DIFFERENT & SHOULD NOT BE SUBSTITUED FOR ANY BUBBLY WATER!

Tonic water contains Quinine, which was used to treat Malaria. It also contains citrus and sweetener. It's a wonderful mixer when used in drinks it is called for.

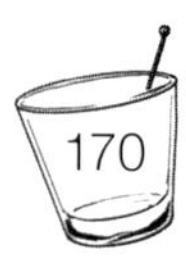

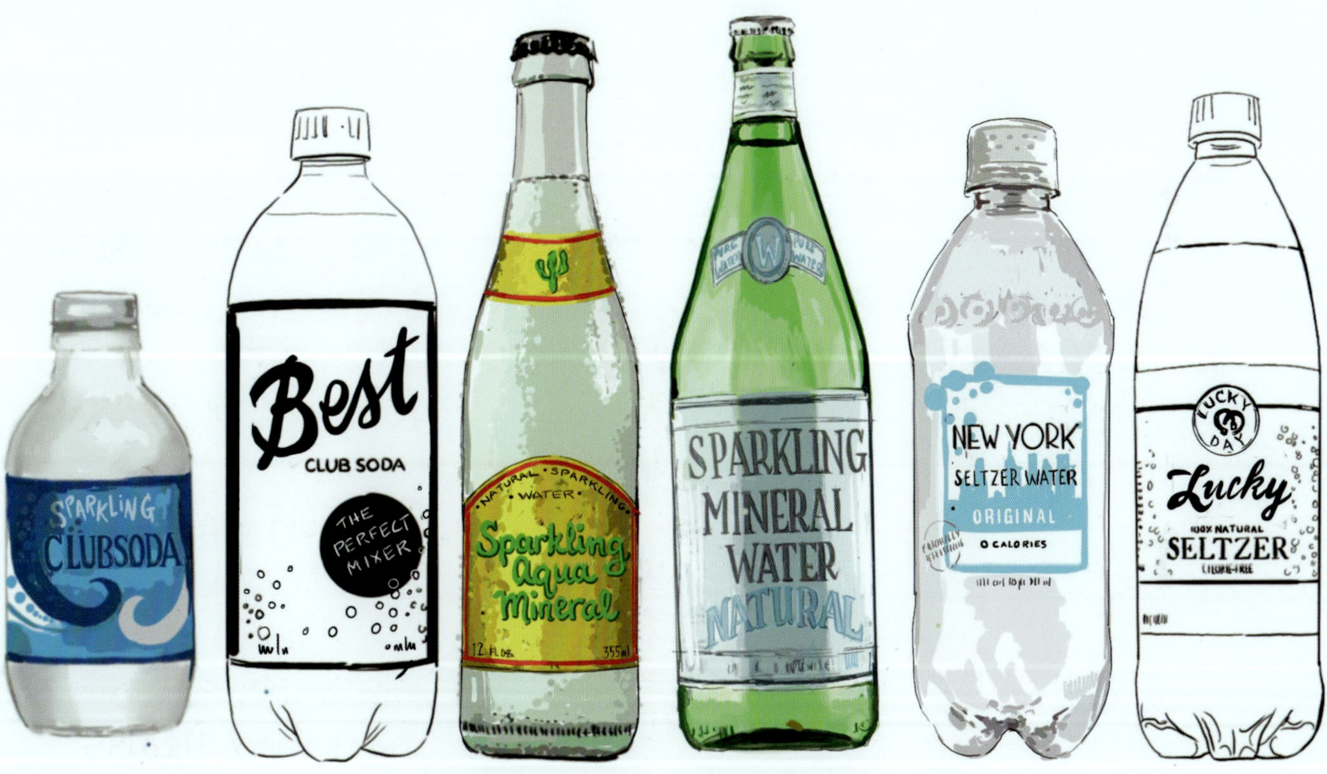
SPARKLING
CLUBSODA
Best
CLUB SODA
THE PERFECT MIXER
NATURAL · SPARKLING · WATER
Sparkling Aqua Mineral
12 FL OZ
355ml
SPARKLING
MINERAL
WATER
NATURAL
NEW YORK
SELTZER WATER
ORIGINAL
0 CALORIES
LUCKY DAY
Lucky
100% NATURAL
SELTZER

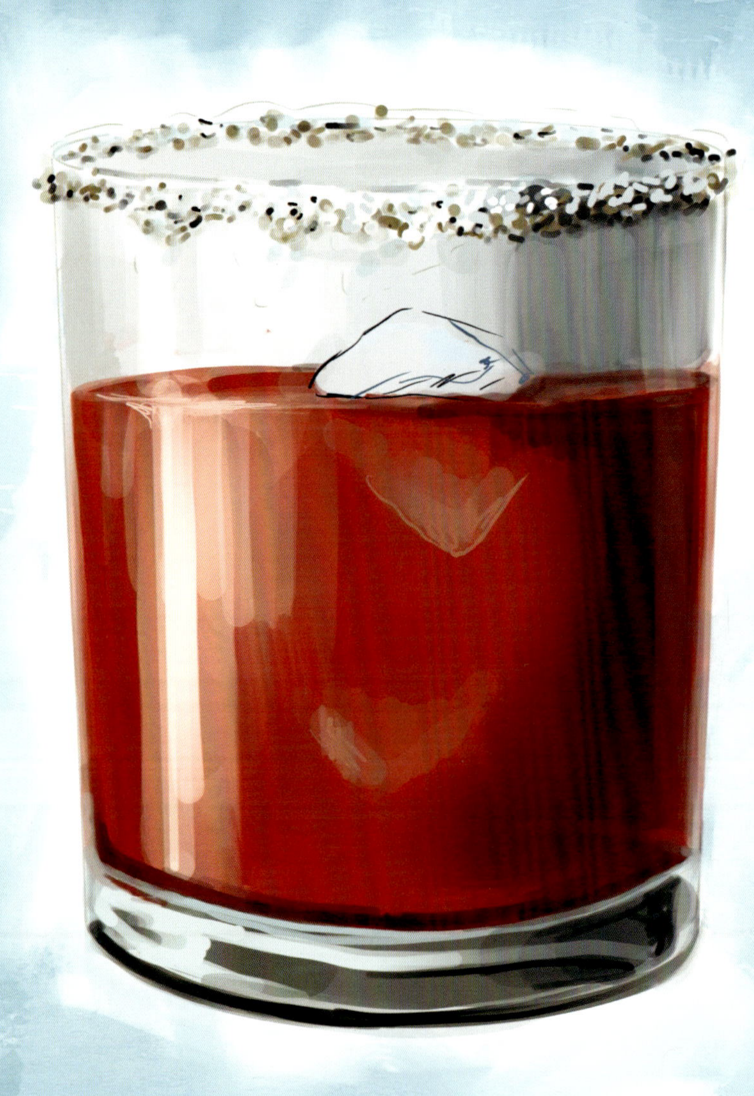

How To Rim A Glass

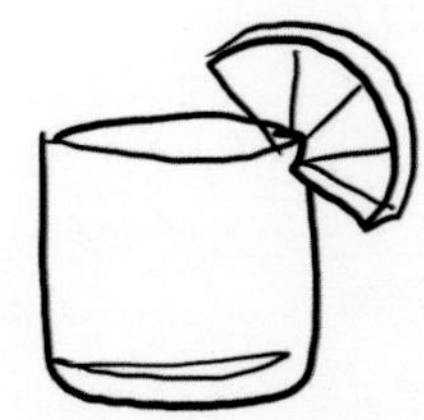

① USE A WEDGE OF FRUIT TO MOISTEN THE EDGE OF THE GLASS. (WATER IS TOO RUNNY)

② PUT YOUR SUGAR, SALT, OR SPICE MIXTURE INTO A SAUCER OR SHALLOW PLATE.

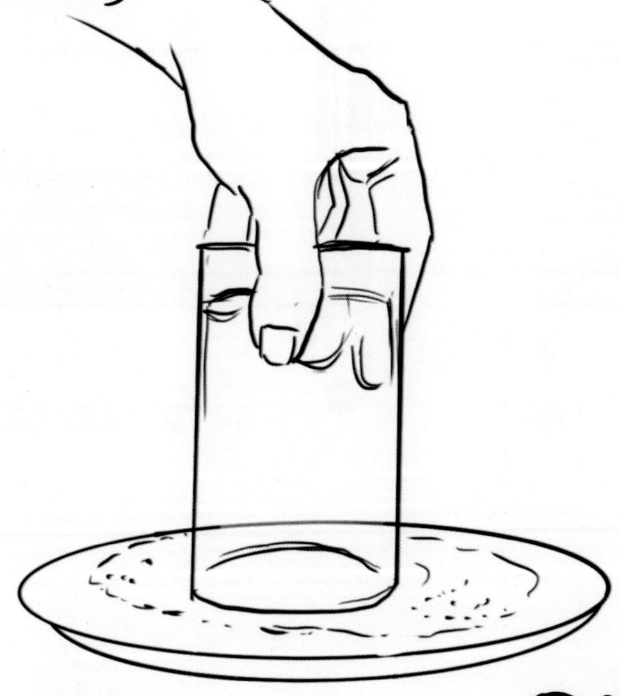

③ INVERT GLASS AND DIP IN SAUCER. DO NOT TWIST! TAP, NOT TWIST.

④ CAREFULLY, ADD YOUR ICE & OTHER INGREDIENTS TO COCKTAIL GLASS. AVOID MESSING UP THE RIM.

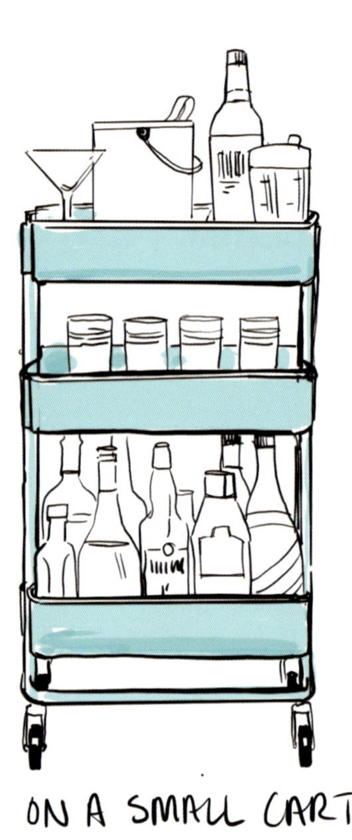

ON A SMALL CART

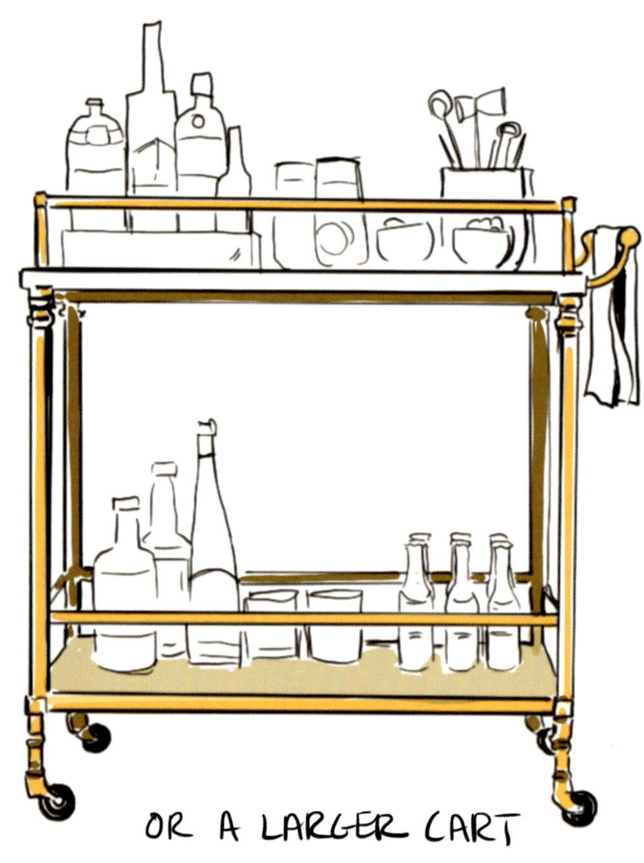

OR A LARGER CART

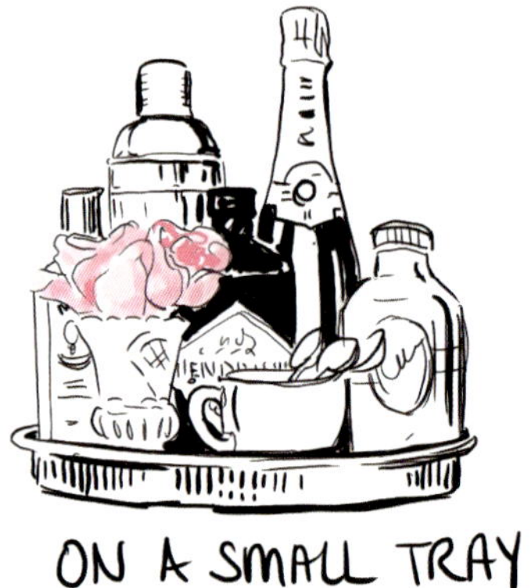

ON A SMALL TRAY

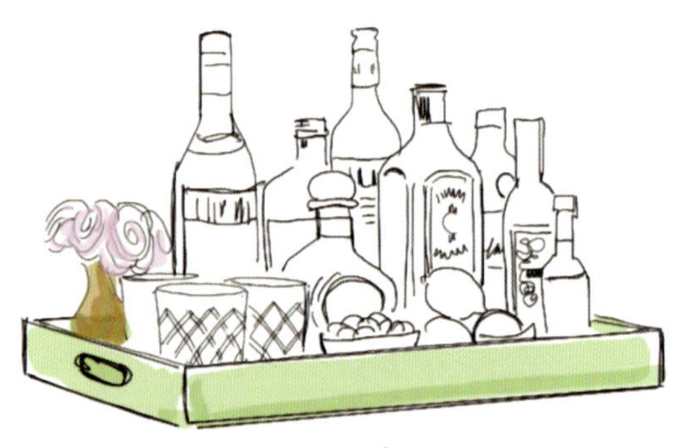

OR A LARGER TRAY

How To Set Up A Home Bar

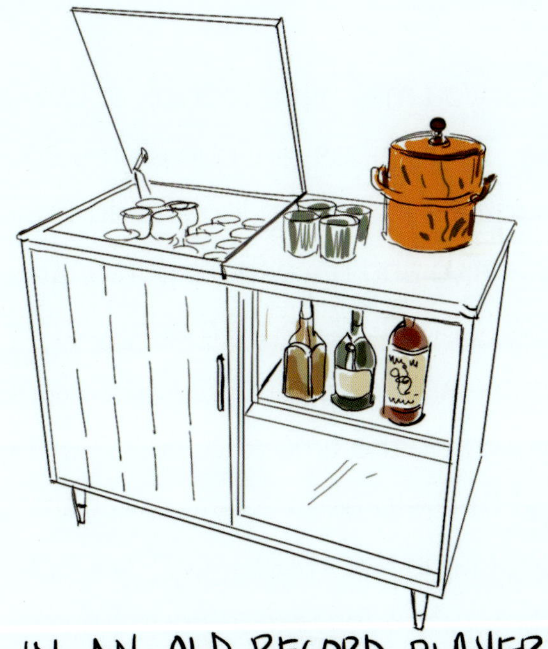

IN AN OLD RECORD PLAYER CONSOLE

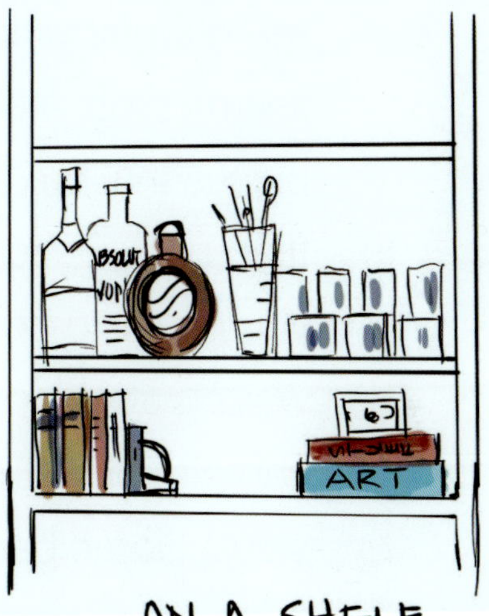

ON A SHELF

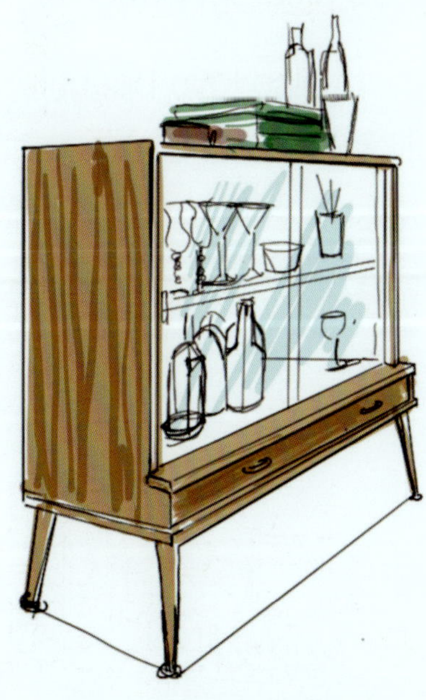

IN A CABINET

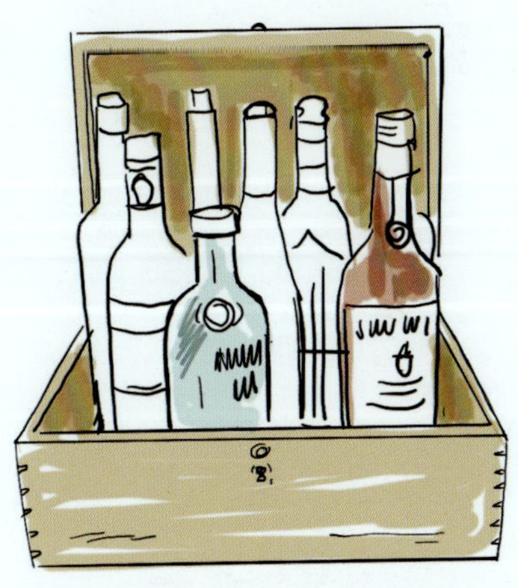

IN A BOX

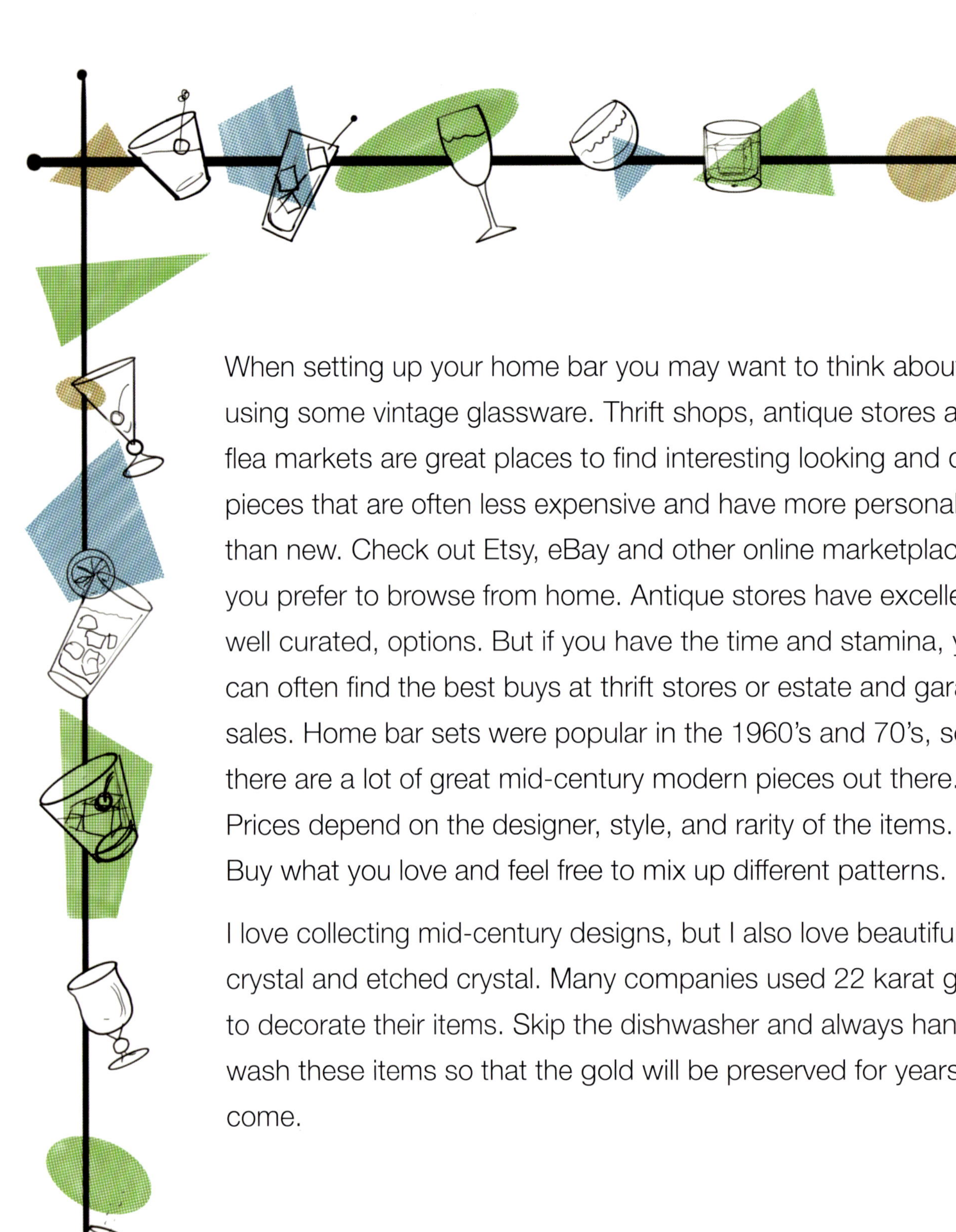

When setting up your home bar you may want to think about using some vintage glassware. Thrift shops, antique stores and flea markets are great places to find interesting looking and quality pieces that are often less expensive and have more personality than new. Check out Etsy, eBay and other online marketplaces if you prefer to browse from home. Antique stores have excellent, well curated, options. But if you have the time and stamina, you can often find the best buys at thrift stores or estate and garage sales. Home bar sets were popular in the 1960's and 70's, so there are a lot of great mid-century modern pieces out there. Prices depend on the designer, style, and rarity of the items. Buy what you love and feel free to mix up different patterns.

I love collecting mid-century designs, but I also love beautiful cut crystal and etched crystal. Many companies used 22 karat gold to decorate their items. Skip the dishwasher and always hand wash these items so that the gold will be preserved for years to come.

FAMOUS MAKERS

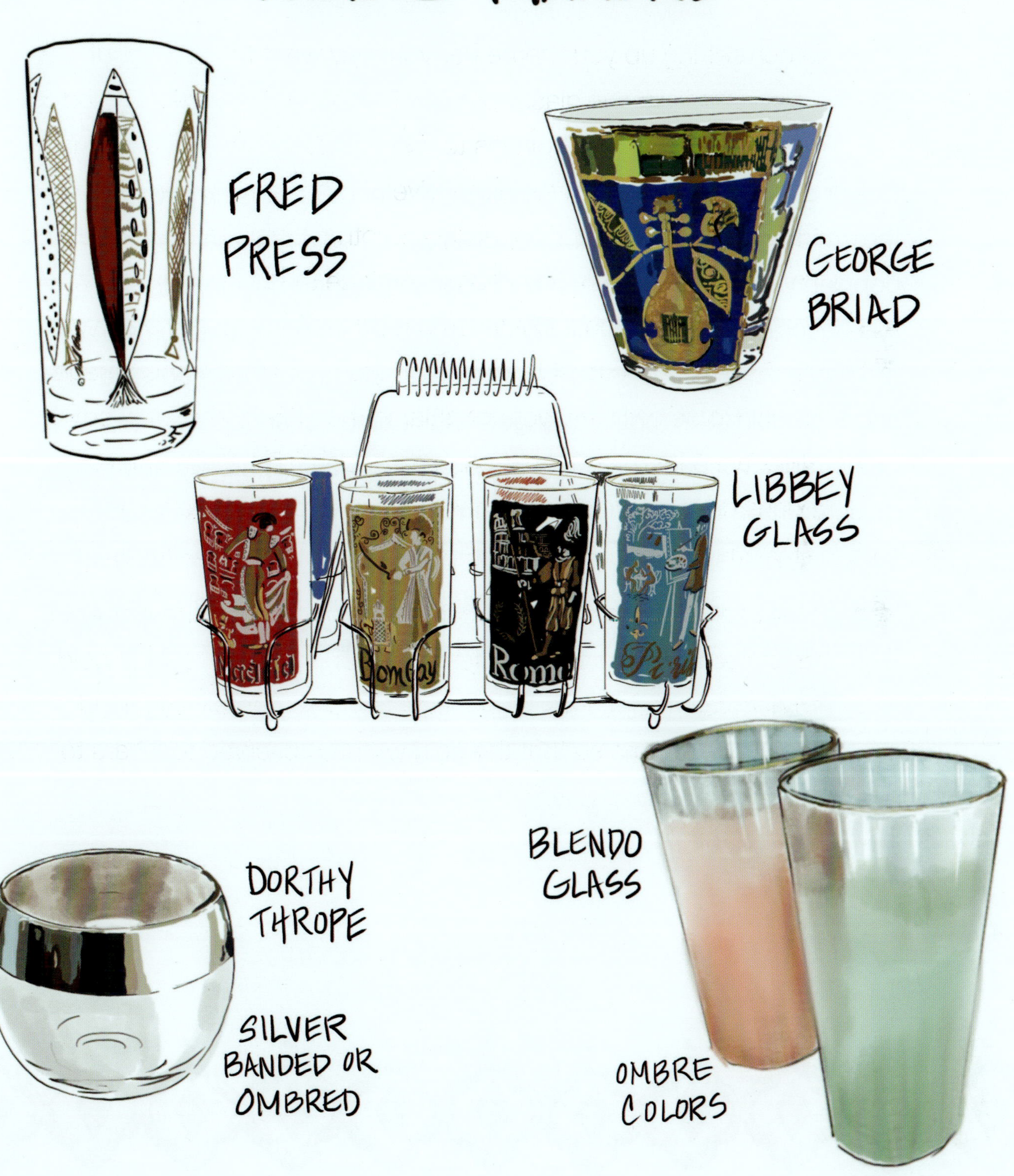

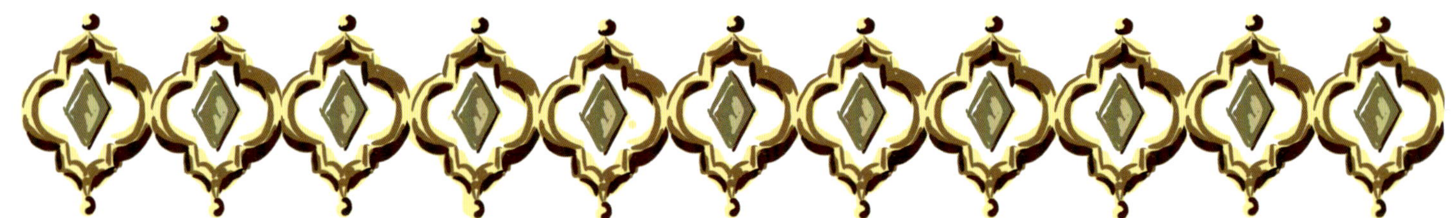

Culver glass was founded in Brooklyn, NY in 1939. Best known for their mid-century designs, Culver glassware had a resurgence of popularity in the 1960's when suburbanites started buying sets of this decorated glass for their home parties. At its peak, the company produced 75 different patterns, most featuring beautiful embossing and 22kt gold. The motifs changed as the times changed, with the more traditional patterns of the 1960's giving way to paisleys and mushrooms in the 70's. Culver also manufactured decorated snack sets, plates, and ice buckets as well as all types of barware. Antique Culver is still a good buy; but if you are lucky you may have a grandparent who has a set stashed somewhere.

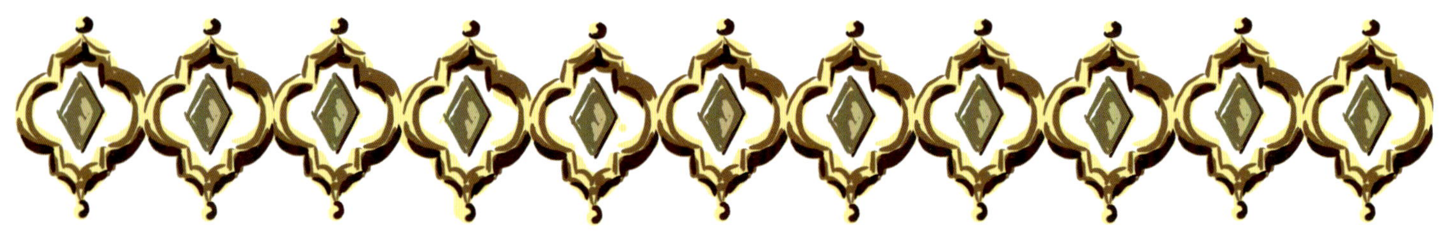

Culver

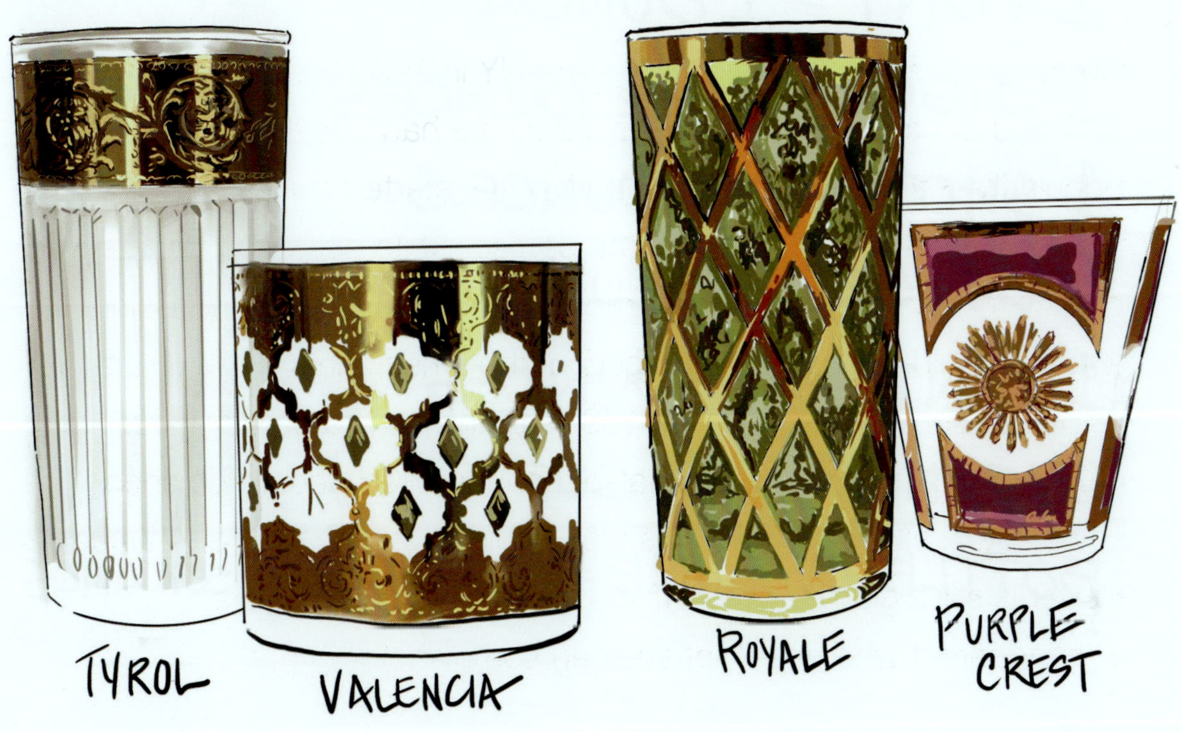

ALWAYS GREAT TO FIND A SET WITH THE ORIGINAL WIRE CADDY

RED SCROLL

MEASUREMENTS

DASH = 1/4 TEASPOON

1 TEASPOON = 1/8 OUNCE

1 PONY = 1 OUNCE

1 JIGGER = 1 1/2 OUNCES

1 SHOT = 1 1/2 OUNCES

8 OUNCES = 1 CUP

1 PINT = 16 OUNCES

2 OUNCES = 1/4 CUP

BOTTLE OF WINE = ABOUT 3-4 SERVINGS

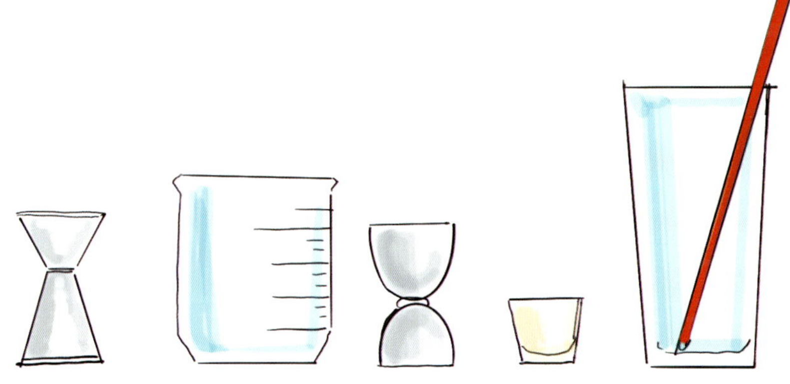

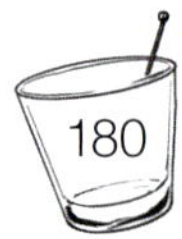

cups	Ounces	milliliters
1	8	240
3/4	6	180
2/3	5	160
1/2	4	120
1/3	3	80
1/4	2	60
1/8	1	30
1/16	1/2	15

Acknowledgements

I want to thank so many people who helped me through this process...

- **Francie Kranzberg**
  you took my words & thoughts & made them smarter, more interesting & witty. Plus you rock at proofreading. Thank you so much for all you do!

- **My Mom & Brother Josh-**
  (my biggest cheerleaders.)
  You guys have never doubted my abilities. I could not have acomplished this book without your support!

- **My Extended Family & Friends**
  Old friends, new ones, people I see a lot & others I haven't spoken to for years. When called on to support this book on Kickstarter, you were there. I am overcome with your generousity!

- **Steve Jurgensmeyer-**
  You believed in this project & reached out to help. The entire process was great. I can't imagine a better book designer.

- **For everyone who offered advice, encouragement, or otherwise.**
  Thank you so much, I listened & took everything into consideration. I learned so much & I am grateful!

- **My Daughters Abby & Tamara**
  You both encouraged, suggested, critcized, and helped spread the word. I am so proud of you both, everyday!

Love,
Rachel

About the Author

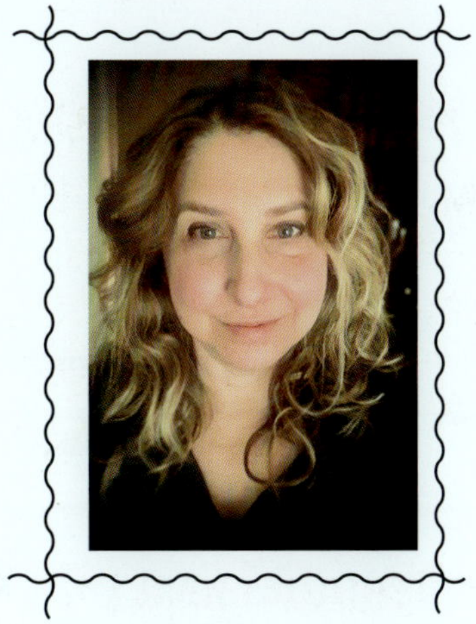

Rachel K Miller has been creating art her entire life. She studied painting at Boston University, sportswear design at the Fashion Institute of Technology and worked as a sportswear designer in New York. Rachel owned and operated a jewelry company and presently works in Interior Design. She lives in St Louis, Missouri.

You can reach Rachel at:

rachelkm62@gmail.com

www.theillustratedcocktail.com

Instagram: @theillustratedcocktail

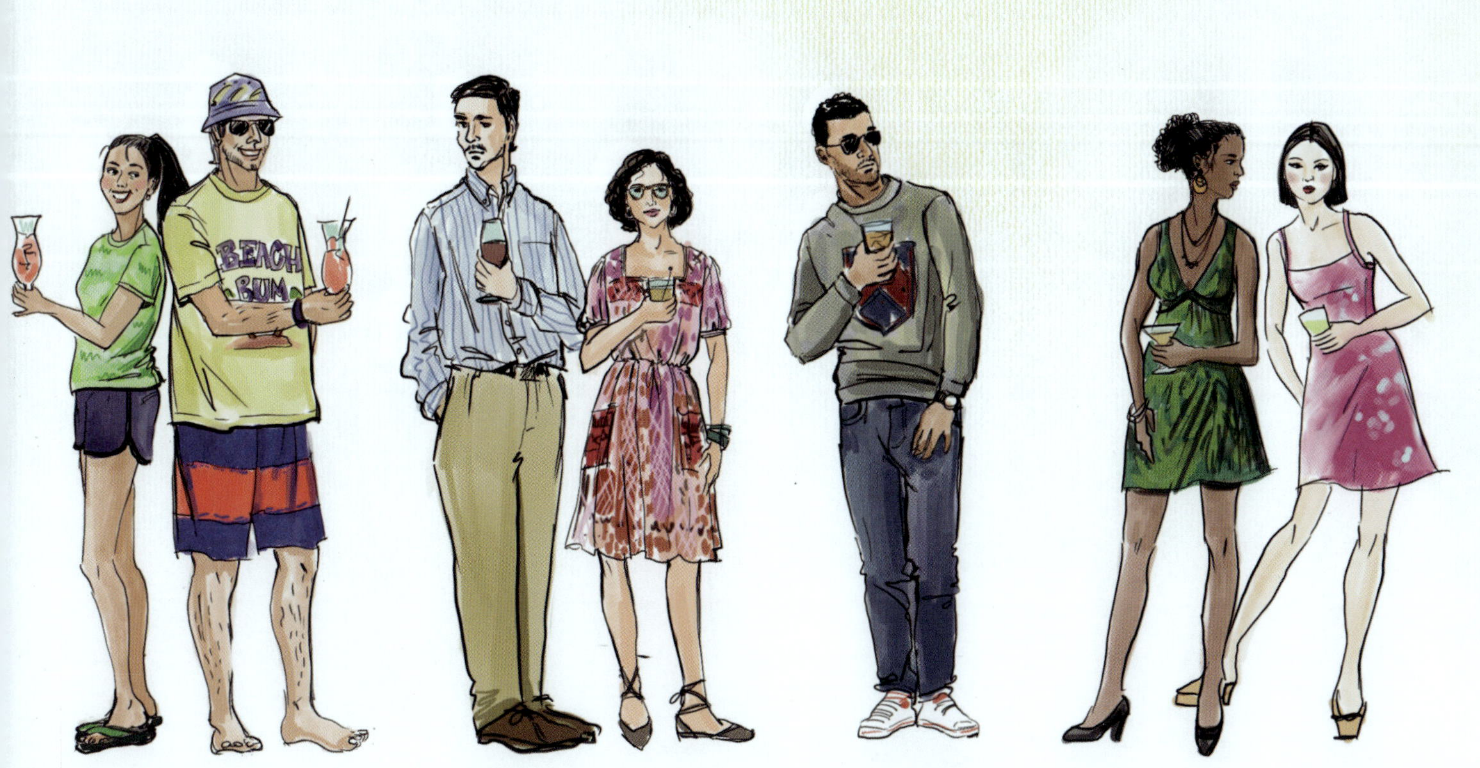
BEACH
BUM

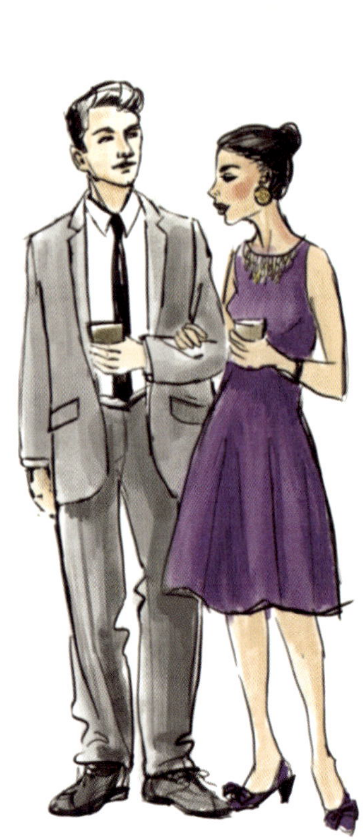
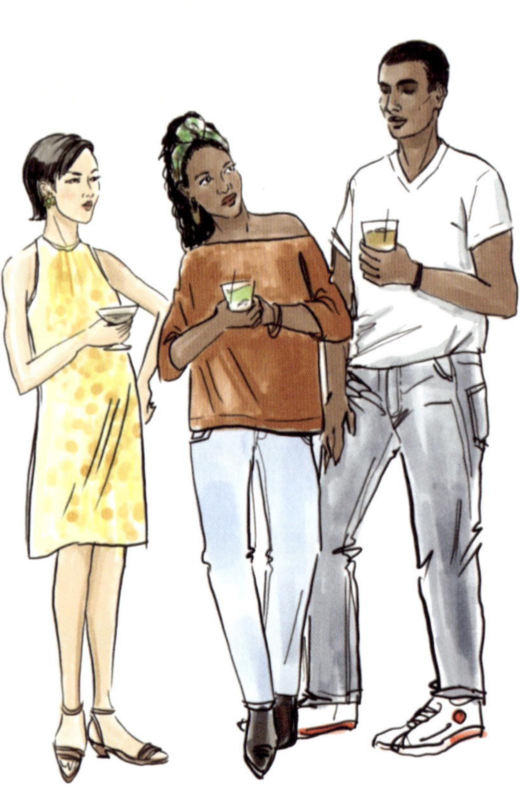